LETTERS AND SKETCHES:

WITH

A NARRATIVE OF A YEAR'S RESIDENCE

AMONG

THE INDIAN TRIBES

OF

The Rocky Mountains.

BY

P. J. DE SMET, S. J.

Philadelphia:
PUBLISHED BY M. FITHIAN, 61 N. SECOND STREET.

1843.

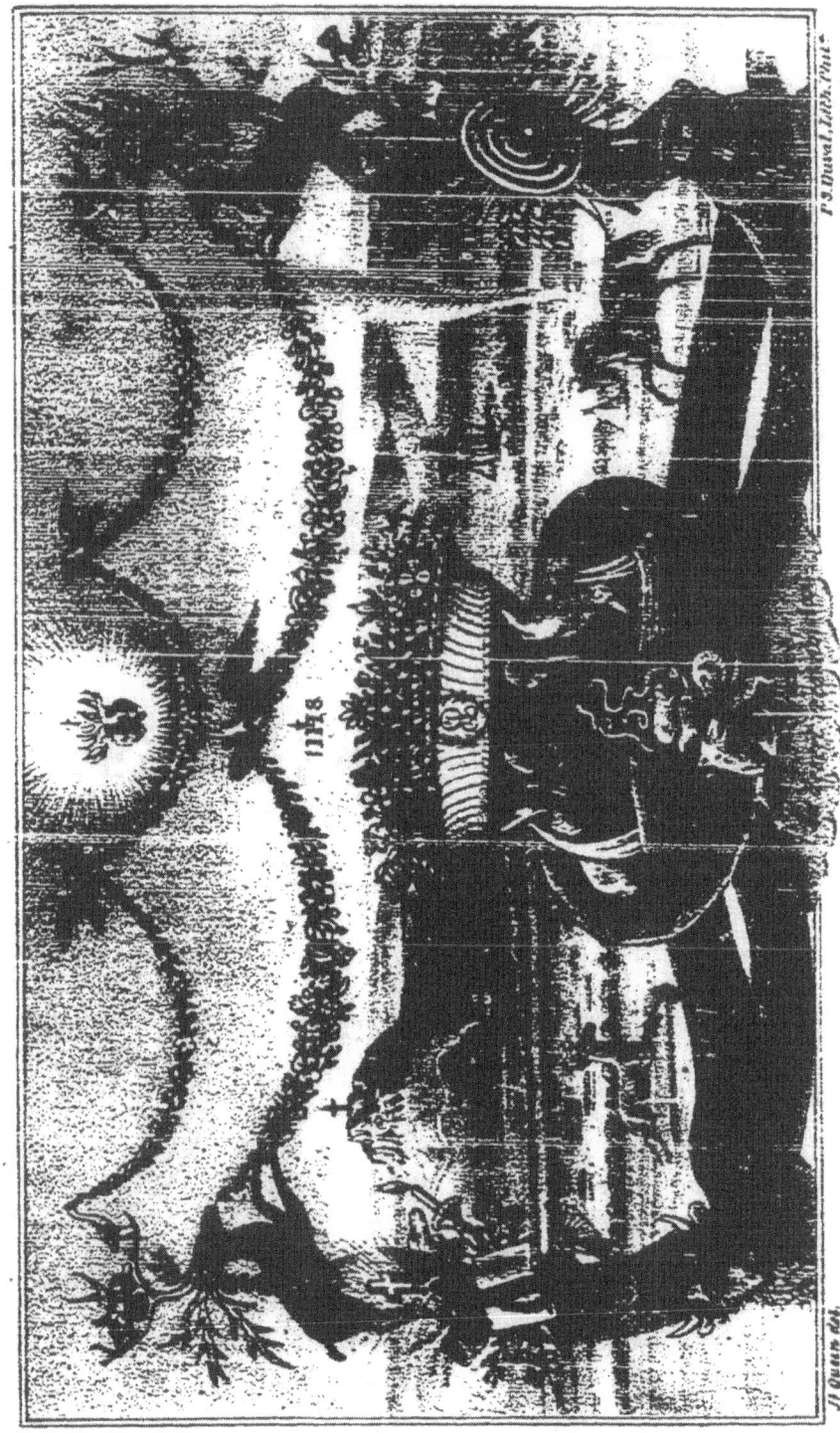

PREFACE.

To those who love their country, and their fellow men, we present this interesting Narrative, with the hope, we might say, the certainty, that its perusal will afford them some moments of the purest gratification. We have seldom met any thing more entertaining. Its simple, manly eloquence enchants the attention. The facts it makes known to us of the " far, far West," the dispositions and habits of the Indian Tribes who roam over the vast region of the Oregon, their present state and future prospects, are such as cannot fail to awaken a lively interest in all who love to look around them beyond the narrow horizon of every-day scenes, and learn what the holy servants of God are doing for His sake and in His name in distant parts of the world. We have conversed with the apostolic man from whose pen we receive this narrative; and as we listened we felt at once honoured and delighted to be so near one who in our days and in his own person brings before us that lofty spirit of missionary devotedness—those thrilling scenes of Indian life and adventure which we so much admire in the pages of Charlevoix and Bancroft.

Truly our country is full of interest to those who watch its progress, and compare it with the past. Who, for example, could have dreamt that the Iroquois, the savage Mohawk,—under which name we best know the tribe, and whose startling yell so often made our forefathers tremble,—would have been chosen to kindle the first faint sparks of civilization and Christianity among a large portion of the Indian tribes beyond the Rocky Mountains? This is one of the singular facts which these pages present to us. They abound in others not less singular and interesting. Many of these Indian nations actually thirst after the waters of life—sigh for the day when the real "Long Gown" is to appear among them, and even send messengers thousands of miles to hasten his coming. Such longing after God's holy truth, while it shames our colder piety, should also enflame every heart to pray fervently that laborers may be found for this vast vineyard—and open every hand to aid the holy, self-devoted men, who, leaving home and friends and country, have buried themselves in these wilds with their beloved Indians, to live for them and God. One of their favourite plans at this moment is to introduce among them a taste for agriculture, with the means to pursue it. They believe it to be the speediest, perhaps the only way by which the Indians may be won from the wandering life they now in general lead and from the idle habits it engenders. To aid them in this philanthropic object is our sacred duty as men, as Americans, as Christians. It is at least one method of atonement for the countless wrongs which these unfortunate races have received from the whites. We should be grateful to have such an opportunity of doing good: let none suffer the occasion to pass unhonoured by some tribute to the noble cause—some evidence of their love for God, their country and their fellow man.

The frontispiece is from the pencil of one of the Indian Missionaries.

It blends the skill of the artist with the fancy of the poet, and will hardly be understood without a word of explanation. In the foreground we see several of the gigantic trees of the Oregon forests, fallen and crossing each other. On these repose two wolves, a squirrel and several serpents. Above, two Indian chiefs, surnamed in baptism after the great Apostles of the Gentiles, Peter and Paul, are supporting a large basket of hearts,—an offering to heaven from the grateful wilderness. On the right are the emblems of Indian life and warfare: the bow and arrows, battle-axe and shield. Below and above these are seen some of the most remarkable animals of the country—the bear, the wild horse, the badger, the graceful antelope, intermingled with the plover, the pigeon, the wood-cock, the bittern, and other birds of the region. On the left are the peaceful symbols of Christianity—the Bible and the Cross, the chalice and altar lights—the anchor, symbol of faith and hope—the trumpet, to proclaim the word of God and bid the desert bless His holy name. Here too we behold several of the noble animals of the territory—the buffalo, the deer and elk, the mountain sheep and different birds. In the distance are seen on the right, Indian mounds, and a water-spout rising from the river Platte, and on the left, the Rocky Mountains surmounted by the Cross. Festoons, composed of the various flowers the Fathers have met on their way over mountains and prairies and through lonely vallies, complete the picture—the whole supported at the extremities by different birds of the country, and in the centre by the American eagle,—fit emblem, we may say, of their own dauntless faith, as well as of the heroic spirit of the nation within whose borders they have their principal station, and from whose genuine piety they have received the most consoling assurances of final success, viz: the Flat Head Indians and the Pends-d'oreilles, who are styled, even by their foes the "nation of chiefs."

Once more we earnestly commend the noble cause of these devoted Missionaries to the charity of every sincere Christian. The short time allowed to prepare the work for the press must be our apology for several imperfections or errors which may meet the eye of the reader.

⁎ Wherever the word "caimut" occurs, read *calumet*.

BOOK I.

*Dies venit, dies tua
In qua reflorent omnia,
Lætemur et nos in viam,
Tua reducti dex-tera.*

The days of spring are drawing near
When all thy flowers will re-appear,
And we redeemed by thy right hand,
Shall walk in gladness thro' the land.

LETTER I.

St. Louis University, Feb. 4, 1841.

TO THE REV. F. J. B.

Rev. and Dear Sir:

I presume you are aware, that in the beginning of last Spring, I was sent by the Right Rev. Bishop of St. Louis, and my Provincial, on an exploring expedition to the Rocky Mountains, in order to ascertain the dispositions of the Indians, and the prospects of success we might have if we were to establish a mission among them. It is truly gratifying to me to have so favorable a report to make.— My occupations do not allow me to enter into all the details; I shall therefore be satisfied at present with giving you a brief sketch of my journey and its result.

I started from Westport on the 30th of April, in company with the Annual Expedition of the American Fur Company, which for this year had appointed the rendezvous on Green River, a tributary of the Rio Colorado of the West. Captain Dripps, who commanded the caravan, treated me on all occasions with the most polite attention. On the 6th day of our journey I was seized with the fever and ague, and have been subject to it for nearly five months. Nothing particularly worth noticing, occurred during the journey, except, when we halted in the village of the Sheyennes. I was introduced to the Chiefs as a minister of the Great

Spirit: they showed me great deference, and I was invited to a feast. I had to pass at through all the ceremonies of the Calmut; the gre' ch' approached me to shake hands, and gave me a 1 felt "How do you do."— "Blackgown," said he, "my heart was filled with joy when I learned who you were. My lodge never received a visitor for whom I feel a greater esteem. As soon as I was apprised of your coming, I ordered my great kettle to be filled, and in your honor, I commanded that my three fattest dogs should be served up." The bravest warriors of the nation partook of the repast, and I availed myself of the opportunity to explain to them the most important tenets of Christianity. I told them the object of my visit, and enquired whether they would not be satisfied to have also Black-gowns among them, who would teach them to love and serve the Great Spirit, as he wished. "Oh yes," they eagerly answered, "we will gladly provide for every thing that they stand in need of; they will not die of hunger amongst us." I have no doubt but a zealous missionary would do a great deal of good among them. They are about two thousand in number. Their language, it is said, is very difficult. On the 30th of June we arrived at the rendezvous. An escort of warriors had been provided for me by the Flat-heads. Our meeting was that of children who come to meet their parent, and in the effusion of their heart, they bestowed upon me the fondest names with a simplicity truly patriarchial. They told me of all the interesting particulars of their nation, and of the wonderful preservation of sixty of their men, in a battle against two hundred Black-feet, which lasted five whole days, and in which they killed fifty of their enemies, without losing a single man of their number. "The Great Spirit watched over them;" they said, "he knew that we were to guide you to our camp, and he wanted to clear the road of all the obstacles that you might have found on your way. We trust we will not be annoyed any more by the Black-feet; they went off weeping like women." We thanked heaven for the signal preservation, and implored its assistance for the new and perilous journey we were on the point of undertaking. The Indians of different nations and the trappers, had assembled at the rendezvous in great numbers, for the sake of the trade. On Sunday, the fifth of July, I had the consolation of celebrating the holy sacrifice of Mass *sub dio*. The altar was placed on an elevation, and surrounded with boughs and garlands of flowers; I addressed the congregation in French and in English, and spoke also by an interpreter to the Flat-head and Snake Indians. It was a spectacle truly moving for the heart of a Missionary, to behold an assembly composed of so many different nations, who all assisted at our holy mysteries with great satisfaction.— The Canadians sung hymns in French and Latin, and the Indians in their native tongue. It was truly a Catholic worship. . . . This place has been called since that time, by the French Canadians, *la prairie de la Messe.*

About thirty of the principal chiefs of the Snake Indians invited me to a council. I explained to them the christian doctrine in a compendious manner—they were all very attentive—they then deliberated among themselves for about half an hour, and one of the chiefs, addressing me in the name of the others, said: " Black-gown, the words of thy mouth have found their way to our hearts; they never will be forgotten. Our country is open for thee; come to teach us what we have to do, to please the Great Spirit, and we will do according to thy words." I advised them to select among themselves a wise and prudent man, who, every morning and evening, should assemble them to offer to Almighty God their prayers and supplications; that there the good chiefs should have an opportunity of exhorting their warriors to behave as they ought. The meeting was held the very same evening, and the great chief promulgated a law, that for the future, the one who would be guilty of theft, or of any other disorderly act, should receive a public castigation. On Monday, 6th, we proceeded on our journey. A dozen Canadians wished to accompany me, to have an opportunity, as they said, to practise their religion. Eight days afterwards we arrived safely in the camp of the Flat-heads, and Ponderas, or Pends d'oreilles.

Immediately the whole village was in commotion; men, women and children, all came to meet me, and shake hands, and I was conducted in triumph to the lodge of the great chief Tjolizhitzay, (the Big face.) He has the appearance of an old patriarch. Surrounded by the principal chiefs of the two tribes, and the most renowned warriors, he thus addressed me: "This day Kaikolinzosten (the Great Spirit) has accomplished our wishes, and our hearts are swelled with joy. Our desire to be instructed was so great, that three times had we deputed our people to the Great Black-gown* in St. Louis, to obtain a father. Now, Father, speak, and we will comply with all you will tell us. Show us the road we have to follow, to come to the place where the Great Spirit resides." Then he resigned his authority to me; but I replied that he mistook the object of my coming among them; that I had no other object in view, but their spiritual welfare; that with respect to temporal affairs, they should remain as they were, till circumstances should allow them to settle in a permanent spot.— Afterwards we deliberated on the hours proper for their

---

* The Bishop.

spiritual exercises and instructions. One of the chiefs brought me a bell, with which I might give the signal.

The same evening about 2,000 persons were assembled before my lodge to recite night prayers in common. I told them the result of my conference with the chiefs; of the plan of instructions which I intended to pursue; and with what disposition they ought to assist at them, etc. Night prayers having been said, a solemn canticle of praise of their own composition, was sung by these children of the mountains, to the Author of their being. It would be impossible for me to describe the emotions I felt at this moment; I wept for joy, and admired the marvellous ways of that kind Providence, who, in his infinite mercy, had deigned to depute me to this poor people, to announce to them the glad tidings of salvation. The next day I assembled the council, and with the assistance of an intelligent interpreter, I translated into their language the Lord's Prayer, the Hail Mary, the Apostles' Creed, the ten Commandments, and four Acts. As I was in the habit of reciting these prayers, morning and evening, and before instructions, about a fortnight after, I promised a beautiful silver medal to the one who would recite them first. One of the chiefs rising immediately, "Father," said he, smiling, "that medal is mine," and he recited all the prayers without missing a word. I embraced him, praised the eagerness which he had evinced of being instructed, and appointed him my Cathecist. This good Indian set to work with so much zeal and perseverance, that in less than a fortnight all knew their prayers.

Every morning, at the break of day, the old chief is the first on horseback, and goes round the camp from lodge to lodge. "Now my children," he exclaims, "it is time to rise; let the first thoughts of your hearts be for the Great

Spirit; say that you love him, and beg of him to be merciful unto you. Make haste, our Father will soon ring the bell, open your ears to listen, and your hearts to receive the words of his mouth." Then, if he has perceived any disorderly act on the preceding day, or if he has received unfavorable reports from the other chiefs, he gives them a fatherly admonition. Who would not think, that this could only be found in a well ordered and religious community, and yet it is among Indians in the defiles and vallies of the Rocky Mountains!!! You have no idea of the eagerness they showed to receive religious instruction. I explained the christian doctrine four times a day, and nevertheless my lodge was filled, the whole day, with people eager to hear more. At night I related those histories of the Holy Scriptures that were best calculated to promote their piety and edification, and as I happened to observe, that I was afraid of tiring them, "oh no," they replied, "if we were not afraid of tiring you, we would gladly spend here the whole night."

I conferred the holy sacrament of Baptism on six hundred of them, and if I thought it prudent to postpone the baptism of others till my return, it was not for want of desire on their part, but chiefly to impress upon their minds a greater idea of the holiness of the sacrament, and of the dispositions that are required to receive it worthily. Among those baptised, were the two great chiefs of the Flatheads and of the Ponderas. As I excited the catechumens to a heartfelt contrition of their sins, the *Walking Bear*, chief of the Ponderas, answered: "Father, I have been plunged for a number of years in profound ignorance of good and evil, and no doubt, during that time, I have often greatly displeased the Great Spirit, and therefore I must humbly beseech his pardon. But when I afterwards conceived that a thing was bad, I banished it from my heart, and I do not recollect to have since deliberately offended the Great Spirit." Truly, where such dispositions are found, we may well conclude that a rich harvest is to be gathered.

I remained two months among these good people, and every day they were adding to my consolations, by their fervor in prayer, by their assiduity in coming to my instructions, and by their docility in putting into practice what they had been taught.

The season being far advanced, and as I had waited in vain for a safe opportunity to return to St. Louis, I resolved to commit myself entirely to Providence, and on the 7th of August, I took leave of my dear Neophytes. I appointed one of the chiefs to replace me during my absence, who should preside in their evening and morning devotions, and on the Sabbath exhort them to virtue, baptize the little children, and those who were dangerously ill. Grief was depicted on the features of all, and tears were glistening in every eye. The old chief addressed me, saying, " Father, the Great Spirit accompany thee in thy long and dangerous voyage; every day, morning and evening, we will address to him our humble supplications, that thou mayest arrive safely among thy brethren. And we will continue to do so, till thou be again among thy children of the mountains. We are now like the trees that have been spoiled of their verdure by winter's blast. When the snow will have disappeared from these vallies, and the grass begins to grow, our hearts will begin to rejoice; when the plants will spring forth our joy will increase; when they blossom, it will still be greater, and then we will set out to meet you. Farewell, Father, farewell."

The Chiefs would not suffer me to depart by myself—

thirty of the bravest warriors were deputed as a safeguard to traverse the country of the Black-feet, who are very hostile to the whites, and they were instructed to accompany me, as far as need would be of their assistance. I resolved to take on my return a different route from the one I had taken in coming. I was induced to do so, in order to visit the Forts of the American Fur Company on the Missouri, and on the Yellow Stone, to baptize the children. After five or six days travelling, we fell in with a war party of the Crow Indians, who received us very kindly, and we travelled together for two days. Then we directed our course to the Big Horn, the most considerable of the tributary streams of the Yellow Stone. There we met another party of the same nation, who were also amicably disposed towards us. As there was question about religion, I availed myself of the opportunity to express to them the main articles of the Christian faith, and as I was depicting in lively colors the torments of hell, and had told them that the Great Spirit had kindled this fire of his wrath, for those who did not keep the commandments I had explained to them, one of the Chiefs uttered a horrid shriek. "If this be the case," said he, "then I believe there are but two in the whole nation who will not go to that place; it is the Beaver and the Mink; they are the only Crows who never stole, who never killed, nor committed all the excesses which your law prohibits. Perhaps I am deceived, and then we must all go together." When I left them on the next day, the Chief put a fine bell on my horse's neck, and invited me to take a turn round the village. Next, he accompanied me for six miles.

After several days of a painful journey over rocks and cliffs, we arrived at last at the fort of the Crows. It is the first the American Fur Company possessed in that country.

My dear Flat-heads edified all the inhabitants by their fervor and their piety. As well in the fort, as on the road, we never missed performing in common, our evening and morning devotions, and singing canticles in honor of the Almighty. Frequently, during my stay with them, they had given me abundant proofs of their trust in Providence. I cannot forbear mentioning one instance that occurred during my travels in this place. One day as dinner was preparing and provisions scarce, a countryman of mine, who accompanied me, suggested the propriety of keeping something in reserve for supper. "Be not uneasy," said the chief, called Ensyla, "I never missed my supper in my life. I trust in the mercy of the Great Spirit, he will provide for all our wants." We had just camped at night, when the chief killed two stags. "Did I not tell you right?" he remarked, smilingly, to my companion. "You see the Great Spirit does not only provide for our wants of this evening, but he gives us also a supply for to-morrow."

Now began the most difficult and most perilous part of our journey. I had to pass through a country supposed to be overrun by war parties, of the Black-feet, Assineboins, Gros Ventres, Arikaras, and Sioux. All these nations entertained the most hostile dispositions towards the Flatheads. I therefore dispensed with their services any farther. I again excited them to continue the good work they had begun; to be steadfast in their faith; regular in their devotions; charitable towards one another. I embraced them all and took my leave. Mr. John de Velder, a native of Ghent in Belgium, had volunteered his services to me at the Rendezvous. In consideration of the bad state of my health, I deemed myself very happy to accept of them; he has never left me since. He was now to be my only travelling companion. As there is no road, we followed the direction of the river; at intervals we were obliged to make immense circuits to avoid the steep and craggy hills that defied our passage. For two hundred miles, we had continually death before our eyes. On the second day, I discovered before daylight a large smoke at a distance of about a quarter of a mile. We hastily saddled our horses and following up a ravine we gained a high bluff unperceived. At night we did not dare to make fire for fear of attracting notice. Again about dinner time, we found on the road the carcase of a Buffalo, killed only two hours before; the tongue and the marrow bones with some other dainty pieces had been taken away. Thus the kind providence of our God took care to supply our wants.

We took a direction contrary to the tracks of the Indians, and spent a safe night in the cliffs of the rocks. The next day we struck upon a spot where forty lodges had been encamped, the fires were yet in full blaze.

Finally, we crossed the Missouri at the same place where, only an hour before, a hundred lodges of ill-minded Assineboins had passed, and we arrived safe and unmolested at Fort Union, situated a few miles above the mouth of the Yellow Stone. In all these Forts great harmony and union prevail; Mr. Kipps, the present administrator of them, is a gentleman well worthy of his station. Every where I was treated by these gentlemen with the greatest politeness and kindness, and all my wants were liberally supplied. As I was relating the particulars of this dangerous trip to an Indian Chief, he answered: " The Great Spirit has his Manitoos; he has sent them to take care of your steps and to trouble the enemies that would have been a nuisance to you." A Christian would have said: Angelis suis mandavit de te, ut custodiant te in omnibus viis tuis.*

---

* " He has given his angels charge of thee, that they guard thee in all thy ways."

On 23d of September we set out for the village of the Mandans, in company with three men of the fort, who had the same destination. We met on the road a party of 19 Assineboins, who were returning to their country from an unsuccessful expedition against the Gros Ventres. Their looks indicated their bad intentions: although we were but five in number, we showed a determined countenance, and we passed unmolested. Next day we crossed a forest, the winter quarters of the Gros Ventres, and Arikaras, in 1835. It was there that those unfortunate tribes were nearly exterminated by the small pox. We saw their bodies wrapped up in Buffalo robes, tied to the branches of the largest trees. It was truly a sad and mournful spectacle. Two days later we met the miserable survivors of these unhappy tribes. Only ten families of the Mandans, once such a powerful nation, now remain. They have united with the Gros Ventres and Arikaras. They received me with great demonstrations of friendship; I spent that night in their camp, and the next day crossed the Missouri in their canoe, made of a buffalo skin. The next day we came to the first village of the Arikaras, and on the following day to their great village, consisting of about a hundred earthen wig-wams. This tribe also received me very kindly. On the 6th of October we started from the Mandan village, for Fort Pierre, on the little Missouri; a Canadian, whose destination lay in the same direction, accompanied us. The Commandant of the Fort had recommended to us in a special manner to be on our guard against the Jantonnois, the Santees, Jantous, Ankepatines, Ampapas, Ogallallas, and Black-feet Scioux, who have often proved very troublesome to white strangers. On the third day of our journey we fell in with an ambuscade of the Jantonnois and Santees; they did not do us any harm, but on the contrary treated us very kindly, and at our departure loaded us with provisions. The next day we fell in with several other parties, who showed us much kindness. On the ninth day we were on the lands of the Black-feet Scioux; this country is undulating and intersected with numberless little streams. For greater caution we travelled in ravines. Towards dinner time, a fine landscape, near a delicious spring, seemed to invite us to take some repose. We had scarcely alighted, when all on a sudden a tremendous yell alarmed us, and from the top of the hill under which we were, the Black-feet darted upon us like lightning. " Why do you hide yourselves?" asked the Chief, in a stern voice. " Are you afraid of us?" Dressed in my cassock with a crucifix on my breast,—a costume I always wear in the Indian country,—it appeared to me that I was the subject of his particular enquiry. He asked the Canadian what kind of a man I was. The Frenchman said I was a Chief, a Black-gown, the man who spoke to the Great Spirit. He assumed immediately a milder countenance, ordered his men to lay down their arms, and we performed the ceremonies of shaking hands and smoking the calmut of peace. He then invited me to accompany them to the village, situated only at a short distance. It consisted of about a thousand souls. I pitched my tent at some distance, in a beautiful pasture, on the margin of a fine stream, and invited the great chief to partake of a supper with me. As I said grace before meal, he enquired of the Canadian what I was about. He is addressing the Great Spirit, was the reply, in gratitude for the food he has granted us. The chief nodded a sign of approbation. Shortly after, twelve warriors, in full costume, stretched a large buffalo robe before the place where I sat. The chief, taking me by the arm, invited me to sit down. I was under the impression that there was question again of smoking the calmut. Judge of my astonishment, when the twelve warriors, seizing each a piece of the robe, took me up, and headed by their chief, carried me in triumph to their village. In the lodge of the great chief the most conspicuous place was assigned me, and he addressed me thus: "This day is the happiest of my life. For the first time do we behold among us a man who is so closely united with the Great Spirit. Black-gown, you see before you the chief warriors of my tribe; I have invited them to this feast, in order that they may keep the remembrance of your coming among us as long as they shall live." Then he invited me to speak again to the Great Spirit, (to say grace) I began in the name of the Father and of the Son, etc., and immediately all present lifted up their hands towards heaven; when I had concluded they all struck the ground. I asked the chief what they meant by this ceremony. "When we lift up our hands," said he, "we signify that all our dependence is on the Great Spirit, and that he in his fatherly care provides for all our wants: we strike the ground to signify that we are only worms and miserable creeping beings in his sight." He asked me in his turn, what I had told to the Great Spirit. Unhappily, the Canadian was a poor interpreter, still I endeavored to make them understand, as well as I could, the Lord's Prayer. The chief showed great eagerness to know what I said.— He ordered his son and two other very intelligent young men to accompany me to the fort, in order to learn the principles of the Christian doctrine, and to be at the same time a safeguard against the Indians who might be inimically disposed towards us. Two days afterwards we met an Indian, whose horse was bending under a load of buffalo meat. Seeing us without provisions, he requested us to accept what we might stand in need of, advising us to take the whole, for, said he, in the vicinity of the fort, game is very scarce. Five days aftewards we arrived at Fort Pierre. Thence I travelled through prairies for nineteen days successively. We were often obliged to cook our victuals with dried herbs—not a stick was to be found. When I arrived at Fort Vermillion, I was apprised that the Santees had been on a warlike expedition against the Pottawatomies, of the Council Bluffs, among whom I had labored the two preceding years.

I invited them to a council, and gave them a severe reprimand for violating the solemn promise they had made me the preceding year, of living with their neighbors on amicable terms. I showed them the injustice of attacking a peaceable nation without being provoked; the dreadful consequences of the Pottawatomies' revenge, that might end in the extinction of their tribe. I was requested to be once more the mediator, and they told me that they had resolved to bury the tomahawk forever.

I had lost two horses on the road; the one I was riding could hardly support me any longer, and I was yet three hundred miles distance from the Council Bluffs. I resolved of course to embark on the Missouri, and engaged a native Iroquois to be my pilot. At first we were favored with fine weather, but this lasted only a few days. Very soon inclement weather set in with frost and snow; and several times as we drifted down the rapid stream, our frail canoe was on the point of being dashed to pieces against the numberless snags that obstruct its navigation. This dangerous trip lasted ten days. We generally spent the night on a sand bar. We had only a few frozen potatoes left when we perceived a beautiful deer gazing at us, and apparently waiting to receive its mortal blow. We shot at it.

At last we arrived safe at the bluffs, and on the same night the river was closed by ice.

So many escapes from the midst of so many dangers thoroughly convinced me that this undertaking is the work of God—omnia disponens fortiter et ad finem suam conducens suaviter. (Who reacheth from end to end mightily, and ordereth all things sweetly.) I am now preparing for my return, and will start early in Spring, accompanied by three Fathers and as many Brothers. You are aware such expeditions cannot be undertaken without the necessary means, and the fact is, I have no other reliance than Providence and the kindness of my friends. I hope they will not be wanting. I know that you must feel deeply interested in this meritorious good work, I therefore take the liberty of recommending it to your generosity, and that of your friends—every little contribution will help. I will be very grateful to you, if you have the kindness to forward to my address at the St. Louis University, Mo., before the end of March, or middle of April, the amount you have collected.

I recommend myself and my dear Neophytes to your good prayers and holy sacrifices, and rest assured that we shall not forget our benefactors.

P. J. De Smet, S. J.

LETTER II.

TO THE REV. FATHER ROOTHAAN, GENERAL OF THE SOCIETY OF JESUS.

University of St. Louis, 7th Feb. 1841.

Very Rev. Father:

In a letter, which I suppose has been communicated to you, I informed the Bishop of St. Louis of the results, as far as they bear on religion, of my journey to the *Rocky Mountains*. But that letter, though lengthy, could give you but a very imperfect idea of the desert which I passed six months in traversing, and of the tribes who make it the scene of their perpetual and sanguinary rivalship. It will, therefore, I think, be useful to resume the history of my mission; and I repeat it the more willingly, since I am called to penetrate again into those deep solitudes, from which, I may, perhaps, never return. To my brethren, who take an interest in my dear Indians, I owe an account of all my observations upon their character and customs, upon the aspect and resources of the country they inhabit, and upon their dispositions, that they may know how far they are favorable to the propagation of the Gospel.

We arrived the 18th of May upon the banks of the *Nebraska*, or *Big Horn*, which is called by the French by the less suitable name of the *Flat River*. It is one of the most magnificent rivers of North America. From its source, which is hidden among the remotest mountains of this vast continent, to the river Missouri, of which it is a tributary, it receives a number of torrents descending from the

Rocky Mountains; it refreshes and fertilizes immense vallies, and forms at its mouth the two great geographical divisions of the upper and lower Missouri. As we proceeded up this river, scenes more or less picturesque opened upon our view. In the middle of the Nebraska, thousands of islands, under various aspects, presented nearly every form of lovely scenery. I have seen some of those isles, which, at a distance, might be taken for flotillas, mingling their full sails with verdant garlands, or festoons of flowers; and as the current flowed rapidly around them, they seemed, as it were, flying on the waters, thus completing the charming illusion, by this apparent motion. The tree which the soil of these islands produces in the greatest abundance, is a species of white poplar, called cotton tree; the savages cut it in winter, and make of the bark, which appears to have a good taste, food for their horses.

Along the banks of the river, vast plains extend, where we saw, from time to time, innumerable herds of wild Antelopes. Further on, we met with a quantity of buffaloes' skulls and bones, regularly arranged in a semicircular form, and painted in different colors. It was a monument raised by superstition, for the Pawnees never undertake an expedition against the savages who may be hostile to their tribe, or against the wild beasts of the forest, without commencing the chase, or war, by some religious ceremony, performed amidst these heaps of bones. At the sight of them our huntsmen raised a cry of joy; they well knew that the plain of the buffaloes was not far off, and they expressed by these shouts the anticipated pleasure of spreading havoc among the peaceful herds.

Wishing to obtain a commanding view of the hunt, I got up early in the morning and quitted the camp alone, in order to ascend a hillock near our tents, from which I might fully view the widely extended pasturages. After crossing some ravines, I reached an eminence, whence I descried a plain, whose radius was about twelve miles, entirely covered with wild oxen. You could not form, from any thing in your European markets, an idea of their movement and multitude. Just as I was beginning to view them, I heard shouts near me; it was our huntsmen, who rapidly rushed down upon the affrighted herd—the buffalos fell in great numbers beneath their weapons. When they were tired with killing them, each cut up his prey, put behind him his favorite part, and retired, leaving the rest for the voracity of the wolves, which are exceedingly numerous in these places, and they did not fail to enjoy the repast. On the following night I was awakened by a confused noise, which, in the fear of the moment, I mistook for impending danger. I imagined, in my first terror, that the Pawnees, conspiring to dispute with us the passage over their lands, had assembled around our camp, and that these lugubrious cries were their signal of attack.— "Where are we," said I, abruptly, to my guide. "Hark ye!—Rest easy," he replied, laying down again in his bed; "we have nothing to fear; it is the wolves that are howling with joy, after their long winter's hunger: they are making a great meal to-night on the carcasses of the buffalos, which our huntsmen have left after them on the plain."

On the 28th, we forded the southern arm of the river Platte. All the land lying between this river and the great mountains is only a heath, almost universally covered with lava and other volcanic substances. This sterile country, says a modern traveller, resembles, in nakedness and the monotonous undulations of its soil, the sandy deserts of Asia. Here no permanent dwelling has ever been erected, and even the huntsman seldom appears in the best seasons of the year. At all other times the grass is withered, the streams dried up; the buffalo, the stag, and the antelope, desert these dreary plains, and retire with the expiring verdure, leaving behind them a vast solitude completely uninhabited. Deep ravines, formerly the beds of impetuous torrents, intersect it in every direction, but now-a-days the sight of them only adds to the painful thirst which tortures the traveller. Here and there are heaps of stones, piled confusedly like ruins; ridges of rock, which rise up before you like impassible barriers, and which interrupt, without embellishing, the wearisome sameness of these solitudes. Such are the Black Hills; beyond these rise the Rocky Mountains, the imposing land-marks of the Atlantic world. The passes and vallies of this vast chain of mountains afford an asylum to a great number of savage tribes, many of whom are only the miserable remnants of different people, who were formerly in the peaceable possession of the land, but are now driven back by war into almost inaccessible defiles, where spoliation can pursue them no further.

This desert of the West, such as I have just described it, seems to defy the industry of civilized man. Some lands, more advantageously situated upon the banks of rivers, might, perhaps, be successfully reduced to cultivation; others might be turned into pastures as fertile as those of the East—but it is to be feared that this immense region forms a limit between civilization and barbarism, and that bands of malefactors, organised like the Caravans of the Arabs, may here practise their depredations with impunity. This country will, perhaps, one day, be the cradle of a new people, composed of the ancient savage races, and of that class of adventurers, fugitives and exiles, that society has cast forth from its bosom—a heterogeneous and dangerous population, which the American Union has collected like a portentous cloud upon its frontiers, and whose force and irritation it is constantly increasing, by transporting entire tribes of Indians from the banks of the Mississippi, where they were born, into the solitudes of the West, which are assigned as their place of exile. These savages carry with them an implacable hatred towards the whites, for having, they say, unjustly driven them from their country, far from the tombs of their fathers, in order to take possession of their inheritance. Should some of these tribes hereafter form themselves into hordes, similar to the wandering people, partly shepherds, and partly warriors, who traverse with their flocks the plains of Upper Asia, is there not reason to fear, that in process of time, they with others, may organize themselves into bands of pillagers and assassins, having the fleet horses of the prairies to carry them; with the desert as the scene of their outrages, and inaccessible rocks to secure their lives and plunder?

On the 4th of June we crossed the Ramee, a tributary river of the Platte. About forty tents erected on its banks, served as dwellings for a part of the tribe of the Sheyennes. These Indians are distinguishable for their civility, their cleanly and decent habits. The men, in general, are of good stature, and of great strength; their nose is aquiline, and their chin strongly developed. The neighboring nations consider them the most courageous warriors of the prairies. Their history is the same as that of all the savages who have been driven back into the West—they are only the shadow of the once powerful nation of the Shaways, who formerly lived upon the banks of the Red River. The Scioux, their irreconcilable enemies, forced them, after a dreadful war, to pass over the Missouri, and to retreat behind the Warrican, where they fortified themselves; but the conquerors again attacked them, and drove them from post to post, into the midst of the Black Coasts, situate upon the waters of the Great Sheyenne River. In consequence of these reverses, their tribe, reduced to two thousand souls, has lost even its name, being now called Sheyennes, from the name of the river that protects the remnant of the tribe. The Sheyennes have not since sought to form any fixed establishment, lest the Scioux should come again to dispute with them the lands which they might have chosen for their country. They live by hunting, and follow the buffalo in his various migrations.

The principal warriors of the nation invited me to a solemn banquet, in which three of the great chief's best dogs were served up to do me honor. I had half a one for my share. You may judge of my embarrassment, when I tell you that I attended one of those feasts at which every one is to eat all that is offered to him. Fortunately, one may call to his aid another guest, provided that the request to perform the kind office be accompanied by a present of tobacco.

In our way from Ramee, the sojourn of the Sheyennes, to the Green River, where the Flat Heads were waiting for me, we successively passed the Black Hills, which owe this name not to the color of the soil and rocks that form them, but to the sombre verdure of the cedars and pines that shadow their sides; the Red Bute, a central point by which the savages are continually crossing, when emigrating to the West, or going up towards the North; and the famous rock, Independence, which is detached, like an outwork, from the immense chain of mountains that divide North America. It might be called the great registry of the desert, for on it may be read in large characters the names of the several travellers who have visited the Rocky Mountains. My name figures amongst so many others, as that of the first priest who has visited these solitary regions. These mountains have been designated the *back-bone* of the world. In fact a fitter appellation could not be given to these enormous masses of granite, whose summit is elevated nearly twenty-four thousand feet above the level of the sea; they are but rocks piled upon rocks. One might think that he beheld the ruins of a world covered, if I may so speak, with a winding-sheet of everlasting snow.

I shall here interrupt the recital of my journey, to give a short account of the different tribes of the mountains, and of the territory they inhabit. I will join with my own personal observations the most correct information that I could possibly obtain.

The Soshonees, or Root-diggers, appeared in great numbers at the common rendezvous, where the deputations from all the tribes assemble every year, to exchange the products of their rude industry. They inhabit the southern part of the Oregon, in the vicinity of California. Their population, consisting of about ten thousand souls, is divided into several parties, scattered up and down in the most uncultivated quarter of the West. They are called Snakes, because in their indigence they are reduced, like such reptiles, to burrow in the earth and live upon roots. They would have no other food if some hunting parties did not occasionally pass beyond the mountains in pursuit of the buffalo, while a part of the tribe proceeds along the banks of the Salmon River, to make provision for the winter, at the season when the fish come up from the sea. Three hundred of their warriors wished, in honor of the whites, to go through a sort of military parade: they were hideously painted, armed with their clubs, and covered over with feathers, pearls, wolves' tails, the teeth and claws of animals and similar strange ornaments, with which each of them had decked himself, according to his caprice. Such as had received wounds in battle, or slain the enemies of their tribe, showed ostentatiously their scars, and had floating, in the form of a standard, the scalps which they won from the conquered. After having rushed in good order, and at full gallop, upon our camp, as if to take it by assault they went several times round it, uttering at intervals cries of joy. They at length dismounted, and came and gave their hands to all the whites in token of union and friendship.

Whilst I was at the rendezvous, the Snakes were preparing for an expedition against the Black-Feet. When a chief is about to wage war, he announces his intention to his young warriors in the following manner. On the evening before his departure, he makes his farewell dance before each cabin; and everywhere receives tobacco, or some other present. His friends wish him great success, scalps, horses, and a speedy return. If he brings back women as prisoners, he delivers them as a prey to the wives, mothers, and sisters of his soldiers, who kill them with the hatchet or knife, after having vented against their unhappy captives the most outrageous insults: " Why are we unable," howl these furies, " to devour the heart of thy children, and bathe in the blood of thy nation !"

At the death of a chief, or other warrior, renowned for his bravery, his wives, children, and relatives cut off their hair: this is a great mourning with the savages. The loss of a parent would seem but little felt, if it only caused his family to shed tears; it must be deplored with blood; and the deeper the incisions, the more sincere is the affection for the deceased. "An overwhelming sorrow," they say, " cannot be vented unless through large wounds." I know not how to reconcile these sentiments respecting the dead with their conduct towards the living. Would you believe that these men, so inconsolable in their mourning, abandon without pity, to the ferocious beasts of the desert, the old men, the sick, and all those whose existence would be a burden to them?

The funeral of a Snake warrior is always performed by the destruction of whatever he possessed; nothing, it seems, should survive him but the recollection of his exploits. After piling up in his hut all the articles he made use of, they cut away the props of the cabin, and set the whole on fire. The Youts, who form a separate people, although they belong to the tribe of the Soshones, throw the body of the deceased upon the funeral pile, together with a hecatomb of his best horses. The moment that the smoke rises in thick clouds, they think that the soul of the savage is flying towards the region of spirits, borne by the *manes* of his faithful coursers; and, in order to quicken their flight, they altogether, raise up frightful yells. But in general, instead of burning the body, they fasten it upon his favourite charger, as on a day of battle; the animal is then led to the edge of a neighboring river, the warriors are drawn up in a semicircular form, in order to prevent his escape; and then, with a shower of arrows, and a universal hurra, they force him to plunge into the current which is to engulf him. They next, with redoubled shouts, recommend him to transport his master without delay to the land of spirits.*

---

* Although this mode of funeral exists amongst the Snakes, it is not, however, common to all the Indian tribes. Amongst the people who live on the borders of lake Abbitibbi, in Lower Canada, as soon as a warrior happens to die, they wrap the body in a shroud, lower it into a grave about a foot and a half deep, and place alongside it a pot, a knife, a gun, and such other articles as are of prime necessity to the savages. Some days after the burial, the relations of the deceased assemble to smoke over his grave. They then hang presents upon the nearest tree, particularly tobacco for the soul of the deceased, which is to come occa-

The Sampeetches are the next neighbours of the Snakes. There is not, perhaps, in the whole world, a people in a

---

sionally and smoke upon the grave, where the body is laid. They suppose that the poor soul is wandering not far from thence, until the body becomes putrified; after which it flies up to heaven. The body of a wicked man, they say, takes a longer time to corrupt than that of a good man; which prolongs his punishment. Such, in their opinion, is the only punishment of a bad life.

In Columbia we find that a different custom prevails. There, so soon as the person expires, his eyes are bound with a necklace of glass beads; his nostrils filled with aiqua (a shell used by the Indians in place of money), and he is clothed in his best suit and wrapped in a winding-sheet. Four posts, fixed in the ground, and joined by cross-beams, support the aerial tomb of the savage: the tomb itself is a canoe, placed at a certain height from the ground, upon the beams I have just mentioned. The body is deposited therein, with the face downwards, and the head turned in the same direction as the course of the river. Some mats thrown upon the canoe finish the ceremony. Offerings, of which the value varies with the rank of the deceased, are next presented to him; and his gun, powder-horn and shot-bag are placed at his sides.

Articles of less value, such as a wooden bowl, a large pot, a hatchet, arrows, &c. are hung upon poles fixed around the canoe. Next comes the tribute of wailing, which husbands and wives owe to each other, and to their deceased parents, and also to their children: for a month, and often longer, they continually shed, night and day, tears, accompanied with cries and groans, that are heard at a great distance. If the canoe happen to fall down in course of time, the remains of the deceased are collected, covered again with a winding-sheet, and deposited in another canoe.— *Extract of a letter from M. Demers, Missionary among the Savages* *****.

Some individuals of other tribes, seen by Father de Smet on his tour, are the following: The Kootenays and the Carriers, with a population of 4,000 souls, the Savages of the Lake, who are computed at about 500, the Cauldrons 600, the Okinaganes 1,100, the Jantons and Santees 300, the Jantonnees 4,500, the Black-Feet Sciouх 1,500, the Two-Cauldrons 800, the Ampapas 2,000, the Burned 2,500, the Lack-Bows 1,000, the Minikomjoos 2,000, the Ogallallees 1,500, the Saoyues 2,000, the Unkepatines 2,000, the Mandans, Big-Bellies, and Arikaras, who have formed of their remnants one tribe, 3,000, the Pierced-Noses, 2,500, the deeper state of wretchedness and corruption; the French commonly designate them "*the people deserving of pity,*" and this appellation is most appropriate. Their lands are uncultivated heaths; their habitations are holes in the rocks, or the natural crevices of the ground, and their only arms, arrows and sharp-pointed sticks. Two, three, or at most four of them may be seen in company, roving over their sterile plains in quest of ants and grasshoppers, on which they feed. When they find some insipid root, or a few nauseous seeds, they make, as they imagine, a delicious repast. They are so timid, that it is difficult to get near them; the appearance of a stranger alarms them; and conventional signs quickly spread the news amongst them. Every one, thereupon, hides himself in a hole; and in an instant this miserable people disappear and vanish like a shadow. Sometimes, however, they venture out of their hiding places, and offer their newly born infants to the whites in exchange for some trifling articles.

I have had the consolation of baptizing some of these unfortunate beings, who have related to me the sad circumstances which I have just mentioned. It would be easy to find guides among these new converts, and be introduced

---

Kayuses 2,000, the Walla-Wallas 500, the Palooses 300, the Spokanes 800, the Pointed-Hearts 700, the Crows, the Assinboins, the Ottos, the Pawnees, the Santees, the Renards, the Aonays, the Kikapoux, the Delawares, and the Shawanons, whose numbers are unknown. The following are the names of the principal chiefs, who received the Missionary in their tents: The Big-Face and Walking-Bear, the Patriarchs of the Flat-Heads and Ponderas; the Iron-Crow, the Good-Heart, the Dog's-Hand, the Black-Eyes, the Man that does not eat cow's flesh, and the Warrior who walks barefooted; the last named is chief of the Black-Feet Scioux.

by them to their fellow countrymen, to announce to them the Gospel, and thus to render their condition, if not happy, at least supportable through the hope of a better futurity. If God allows me to return to the Rocky Mountains, and my superiors approve of it, I shall feel happy to devote myself to the instruction of these *pitiable people*.

The country of the Utaws is situated to the east and south east of the Soshonees, at the sources of the Rio Colorado. The population consists of about 4,000 souls. Mildness, affability, simplicity of manners, hospitality towards strangers, constant union amongst themselves, form the happy traits in their character. They subsist by hunting and fishing, and on fruits and roots; the climate is warm, and the land very fit for cultivation.

I shall join to this account a brief exposition of the belief of the savages. Their religious tenets are composed of a few primitive truths and of gross errors: they believe in the existence of a Supreme Being, the source of every good, and consequently that he alone is adorable; they believe that he created whatever exists, and that his providence over-rules the principal events of life, and that the calamities which befall the human race are chastisements inflicted by his justice on our perversity. They suppose, that with this, their God, whom they call the *Great Spirit*, there exists an evil genius, who so far abuses his power as to oppress the innocent with calamities. They also believe in a future life, where every one shall be treated according to his works; that the happiness reserved for the virtuous will consist in the enjoyment of such goods as they most anxiously desired upon earth; and that the wicked shall be punished by suffering, without consolation, the torments invented by the spirit of evil. According to their opinion, the soul, upon its entry into the other world, resumes the form which our bodies have had in the present life.*

---

* A Canadian Missionary, who lived for a long time among the savages, gives the following account of the popular tradition of the Indians respecting the creation of the world:—"Water, they say, was every where formerly; and Wiskain, a spirit, or subordinate deity, commanded the castor to dive into it, in order to procure some earth. The castor obeyed the order, but he was so fat that he could not possibly descend to the bottom, and he had to return without any earth. Wiskain, nothing discouraged, charged the musk-rat with the commission which the castor was unable to perform. The new messenger having remained a long while under water, and with as little success as the castor, returned almost drowned. The rat expected that he should not be required a second time, as he had already nearly lost his life. But Wiskain, who was not discouraged by obstacles, directed the rat to dive again, promising him, that if he should happen to be drowned, he (Wiskain) would restore him to life. The rat dived a second time, and made the greatest efforts to comply with Wiskain's orders. After remaining a considerable while under the water, he arose to the surface, but so exhausted by fatigue that he was insensible. Wiskain, upon a careful and minute examination, finds at length in the claws of the poor animal a little earth, upon which he breathes with such effect, that it begins to augment rapidly. When he had thus blown for a long time, feeling anxious to know if the earth was large enough, he ordered the crow, which at that period was as white as the swan, to fly round it, and take its dimensions. The crow did accordingly, and returned, saying that the work was too small. Wiskain set about blowing upon the earth with renewed ardour, and directed the crow to make a second tour round it, cautioning him, at the same time, not to feed upon any carcass that he might see on the way. The crow set off again without complaint, and found, at the place which had been pointed out, the carcass which he was forbidden to touch. But, having grown hungry on the way, and being also, perhaps, excited by gluttony, he filled himself with the infected meat, and on his return to Wiskain, informed him that the earth was large enough, and that he need not, therefore, resume his work. But the unfaithful messenger, at his return, found himself as black as he had been white at his setting out, and was thus punished for his disobedience, and the black colour communicated to his descendants." The above tradition, which bears some striking vestiges of the tradition respecting original sin,

What I am going to add applies chiefly to the tribe that I have been lately instructing. Besides my escort of Flat Heads, I had also with me an intrepid Fleming, John Baptist de Velder, who formerly served as a grenadier under Napoleon. From the battle fields of Europe he betook himself to the forests of the New World, where he has passed thirty years of his life in pursuit of beavers and bears. During the Missionary's journey, he was his devoted friend, and the faithful companion of his dangers. He has now taken the resolution to traverse the desert only as a guide to the apostles of the Gospel. He had almost forgotten his native language, except his prayers, and a hymn in honour of Mary, which his mother taught him when a child, and which he daily recited, when engaged in the adventurous chase.

I found the Flat Heads and the Ponderas assembled, to the number of sixteen hundred, in the beautiful Peters' Valley. You know already the reception they gave me, and I shall never forget it. The enthusiastic joy with which they welcomed my arrival—the exulting shouts of the young warriors—the tears of the aged, returning thanks to the Great Spirit, for having granted them the favour to see and hear a Black-Gown before their death—that scene, I repeat it, I can never forget. I shall not recount the religious exercises of my mission, as the consoling results of them have been already communicated to you. You will,

---

and several circumstances of the deluge, makes no mention whatever of the creation of man and woman; and, however illogical it may be, it is, perhaps, not more ridiculous than the systems of certain pretended philosophers of the last century, who, in hatred of revelation, have endeavoured to explain the formation of the earth, by substituting their extravagant reveries for the Mosaic account.

perhaps, take an interest in reading the notes I have collected regarding the character and habits of my neophytes during a sojourn of three months amongst them; living like them, by the chase and on roots, having only a buffalo's hide for my bed, passing my nights under the canopy of heaven, when the weather was calm, or taking shelter under a small tent against the fury of the tempest.

With regard to the character of these Indians, it is entirely pacific. They never fight, except in circumstances of lawful defence; but they are, unfortunately, often reduced to this said necessity, in consequence of the warlike temper of the Black Feet tribe, who are their neighbours and implacable enemies. That marauding people appear to live only for murder and pillage. They are the terror of the savages of the west, who endeavour, as much as possible, to avoid their fatal encounter. But should the Flat Heads, notwithstanding such precaution, be forced to fight, their courage is as conspicuous as their love of peace; for they rush impetuously on their adversaries, whom they prevent from escaping, and generally make them pay dear for their cruel attacks.

It is a truth which has become proverbial in the mountains, that one Flat Head, or one of the Ear Rings, is worth four Black Feet. If the band of the latter meets a detachment of Flat Heads, of equal or superior numbers, they forthwith appear disposed for peace, unfurl a standard, and present a pipe, in token of friendship. The Flat Heads always accept these tokens of amity; but they take care to make their enemies sensible that the motives which influence their conduct on such occasions are fully understood. "Black Foot," they say, "I take your pipe, but be assured that I am aware that your heart is disposed for war, and that your hands are stained with murder. Let us smoke together, as you desire it, though I am convinced that blood will soon be made to flow."

The greatest reproach that could be made to the Flat Heads was their excessive love for games of chance, in which they often risked all they possessed. The Indians of Colombia carried this passion to an almost inconceivable degree; for, after losing their goods, they would stake their own persons, at first playing for one hand, then for the other; and if the game continued unfavorable to them, they played successively for every one of their limbs, and, lastly, for their head, which, if they lost, they, together with their wives and children, became slaves for life.

The government of the nation is confided to chiefs, who have merited this title by their experience and exploits, and who possess more or less influence, according to the degree of wisdom and courage they have displayed in council or battle. The chief does not command, but seeks to persuade; no tribute is paid to him, but, on the contrary, it is one of the appendages of his dignity to contribute more than any other to the public expense. He is generally one of the poorest in the village, in consequence of giving away his goods for the relief of his indigent brethren, or for the general interests of his tribe. Although his power has nothing imperious in it, his authority is not the less absolute; and it may, without exaggeration, be asserted, that his wishes are complied with as soon as known. Should any mutinous individual be deaf to his personal command, the public voice would soon call him to account for his obstinacy. I know not of any government where so much personal liberty is united with greater subordination and devotedness.

All the mountain tribes differ somewhat from each other in their dress. The men wear a long robe, made of the skins of the antelope or sheep, with shoes and gaiters of doe or dog's skin, and a buffalo hide cloak, covered with woollen cloth, painted in various colours. The Indian loves to add ornament to ornament: his long hair is decked with various kinds of feathers, and a great number of ribbands, rings and shells. In order to give suppleness to his limbs, he rubs his body with bear's grease, over which he spreads a thick layer of vermillion. Children under seven years of age are scarcely ever clothed, except in winter; they are afterwards dressed in a sort of tunic, made of skins, which is open under the arms. They spend whole days amusing themselves in the water, and sometimes even in the mire. The women wear a large pelerine, adorned with elks' teeth and several rows of pearls. Amongst the Arikaras, their grand dress consists of a fine chemise, with doe-skin shoes and gaiters, embroidered in brilliant colours. A quiver filled with arrows is suspended from the left shoulder; and a cap of eagles' feathers adorns the brow of warriors and huntsmen. He that has killed an enemy on his own land is distinguished by having the tails of wolves tied on his legs; the bear-killer wears, for a trophy, the claws of that animal as a necklace; the privilege of a savage who has taken in battle one or more scalps, is to have a red hand painted on his mouth, to show that he has drunk the lood of his enemies. The Indian is not less proud of his horse, the companion of all his excursions and of all his dangers, and the friend to which he becomes extremely attached. The head, breast, and the flanks of the noble animal are covered with scarlet cloth, adorned with pearls and fringes, to which are attached a multitude of little round bells. Cleanliness is a quality not possessed by the savage, nor are the women more particular in this respect than the men; for they never wash their pots or saucepans; and at their meals they often make use of their straw hats, which have no leaf, instead of bowls.

As I before mentioned, the only prevailing vice that I found amongst the Flat Heads was a passion for games of chance—it has since been unanimously abolished. On the other hand, they are scrupulously honest in buying and selling. They have never been accused of stealing. Whenever any lost article is found, it is immediately given to the chief, who informs the tribe of the fact, and restores it to the lawful owner. Detraction is a vice unknown even amongst the women; and falsehood is particularly odious to them. A forked-tongue (a liar) they say, is the scourge of a people. Quarrels and violent anger are severely punished. Whenever any one happens to fall into trouble, his neighbors hasten to his aid. The gaiety of their disposition adds a charm to their union. Even the stranger is received as a friend; every tent is open to him, and that which he prefers is considered the most honored. In the Rocky Mountains they know not the use of locks or bolts.

In looking at this picture, which is in nowise overdrawn, you will perhaps ask, are these the people whom civilized men call barbarians? We have been too long erroneously accustomed to judge of all the savages by the Indians on the frontiers, who have learned the vices of the whites. And even with respect to the latter, instead of treating them with disdain, it would perhaps be more just not to reproach them with a degradation, of which the example has been given them, and which has been promoted by selfish and deplorable cupidity.

The country inhabited by the Flat Heads is as picturesque as their lives are innocent. We often met in the neighborhood of the several encampments of the tribe, majestic torrents, forests with trees that have been growing for ages, and pastures covered with the *traveller's tea*, which, although trampled by numberless horses, embalms the air with its delightful fragrance. We continually beheld a grand succession of lofty mountains; some delighted the sight by their blooming verdure and the imposing appearance of the woods that crowned their summits, while others, as red as brick, bore the impressions of some great convulsion of nature. At the base of the latter may be seen piled up layers of lava, and at their tops the ancient craters are easily distinguished. One day, as the tribe was proceeding towards the banks of the lake Henry, I felt a desire to ascend to the top of a mountain, situate between the waters of the Colombia and the Missouri, in the hope of discovering the exact place where those two great rivers rise, and the distance between them. I succeeded in finding one of their sources: they form two torrents, which, being divided where they rise, by the distance of scarce a hundred paces, continually diverge as they descend towards the plain. Their course over the rocks presents an enchanting sight: they do not flow along, but roll from cascade to cascade; and nothing is comparable to the beauty of their bounding waters, except the distant noise of their fall, repeated by the echoes of the solitary mountains.

Finding it impossible to get to the highest top of the mountain that overlooks these sources, I stopped when I had reached an elevation of 5,000 feet. I then cast my eyes upon the immense region that lay extended at my feet; I contemplated to myself all the tribes upon the banks of the Missouri, as far as Council Bluffs: I thought on my dear colleagues, who are sent by Providence, like angels of salvation, amongst these savage hordes; and I considered, with mixed feelings of joy and grief, their labors, consolations, and hopes, and how disproportionate is their number to the people requiring the aid of their ministry. Kind people, what futurity awaits thee? Holy Missioners, what recompense is reserved for your self-devotion? I remembered that they and I have in heaven a powerful intercessor, in the illustrious founder of our Society; and in order to interest him in our dear missions, from the summit of that mountain from which I could nearly view them all, I placed them under his protection. I would fain persuade myself that he will not prove forgetful of his followers, who are endeavoring to plant the Gospel in these countries where it has hitherto been unknown. Additional apostolic teachers will come hither to assist us by their zeal, before the vices of civilization and the proselytism of error have multiplied the obstacles to the propagation of that faith which all the savages so anxiously desire to know, and which, like the Flat Heads and the Ponderas, they would practise with gratitude and fidelity.

The 27th of August was the day I fixed upon for my departure. Seventeen warriors, chosen from amongst the bravest of the two nations, and under the command of three chiefs, arrived early in the morning, before the entrance of my cabin.* The council of the ancients appointed them to

---

* As a beautiful specimen of an affecting farewell address, we take from the journal of a Canadian Missionary the following discourse spoken by one of the savages of the Red River, to the Black-Gown who had converted them, when he was about leaving them. After expressing, in the name of all the Indians of his locality, the grief which they felt at the Missionary's departure, he added the following words, which prove their gratitude to the worthy Priest, who had brought to them the truths of salvation, and to the members of the Society for the Propagation of the Faith, whose charity had procured them so great a benefit:—

" Dear Father, you are going to leave us, but we hope to see you again. We are quite sensible that you naturally wish to see your relations and friends, your towns and country—we shall find

serve as my escort while I should be in the country of the Black Feet and of the Crows. Of these two tribes, so hostile to the whites, the former never gives them quarter, and the latter will sometimes spare their lives only to leave them, after having robbed them of every thing, to die of hunger in the desert. As we were liable, every instant, to fall into some ambush, we had scouts sent in all directions to reconnoitre the place and examine the defiles; and the smallest trace of a man having passed before us, was minutely examined. And here we cannot sufficiently admire the wonderful sagacity with which Providence has endowed the savage: he will tell you, from the mere footmarks, the exact day on which the Indian had erected his tent on the spot, and how many men and horses had been there; whether it was a detachment of warriors or a company of hunters, and the nation to which they belong. We selected, every evening, a favorable site for our camp, and raised around it a little fort with the trunks of dry trees, in order to protect ourselves against any surprise during the night.

---

the time of your absence very long, but the winter is soon over.—We conceived it to be our duty to assemble before your departure, and to express our feelings. We shall only say these few words: we formerly led very wicked lives, and we know this day to what destruction we were hastening. There was a thick cloud before our eyes; you have dispersed it; we see the sun. We shall never forget what you have done and suffered for us.—Go now, go and tell the Prayers, those kind Prayers, who take pity on us; who love us without knowing us; and who send as priests; go and tell them that savages know how to remember a benefit; go and tell them that we also pray for them, in the desire which we feel to know them, one day, in the abode of our common Father. Set out, but return and instruct those whom you have baptized: leave us not forever in affliction; depart, and in the meanwhile remember that we are counting the days."

This region is the retreat of grizzly bears, the most terrible animals of the desert, whose strength equals their daring and voracity. I have been assured that by a single stroke of his paw, one of these animals tore away four ribs of a buffalo, which fell dead at his feet. He seldom attacks man, unless when he has been surprised and wounded.— An Indian, however, belonging to my escort, in passing by a thick wood of sallow trees, was assailed by one of these ferocious beasts, that sprung furiously upon his horse, fixed his formidable claws in his back, and brought him to the ground. The horseman fortunately was not mounted at the time, and having his gun in his hand, the bear instantly disappeared in the depths of the forest.

On the 5th of September we crossed a defile, which had been passed shortly before by a numerous troop of horsemen. Whether they were allies or enemies, we had no means to discover. I will here observe, that in these immense solitudes, although the howling of wolves, the hissing of venomous serpents, the roaring of the tiger and the bear be calculated to affright, yet this terror is nothing in comparison with the dread excited in the traveller's soul, upon seeing the fresh tracks of men and horses, or columns of smoke rising in the neighborhood. At such a sight, the escort at once assembles and deliberates; each one examines his fire-arms, sharpens his knife and the point of his arrow, and makes, in a word, every preparation for a resistance, even to death; for, to surrender, in such circumstances, would be to expose one's-self to perish in the most frightful torments. The path that we were following led us to a heap of stones, piled upon a small eminence; they were stained with blood, lately spilt; my escort examined them with a mournful attention. The principal chief, a man possessed of much sense, said to me, in a solemn tone, "Father, I think I ought to give you an explanation of what we are looking at. The Crows are not far off: in two hours we shall see them. If I be not mistaken, we are upon one of their fields of battle; and here their nation must have met with some great loss. This monument has been erected to the memory of the warriors, who fell beneath the blows of their enemies. Here the mothers, wives and daughters of them that died, have been weeping over their tombs. It is customary for the women to tear their faces, to make deep cuts in their legs and arms, and to water these tumulary piles with streams of blood. Had we arrived sooner, we should have heard their cries and funeral lamentations." He was not mistaken, as we immediately perceived a considerable troop of savages at a league's distance. They were the Crows, who were returning to their camp, after having paid the tribute of blood to forty of their warriors, who were massacred two years before by the tribe of the Black Feet. Being at present the allies of the Flat Heads, they received us with transports of joy. There were groups of women with them, and so disfigured as to excite both pity and horror. This scene of grief is renewed every year, when they pass near the tombs of their relations.

The chiefs of the Crows wished to cement, by a great feast, their alliance with the tribe of our neophytes. As the language of the two nations is very different, the conversation was made by signs. I shall endeavor to describe this dumb language, by mentioning to you how a bargain, at which I was present, was concluded. A young Crow, of gigantic size, and clad in his best garments, advanced into the midst of the assembly, leading his horse by the bridle, and placed him before the Flat Head, with whose horse he offered to make an exchange. The Flat Head took no notice of him, and kept in an immovable attitude. The

Crow then placed, successively, at the feet of the seller, his gun, his scarlet mantle, his ornaments, his gaiters, and, lastly, his shoes. The Flat Head then took the horse by the bridle, picked up the clothes, &c., and the sale was concluded without saying a word. The Crow, though so divested, joyfully mounted his new courser, and rode several times round the camp, shouting in triumph, and putting his horse through all his paces.

The principal wealth of the savages of the west consists in horses, of which each chief and warrior possesses a great number, that may be seen grazing about their camp. The horses of the Crows are principally of the Maroon race of the prairies. They have also many horses which they have stolen from the Scioux, the Sheyennes, and other Indians of the south-west, which they had in their turn stolen from the Spaniards of Mexico. The Crows are considered the most indefatigable marauders of the desert; they traverse the mountains in all directions, bringing to one side what they have taken at the other. The name of Atsharoke, or Crow, has been given to them on account of their robberies. They are practised from their infancy in this sort of larceny, and they acquire a surprising dexterity in it; their glory augments with the number of their captures, so that a finished robber is in their eyes a hero. I accompanied for two days, these savages, who, I think, were the finest Indians I had met in all my travels. They passed the whole time in rejoicings and feasting. You will not be scandalized, I trust, when I tell you that I was present at twenty different banquets. I was scarcely seated in one cabin, when I was called to partake of the festive entertainment in another.

We arrived, at last, at the first fort belonging to the Fur Company. The Americans, who have here a trading post, received us most cordially. At this place I was to part with my faithful Flat Heads. I therefore told them, that, having before me a country still more exposed to the incursions of the Black Feet, the Assiniboins, the Big Bellies, the Arikaras, and Sioux, all of whom are declared enemies of their tribe, I would no longer peril their lives, on account of my personal safety; that as for my life, I placed it in the hands of God, and that I felt a persuasion it would be preserved, in order that, accompanied by new Missionaries, I might immediately return to them. I exhorted them for the last time to remain faithful to the Great Spirit. We embraced each other, wishing, mutually, a happy return; and shortly after, accompanied by my faithful Fleming, I disappeared from their sight amidst the solitary defiles. We were to pass over several hundred miles of country, where no road is yet traced, and, like the navigator on the boundless ocean, with no other guide than the compass. For a long time we followed the course of the Yellow Stone, except when perpendicular rocks arrested our progress and obliged us to take a circuit. In many places we discovered forts which the savages are in the habit of raising for defence, or for concealing themselves, when they are at war, or waiting for their prey. Perhaps, at the moment of our passing, they were not without enemies. What a solitude, with its horrors and dangers! but it possesses one real advantage: with death constantly before our eyes, we irresistibly feel, without the possibility of illusion, that we are entirely in the hands of God, without any support but Him, without any other refuge than his paternal providence; it is then easy to make to Him the sacrifice of a life which belongs less to us than to the first savage who wishes to take it, and to form the most generous resolutions of which man is capable. It was really the best spiritual retreat that I made in my life.

The second day of the journey, on awaking, I perceived, at the distance of a quarter of a mile, the smoke of a great fire—a point of a rock was all that separated us from a detachment of Indians. Without a moment's delay we saddled our horses and set off, galloping with all speed along the ravines and beds of dried up torrents. We rode that day, without resting, more than fifteen leagues, and we did not encamp until two hours after sunset, lest the savages, having observed our track, should think of pursuing us.— The same fear prevented us from lighting a fire, which obliged us to dispense with supper. I wrapped myself in my blanket, stretched myself on the grass beside my companion, and having recommended myself to God, I endeavored to beguile hunger by sleep. My grenadier, more courageous than I, soon snored like a steam engine in full play.

The next morning we were on our way at day-break; we advanced with caution, for the country appeared full of danger. Towards mid-day we met a new subject of alarm —we found a buffalo, which had been killed about two hours previously. We thrilled at the sight, when we thought that the enemy was not far off; and yet we had reason to thank the Lord for having prepared the food for our evening meal. The following night we encamped among rocks, which are the retreat of tigers and bears. I have already said that the dens of the wild beasts inspire incomparably less terror to the traveller than the hut of the savage. I this time slept heavily and well. We always commenced our journey early in the morning, and each day had new dangers to face, and to meet occasionally the fresh traces of men and horses. One day we had to cross a field of tents, which had been recently abandoned; the fires were not quite extinguished; but happily we met no one. At length we saw again the Missouri at the very place, where an hour before, a hundred families of the Assiniboins had passed over it. The foregoing is only a sketch of the long and perilous journey which we made from the fort of the Crows to fort Union, situated at the mouth of the Yellow Stone river.

All the country watered by this river abounds in game; I do not think that there is in all America another place better suited for hunting: we were continually amidst vast herds of buffalos; we frequently discovered groups of majestic elks bounding over the plains, whilst clouds, if I may say so, of antelopes were flying before us with the swiftness of the wind. The Ashata, or Big Horn, alone appeared not to be disturbed at our presence: we saw them in groups, reposing on the edges of the precipices, or sporting on the points of the steep rocks. The black-tailed roebuck, so richly dressed in its brown coat, frequently excited our admiration, by its elegant shape, and abrupt, animated movements, in which it appears scarcely to touch the earth with its feet. I have already spoken of the grizzly bears, which are here to be met with in abundance, as well as the wolves, panthers, badgers and wild cats. Often the traveller sees the prairie hen and the cock of the mountain start up from the midst of the heath. The lakes and rivers are covered with swans, geese and ducks: the industrious beaver, the otter, and the muskrat, together with the fishes, are in peaceable possession of their solitary waters.

The Arikaras and the Big Bellies, who had been described to us as most dangerous, received us as friends, whenever we met them on our way. Before setting out for war, they observe a strict fast, or rather they abstain from all food for four days. During this interval their imagination is excited to madness; and, either from the effect of weakness, or the warlike projects which fill their minds, they pretend that they have extraordinary visions. The elders and sages of the tribe are called upon to interpret these reveries; and they pronounce them to be more or less favorable to the undertaking. Their explanations are received as oracles, according to which the expedition is scrupulously regulated. Whilst the preparatory fast endures, the warriors make incisions in their bodies, and bury in the flesh, under the shoulder-blade, pieces of wood, to which they attach leather thongs, by which they are suspended from a stake, fixed horizontally over the brink of a chasm a hundred and fifty feet deep. They even sometimes cut off one or two fingers, which they offer as a sacrifice to the Great Spirit, in order that they may return loaded with scalps.

In a recent expedition against the Scioux, the Arikaras killed twenty warriors of the hostile tribe, and piled up the corpses in the middle of their village. The solemn dance of victory then commenced, at which men, women, the aged, and children assisted. After having celebrated, at length, the exploits of the brave, they rushed, like wild beasts, upon the mangled and bloody bodies of the Scioux, parcelled them amongst themselves, and fixed the hideous trophies to the end of long poles, which they carried in proud triumph around the village.

It is impossible to form an idea of the cruelty that presides over the barbarous revenge of those tribes, who are constantly occupied in mutual destruction. As soon as the savages learn that the warriors of a rival nation have set out for the chase, they unexpectedly attack the enemy's defenceless camp, and massacre the women, old men, and children in the cradle. Wo to the men who are spared; their agony is deferred in order to render it more terrible. At other times they lie in wait in their enemy's path, and allow the detachment to pass on, until they have in their power such a portion of it as must infallibly become their prey; whereupon they raise the death cry, and pour upon the enemy a shower of balls, arrows, and pieces of rock; this movement is the signal of extermination: the battle becomes a massacre: the sights of horror which would freeze the heart of any civilized man, serve only to inflame the fury of the savage: he outrages his prostrate rival, tramples on his mangled carcass, tears off his hair, wallows in his blood with the delight of a tiger, and often devours the quivering limbs of the fallen, while they have scarcely ceased to exist.

Such of the vanquished as have not fallen in the combat are reserved to adorn the triumph, and are conducted prisoners to the village of the conquerors. The women come to meet the returning warriors, amongst whom they seek with anxious looks their husbands and brothers: if they discover them not, they express their grief by terrific howling. One of the warriors soon commands silence; he then gives the details of the fortunate expedition; describes the place selected for the ambuscade, the consternation of the waylaid tribe, the bravery of the assailants, and recounts the number of the dead and of the captives. To this recital, which is made with all the intoxication of victory, succeeds the calling over the names of the warriors: their absence tells they are no more. The piercing cries of the women are then renewed; and their despair presents a scene of frenzy and grief, which exceeds all imagination. The last ceremony is the proclaiming of victory. Every one instantly forgets his own misfortunes; the glory of the nation becomes the happiness of all; by an inconceivable transition, they pass in a moment from frantic grief to the most extravagant joy.

I know not what terms to use in order to describe the torments which they inflict on the wretched prisoners: one plucks off their nails, another tears away their flesh; red hot irons are applied to every part of their bodies; they are flayed alive, and their palpitating flesh is devoured as food. The women, who, in other nations, are more accessible to the feelings of pity than the men, here shew themselves more thirsty for revenge, and more ingenious in the barbarous refinement of cruelty. Whilst this horrible drama goes on, the chiefs are gravely seated about the stake at which the victim is writhing. The latter appears to be only intent on conquering his anguish: often has the prisoner been seen to brave his executioners, and with a stoic coolness exclaim, "I fear not death; those who are afraid of your torments are cowards; a woman of my tribe would despise them. Shame upon my enemies; they have not even the power to force from me a tear. In order to take me, they supplied their weakness by stratagem; and now, to revenge themselves, they have assembled an entire people against one man, and they are unable to triumph over him—the cowards! Oh, if they were in my place, how I would devour them, how I would sip from their accursed skulls the last drop of their blood!"

The great village of the Arikaras is only ten miles distant from that of the Mandans. I was surprised to see around their habitations large and well cultivated fields of maiz. The latter Indians still manufacture earthern vases, similar to those which are found in the ancient tombs of the savages of the United States, and which, according to antiquaries, are presumed to have belonged to a race much more ancient than that which now peoples the desert of the west. The jugglers of the Arikaras enjoy a good reputation, and exercise considerable influence over their credulous countrymen; they pretend to have communication with the spirit of darkness. They will fearlessly plunge their arm into boiling water, having previously rubbed it with a certain root; they also swallow, without any ill effect, substances on fire, as well as shoot arrows against themselves. The following is one of the most singular of their tricks, and one which the Indian sorcerer was unwilling to perform in my presence, because *my medicine* (meaning my religion) *was superior to his*. He had his hands, arms, legs, and feet, tied with well-knotted cords; he was then enclosed in a net, and again in a buffalo's skin. The person who tied him had promised him a horse if he extricated himself from his bonds. In a minute after, the savage, to the amazement of the spectators, stood before him perfectly free. The commandant of the neighbouring fort offered him another horse, if he would reveal to him his secret. The sorcerer consented, saying, "Have thyself tied; I have at my command ten invisible spirits: I will detach three of them and put them at thy service: fear them not, they will accompany thee everywhere, and be thy tutelary genii." The commandant was disconcerted, or unwilling to make the trial, and thus the matter terminated.*

The last observation which I have to make concerns the redoubtable tribe of the Scioux. Whoever, amongst these savages, dies in a quarrel provoked by drunkenness, or as

---

* Juggleries are much practised among the savages, although many of them consider them as so many impostures. Mr. Belcourt, who witnessed a great many of them, always succeeded in discovering the deception. One of the most celebrated jugglers acknowledged, after his conversion to Christianity, that all their delusion consists in their cleverness in preparing certain tricks, and in the assurance with which they predict to others what they themselves know not, and, above all, in the silly credulity of their admirers. They are like our own calculators of horoscopes.—*Extract from the Journal of a Missionary in Canada.*

the victim of the revenge of a fellow countryman, receives not the ordinary honours of burial; he is interred without ceremony and without provisions. The most glorious death for them is to expire in fighting the enemies of their nation. Their bodies are, in that case, rolled in buffaloes' skins and placed upon a raised platform, near their camps or highways. From some conversations I have had with the chiefs of this tribe, I have every reason to believe that a mission would produce amongst them the most consoling effects.

I arrived, at length, at Council Bluffs. It would be vain for me to attempt to express what I felt, on finding myself again in the midst of my brethren: I had travelled two thousand Flemish leagues amongst the most barbarous nations, where I had no sooner escaped one danger than I met with another. From Council Bluffs to Westport, a frontier city of the Missouri, I pursued my journey without obstacle or accident. At Independence, I took the public conveyance, and on the eve of the new year, I embraced my dear Fathers of the University of St. Louis.

Recommending myself to your prayers,
    I am yours, &c.
        P. J. DE SMET.

LETTER III.

Banks of the Platte, 2d June, 1841.

Rev. and Very Dear Father Provincial:

Behold us at last on our way towards the long wished for "Rocky Mountains," already inured to the fatigues of the journey and full of the brightest hopes. It is now afternoon and we are sitting on the banks of a river, which, it is said, has not its equal in the world. The Indians call it Nebraska or Big Horn; the Canadians give it the name of la Platte, and Irving designates it as the most wonderful and useless of rivers. The sequel will show that it deserves these various affixes. It was to enjoy the freshness and beauty of its scenery that we travelled more than twenty miles this morning, without breaking our fast, through a wilderness without a single rivulet to water our jaded horses, who must therefore rest where they are till to-morrow. I am far from regretting the delay as it will give me an opportunity of commencing a letter which, I know, will interest you.

Like all the works of God, our humble beginnings have not been unattended with trials: our journey had even well nigh been indefinitely postponed by the unexpected non-arrival of two caravans on which we had confidently relied; one of hunters, for the American Fur Company; the other an exploring expedition belonging to the United States, at the head of which we expected to see the celebrated M. Nicolet. Happily God inspired two estimable travellers, of whom more hereafter, and afterwards sixty others, to take the same route as ourselves, some for health, others for science, or pleasure; but the greater number to seek their fortune in the too highly boasted land of California. This caravan formed an extraordinary mixture of different nations, every country of Europe having in it a representative, my own little band of eleven persons hailing from eight.

The difficulties of setting out once overcome, many others followed in succession. We had need of provisions, firearms, implements of every kind, waggons, guides, a good hunter, an experienced captain,—in a word, whatever becomes necessary when one has to traverse a desert of eight hundred leagues, and expects nothing but formidable obstacles to surmount, and thieving, and sometimes murderous, enemies to combat,—and swamps, ravines and rivers to cross, and mountains to climb, whose craggy and precipitous sides suddenly arrest our progress, compelling us to drag our beasts of burden up their steep ascents. These things are not done without toil and money, but thanks to the generous charity of our friends in Philadelphia, Cincinnati, Kentucky, St. Louis and New Orleans, which place I visited in person and which is always at the head of the others when there is a question of relieving the necessities of the poor, or showing compassion and munificence to any who may be in need of assistance, we were enabled by the resources thence supplied, and by a portion of the funds allowed by the Lyons Association in behalf of the Indian Missions, to undertake this long journey.

You have already learned from my letters of the past year, that I was specially sent among the Flat Heads to ascertain their dispositions towards the " Black Robes," whom they had so long desired. I therefore started from

St. Louis in April, 1840, and arrived on the banks of the Colorado precisely at the moment when a band of Flat Heads reached that point on their way to meet me. It was the rendezvous I had given them. Besides the Flat Heads I visited during that journey, many other tribes, such as the Pends-d'oreilles (Ear Rings), Nez Perces (Pierced Noses), Cheyennes, Serpents, Crows, Gos ventres or Minatarees, Ricaras, Mandans, Kanzas, the numerous nations of the Sioux, &c. Finding every where such good dispositions, I resolved, notwithstanding the approach of winter and frequent attacks of fever, in order to second the visible designs of the divine mercy in favor of so many souls, to commence my journey across the immense ocean of mountains and prairies. I have travelled without any other guide than a compass, without any protection from nations hostile to the whites, but a veteran from Ghent, formerly a grenadier of the Empire, any other provisions in an arid desert, than what powder and ball and a strong confidence in God might procure us. I shall not here repeat what I have already communicated to you, of my adventures and the result of this mission. It will suffice to say, that the unexpected quickness of my return to St. Louis, the excellent health I enjoyed, even though it was the midst of winter, and the consoling accounts I had to give of my reception by the Flat Heads, &c. &c., all contributed to make the most lively impression on the hearts of our brethren. Almost every one thought himself called to share the labors of a mission which offered so many attractions to their zeal. After due deliberation, the fellow-laborers allotted me were five in number, namely two Fathers, Rev. Mr. Point of La Vendee, as zealous and courageous for the salvation of souls as his compatriot, La Roche Jacquelin was in the service of his lawful sovereign; Rev. Mr. Mengarini, recently from

Rome, specially selected by the Father General himself, for this mission, on account of his age, his virtues, his great facility for languages and his knowledge of medicine and music; and three lay-brothers, two Belgians. Claessens and Huet, and one German, of whom the first is a blacksmith, the second a carpenter, and the third a tinner, or a sort of *factotum;* all three industrious, devoted to the Missions and full of good will. They had long ardently desired to be employed on these missions and I thank God that had the choice been left to myself, I could have made none better. Thus launched into the midst of this interminable Far West, how often did I repeat these beautiful lines of Racine:

O Dieu, par quelles routes inconnues aux mortels
Ta Sagesse conduit tes desseins eternels!

In seven days from my departure from St. Louis, namely, on the 30th of April, I arrived at Westport, a frontier town on the West of the United States. It took us seven days, on board a steamboat, to perform this journey of 900 miles, no unfair average of the time required to travel such a distance on the Missouri, at the breaking up of the winter, when, though the ice is melted, the water is still so low, the sand banks so close together and the snags so numerous that boats cannot make greater headway . . . . We landed on the right bank of the river, and took refuge in an abandoned little cabin, where a poor Indian woman had died a few days before, and in this retreat, so like to that which once merited the preference of the Saviour and for which was thenceforth to be substituted only the shelter of a tent in the wilderness, we took up our abode until the 10th May—occupied as well we might be in supplying the wants created by the burning of our baggage waggon on board the steamboat, the sickness of one of our horses which we were compelled to leave after us, and the loss of another that escaped from us at the moment of landing.

We started, then, from Westport, on the 10th of May, and after having passed by the lands of the Shawnees and Delawares, where we saw nothing remarkable but the college of the Methodists, built, it is easy to divine for what, where the soil is richest; we arrived after five day's march on the banks of the Kanzas river, where we found those of our companions, who had travelled by water, with a part of our baggage. Two of the relatives of the grand chief had come twenty miles from that place to meet us, one of whom helped our horses to pass the river in safety, by swimming before them, and the other announced our arrival to the principal men of the tribe who waited for us on the opposite bank. Our baggage, waggons and men crossed in a pirogue, which, at a distance, looked like one of those gondolas that glide through the streets of Venice. As soon as the Kanzas understood that we were going to encamp on the banks of the Soldier's River, which is only six miles from the village, they galloped rapidly away from our Caravan, disappearing in a cloud of dust, so that we had scarcely pitched our tents when the great Chief presented himself with six of his bravest warriors, to bid us welcome. After having made me sit down on a mat spread on the ground, he, with much solemnity, took from his pocket a Portfolio containing the honorable titles that gave him a right to our friendship and placed them in my hands. I read them, and having, with the tact of a man accustomed to the etiquette of savage life, furnished him the means of smoking the Calmet, he made us accept for our guard the two braves who had come to meet us. Both were armed like warriors, one carrying a lance and a buckler, and the other a bow and arrows, with a naked sword and a collar

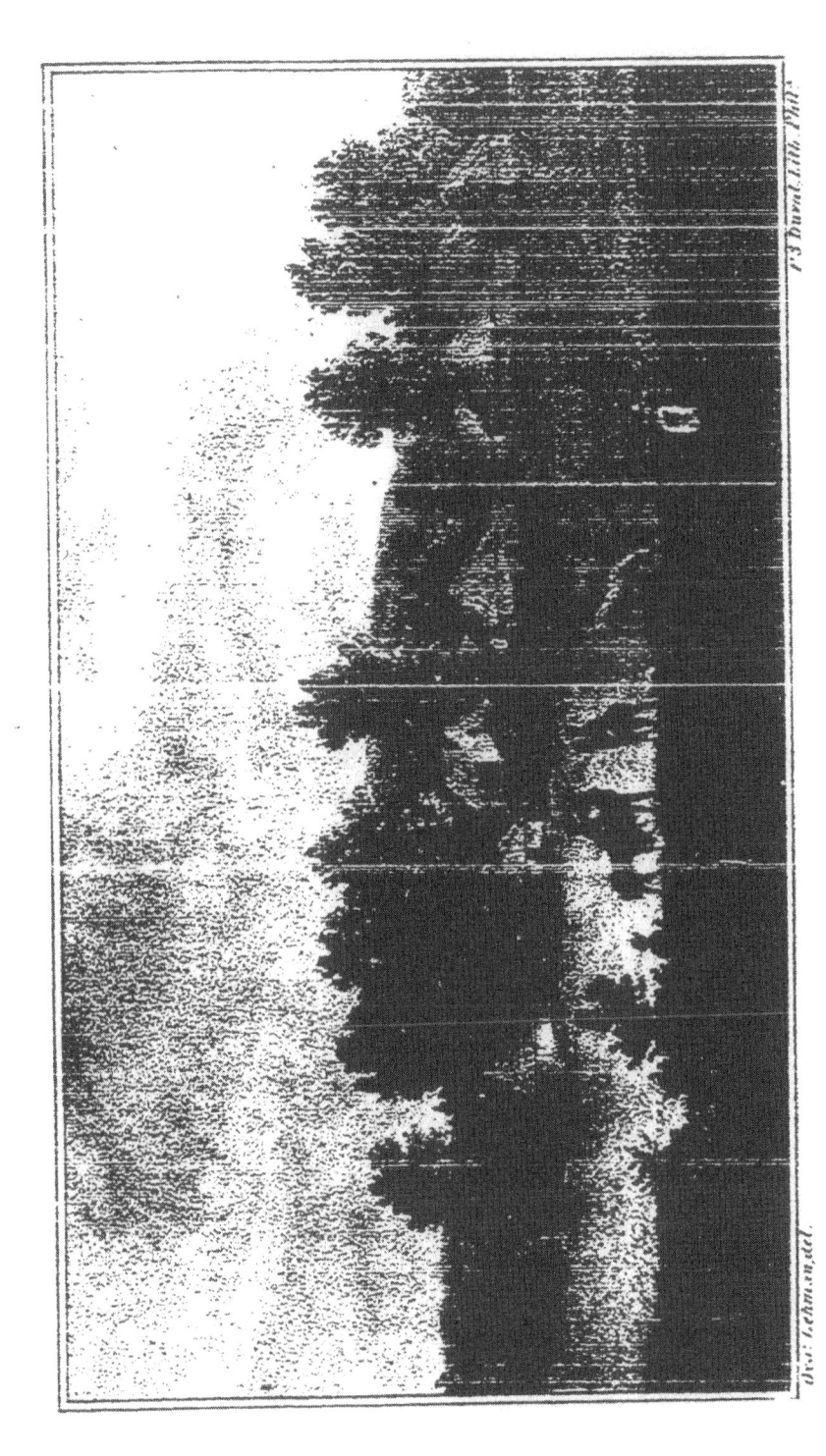

KANZA VILLAGE.

made of the claws of four bears which he had killed with his own hand. These two braves remained faithful at their post during the three days and three nights that we had to wait the coming up of the stragglers of the caravan. A small present which we made them at our departure, secured us their friendship.

On the 19th we continued our journey to the number of seventy souls, fifty of whom were capable of managing the rifle—a force more than sufficient to undertake with prudence the long march we had to make. Whilst the rest of our company inclined to the West, Father Point, a young Englishman and myself turned to the left, to visit the nearest village of our hosts. At the first sight of their wigwams, we were struck at the resemblance they bore to the large stacks of wheat which cover our fields in harvest-time. There were of these in all no more than about twenty, grouped together without order, but each covering a space of about one hundred and twenty feet in circumference, and sufficient to shelter from thirty to forty persons. The entire village appeared to us to consist of from seven to eight hundred souls—an approximation which is justified by the fact that the total population of the tribe is confined to two villages, together numbering 1900 inhabitants. These cabins, however humble they may appear, are solidly built and convenient. From the top of the wall, which is about six feet in height, rise inclined poles, which terminate round an opening above, serving at once for chimney and window. The door of the edifice consists of an undressed hide on the most sheltered side, the hearth occupies the centre and is in the midst of four upright posts destined to support the *rotunda;* the beds are ranged round the wall and the space between the beds and the hearth is occupied by the members of the family, some standing, others sitting or lying on skins, or yellow colored mats. It would seem that this last named article is regarded as a piece of extra finery, for the lodge assigned to us had one of them.

It would be difficult to describe all the curiosities we beheld during the hour we passed among these truly strange beings; a Teniers would have envied us. What most excited our attention was the peculiar physiognomy of the greater number of these personages, their vivacity of expression, singular costume, diversity of amusement and fantastic attitudes and gestures. The women alone were occupied, and in order to attend to their various duties with less distraction, they had placed those of their papooses who were unable to walk, on beds or on the floor, or at their feet, each tightly swathed and fastened to a board, to preserve it from being injured by surrounding objects.—This machine, which I shall not call either cradle or chair, is carried, when they travel, either on the back, after the fashion of the gypsies and fortune-tellers in Europe, or at their side, or more frequently, suspended from the pummel of the saddle, while they lead or drive their ponies, laden with the rest of their goods and chattels. With such encumbrances they manage to keep pace with their husbands, who generally keep their horses at a gallop. But let us return to our wigwam. How were the men occupied? When we entered, some were preparing to eat, (this is their great occupation when they are not asleep) others were smoking, discharging the fumes of the tobacco by their mouths and nostrils, reminding one of the funnels of a steamboat; they talked, they plucked out their beard and the hair of their eye-brows, they made their toilette; the head receiving particular attention. Contrary to the custom of the other tribes, who let the hair on their heads grow, (one of

INTERIOR OF A KANZA LODGE.

the Crows has hair eleven feet long) the Kanzas shave theirs, with the exception of a well curled tuft on the crown, destined to be wreathed with the warrior's plume of eagle's feathers, the proudest ornament with which the human head can be adorned. While we were smoking I could not help watching the motions of a young savage, a sort of dandy, who ceased not to arrange, over and over again, his bunch of feathers before a looking glass, apparently unable to give it the graceful finish he intended.— Father Point, having suffered his beard to grow, soon became an object of curiosity and laughter, to the children—a beardless chin and well picked brows and eye-lashes being, among them, indispensable to beauty. Next come the Plume and Slit-ears, with their pendants of beads and other trinkets. This is but a part of their finery, and the pains thus taken to reach the *beau-ideal* of personal decorations, are but a faint specimen of their vanity. Do you wish to have an idea of a Kanza satisfied with himself in the highest degree? Picture him to yourself with rings of vermillion encircling his eyes, with white, black, or red streaks running down his face, a fantastic necklace, adorned in the centre with a large medal of silver or copper, dangling on his breast; bracelets of tin, copper, or brass, on his arms and wrists; a cincture of white around his waist, a cutlass and scabbard, embroidered shoes or mocasins on his feet; and, to crown all, a mantle, it matters not for the color, thrown over the shoulders and falling around the body in such folds or drapery as the wants or caprice of the wearer may direct, and the individual stands before you as he exhibited himself to us.

As for dress, manners, religion, modes of making war, &c., the Kanzas are like the savages of their neighborhood, with whom they have preserved peaceful and friendly relations from time immemorial. In stature, they are generally tall and well made. Their physiognomy is manly, their language is gutural, and remarkable for the length and strong accentation of the final syllables. Their style of singing is monotonous, whence it may be inferred that the enchanting music heard on the rivers of Paraguay, never cheers the voyager on the otherwise beautiful streams of the country of the Kanzas.

With regard to the qualities which distinguish man from the brute, they are far from being deficient. To bodily strength and courage they unite a shrewdness and address superior to other savages, and in their wars or the chase, they make a dexterous use of fire arms, which gives them a decided advantage over their enemies.

Among the chiefs of this tribe are found men really distinguished in many respects. The most celebrated was " White Plume," whom the author of the Conquest of Grenada represents as a man of great powers of mind and chivalrous character. He was endowed with uncommon intelligence, frankness, generosity and courage. He had been particularly acquainted with Rev. Mr. De la Croix, one of the first Catholic Missionaries that visited that part of the West, and conceived for him and his colleagues, the " Black Robes" profound esteem. His feelings towards the Protestant Missionaries were far different. He had neither esteem nor veneration for them or their reformation. When on a certain occasion one of them spoke to him of conversion; " conversion," said the unsophisticated savage, " is a good thing when the change is made for something good. For my part, I know none such but what is taught and practised by the Black Robes. If then you desire me to change, you must first quit your wife and then put on the habit I shall show you, and then we shall see further." This habit was a priest's cassock, which a missionary had left him with the memory of his virtues.— We presume we need not add that these hard conditions were not complied with by the preacher.

It is not to be inferred from the apparent pleasantry of this remark that the chief spoke lightly of Religion; on the contrary, the Kanzas, like all the Indian tribes, never speak on the subject without becoming solemnity. The more they are observed the more evident does it become that the religious sentiment is deeply implanted in their souls, and is, of all others, that which is most frequently expressed by their words and actions. Thus, for instance, they never take the calmut, without first rendering some homage to the Great Spirit. In the midst of their most infuriate passions they address him certain prayers, and even in assassinating a defenceless child, or a woman, they invoke the Master of life. To be enabled to take many a scalp from their enemies, or to rob them of many horses, becomes the object of their most fervid prayers, to which they sometimes add fasts, macerations and sacrifices. What did they not do last spring, to render the heavens propitious? And for what? To obtain the power, in the absence of their warriors, to massacre all the women and children of the Pawnees! And in effect they carried off the scalps of ninety victims, and made prisoners of all whom they did not think proper to kill. In their eyes, revenge, far from being a horrible vice, is the first of virtues, the distinctive mark of great souls, and a complete vindication of the most atrocious cruelty. It would be time lost to attempt to persuade them that there can be neither merit, nor glory, in the murder of a disarmed and helpless foe. There is but one exception to this barbarous code, it is when an enemy voluntarily seeks a refuge in one of their villages. As long as he remains in it, his asylum is inviolable—his life is more safe than it would be in his own wigwam. But wo to him if he attempt to fly—scarcely has he taken a single step, before he restores to his hosts all the imaginary rights which the spirit of vengeance had given them to his life! However cruel they may be to their foes, the Kanzas are no strangers to the tenderest sentiments of piety, friendship and compassion. They are often inconsolable for the death of their relations, and leave nothing undone to give proof of their sorrow. Then only do they suffer their hair to grow—long hair being a sign of long mourning. The principal chief apologised for the length of his hair, informing us, of what we could have divined from the sadness of his countenance, that he had lost his son. I wish I could represent to you the respect, astonishment and compassion, expressed on the countenances of three others, when they visited our little Chapel for the first time. When we showed them an "Ecce Homo" and a statue of our Lady of the seven Dolours, and the interpreter explained to them that that head crowned with thorns, and that countenance defiled with insults, were the true and real image of a God who had died for the love of us, and that the heart they saw pierced with seven swords, was the heart of his mother, we beheld an affecting illustration of the beautiful thought of Tertullian, that the soul of man is naturally Christian! On such occasions, it is surely not difficult, after a short instruction on true faith and the love of God, to excite feelings of pity for their fellow creatures in the most ferocious bosoms. What were the Iroquois before their conversions, and what have they not since become? Why do the Kanzas and so many other tribes on the confines of civilization, still retain that savage ferocity of manners? Why have the great sums expended in their behalf by Protestant philanthropy produced no satisfactory results? Why are the germs of civilization so thickly scattered among these tribes, as it were, stricken with sterility? Ah! it is doubtless, because something more than human policy and zeal of Protestantism is necessary to civilize the savage and make them Christians. May the God of Mercies, in whom we alone place all our trust, bless our undertaking and enable us to predict that our sweat, mixed with the fertilizing dew of heaven, will fall auspiciously on this long barren earth, and make it produce something else besides briars and thorns! When we took leave of our hospitable hosts, two of their warriors, to one of whom they gave the title of Captain, escorted us a short distance on the road, which lay through a vast field which had been cleared and planted for them by the United States, but which had been ravaged before the harvest home—sad proof of what we have stated above.

Our escort continued with us until the day following, and would have remained with us still longer, did they not fear the terrible reprisals of the Pawnees, for the massacre committed some months previously. Having therefore received our thanks and a portion of tobacco, they resumed the road to their village, just in time to escape the vengeance of a party of Pawnees, whom we met two days later, in quest of the Kanzas!

The Pawnees are divided into four tribes, scattered over the fertile borders of the Platte River. Though six times more numerous than the Kanzas, they have almost on every occasion been conquered by the latter, because they are far inferior to them in the use of arms, and in strength and courage. Yet as the party just mentioned seemed to have adopted decisive measures, and as their thirst of revenge had been stimulated to the highest degree by the still fresh recollection of what their mothers, their wives and children had suffered, we had reason to fear for the Kanzas. Already we fancied that we saw the blood streaming on all sides, when, two days after we had passed them, we saw them return to meet us. The two first who approached us, excited our attention, the one by a human scalp, which hung suspended from the neck of his horse, the other by an American flag, which he had wrapped around his body, in the form of a cloak. This kind of attire made us tremble for the fate of our hosts; but the captain of the caravan having asked them by signs concerning the result of their expedition, they informed us that they had not even seen the enemy, and that they suffered much from the cravings of hunger. We gave to them, and to about fifteen others who followed them, both victuals and tobacco. They devoured the victuals, but did not smoke; and, contrary to the custom of the Indians, who generally expect to get a second meal after the first, they left us in a manner which indicated that they were dissatisfied. The suddenness of their departure, their refusal to smoke the calmut, the unexpected return of their party, the neighborhood of their villages, and their well known love of plunder—in short, every thing induced us to fear that they had some design to make an attempt, if not upon our persons, at least upon the baggage; but, God be praised, not one re-appeared after the departure of the party.

Though addicted to the practice of lying and stealing, yet, what must appear wonderful, the Pawnees are in some respects true believers, with regard to the certainty of a future life, and display a pharisaical punctuality in the observance of their superstitious rites. Dancing and music, as well as fasting, prayer and sacrifice, form an essential part of their worship. The most common worship among them is that which they offer to a stuffed bird, filled with herbs and roots, to which they attribute a supernatural virtue. They protest that this Manitoo had been sent to their ancestors by the Morning Star, to be their mediator when they should stand in need of some particular favor.—Hence, whenever they enter upon some important undertaking, or wish to avert some great evil, they expose the Mediator-bird to public veneration; and in order to render both him and the Great Manitoo (or Spirit) by whom he is sent, propitious to them, they smoke the calmut, and blow the first smoke that issues from it towards the part of the sky where shines their protectress.

On the most solemn occasions, the Pawnees add a bloody sacrifice to the oblation of the calmut; and according to what they pretend to have learned from the bird and the Star, the sacrifice most agreeable to the Great Spirit is that of an enemy immolated in the most cruel manner. It is impossible to listen without horror to the recital of the circumstances that attended the sacrifice of a young female, of the Scioux tribe, in the course of the year 1837. It was about seed time, and they thus sought to obtain a plentiful harvest. I shall here give the substance of the detailed account, which I have given of it in a former letter. This young girl, was only aged fifteen; after having been well treated and fed for six months, under pretence that a feast would be prepared for her at the opening of the summer season, felt rejoiced when she saw the last days of winter roll by. The day fixed upon for the feast having dawned, she passed through all the preparatory ceremonies, and was then arrayed in her finest attire, after which she was placed in a circle of warriors, who seemed to escort her for the purpose of showing her deference. Besides their wonted arms, each one of these warriors had two pieces of wood, which he had received at the hands of the maiden. The latter had on the preceding day carried three posts, which she had helped to fell in the neighboring forest: but supposing that she was walking to a triumph, and her mind being filled with the most pleasing ideas, the victim advanced towards the place of her sacrifice with those mingled feelings of joy and timidity, which, under similar circumstances, are naturally excited in the bosom of a girl of her age.

During their march, which was rather long, the silence was interrupted only by religious songs and invocations to the Master of life, so that whatever affected the senses, tended to keep up the deceitful delusion under which she had been till that moment. But as soon as she had reached the place of sacrifice, where nothing was seen but fires, torches, and instruments of torture, the delusion began to vanish and her eyes were opened to the fate that awaited her. How great must have been the surprise, and soon after the terror which she felt, when she found it no longer possible to doubt of their intentions? Who could describe her poignant anguish? She burst into tears; she raised loud cries to heaven—she begged, entreated, conjured her executioners to have pity on her youth, her innocence, her parents, but all in vain: neither tears, nor cries, nor the promises of a trader who happened to be present, softened the hearts of these monsters. She was tied with ropes to the trunk and branches of two trees, and the most sensitive parts of her body were burnt with torches made of the wood which she had with her own hands distributed to the warriors.—When her sufferings lasted long enough to weary the fanatical fury of her ferocious tormentors, the great chief shot an arrow into her heart; and in an instant this arrow was followed by a thousand others, which, after having been violently turned and twisted in the wounds, were torn from them in such a manner that her whole body presented but one shapeless mass of mangled flesh, from which the blood streamed on all sides. When the blood had ceased to flow, the greater sacrificator approached the expiring victim, and to crown so many atrocious acts, tore out her heart with his own hands, and after uttering the most frightful imprecations against the Scioux nation, devoured the bleeding flesh, amid the acclamations of his whole tribe. The mangled remains were then left to be preyed upon by wild beasts, and when the blood had been sprinkled on the seed, to render it fertile, all retired to their cabins, cheered with the hope of obtaining a copious harvest.

Such horrid cruelties could not but draw down the wrath of heaven upon their nation. And in fact, as soon as the report of the sacrifice reached the Scioux, they burned with the desire to avenge their honor, and swore to a man that they would not rest satisfied till they should have killed as many Pawnees as the young victim had bones in her fingers and joints in her body. More than a hundred Pawnees have at length fallen beneath their tomahawks, and their fury was afterwards more increased by the massacre of their wives and children, of which I have spoken before.

At the sight of so much cruelty, who could mistake the agency of the enemy of mankind, and who would refuse to exert himself for the purpose of bringing these benighted nations to the knowledge of the true Mediator, and of the only true sacrifice, without which, it is impossible to appease the divine justice.

Rev. and dear Father, yours,

P. J. DE SMET, S. J.

LETTER II.

Eau Sucree, 14th July, 1841.

Very Rev. and Dear Father Provincial:

ALREADY two long months have elapsed since we began our journey; but we are at length in sight of those dear mountains that have so long been the object of our desires. They are called Rocky, because they are almost entirely formed of granite and silex, or flint stone. The length, position, and elevation of this truly wonderful chain of mountains, have induced geographers to give to it the appellation of "the back-bone of the western hemisphere." Traversing almost the whole of North America, from north to south, containing the sources of some of the largest streams of the world, this chain has for its branches, towards the west, "the spur of the Cordilleras," which divide the Empire of Mexico, and towards the east the less known but not less wonderful mountains of the Wind River, where are found the sources of the large streams that empty themselves into the Pacific and Atlantic Oceans. The Black Hills and the table lands, called Prairie hills, which separate the sources of the upper Missouri from those of the Mississippi, the Ozark and the Masserne ridges may all be considered as so many collateral chains of the Rocky Mountains.

According to trigonometrical calculations, and observations, made by means of the barometer, Mr. Boneville, in his Memoirs, asserts that the summits of some of these mountains are 25,000 feet high. This height would appear much exaggerated, if we consulted only the testimony of the eyes, but it is well known that the mountains which are found in immense plains, are not unlike ships seen on the ocean; they appear much less elevated than they are in reality. Whatever may be the height of these colossal mountains, it was at their base that we hoped to meet our dear neophytes. But a messenger we had sent to acquaint them with our arrival, has just returned, and informed us that the Indians who lay encamped there, about a fortnight ago, went in a southerly direction to hunt the buffalo. We know not whether those Indians were Flat Heads or belong to another nation, and it is to obtain information on this subject, that we are going to despatch a second messenger. In the mean time, I shall continue my journal. The numerous notes, which, on account of our slow progress, we have been enabled to take on the spot, will warrant that exactness of description, which is the more desirable, as it is a quality frequently wanting in the accounts given of these distant regions. Not to exceed the bounds of a lengthy letter, I shall say but little concerning perspectives, flowers, birds, animals, Indians, and adventures.

With the exception of the mounds which run parallel to each other on both sides of the Platte river, and after passing under the Black Hills, disappear at the base of the Rocky Mountains, the whole plain which we traversed for 1500 miles after we had left Westport, might be called the Prairie Ocean. In fact, nearly the whole of this territory is of an undulating form, and the undulations resemble the billows of the sea when agitated by the storm. On the tops of some of these elevations we have seen shells and petrifactions, such as are found on several mountains in

Europe. No doubt, some impartial geologists may discover here, as they have done elsewhere, incontestible proofs of the deluge. A petrified fragment which I have in my possession, seems to contain a number of these shells.

In proportion as one removes from the banks of the Missouri or penetrates into the Western regions, the forests lose much in height, density and depth, in consequence of the scarcity of water. Soon after, only the rivers are lined with narrow skirts of wood, in which are seldom seen any lofty creeks. In the neighborhood of creeks and rivulets we generally find willow bushes, and where there is no water it would be vain to look for any thing but grass, and even this grass is only found in the fertile plains that lie between Westport and the Platte river.

This intimate connexion between rivers and forests is so striking to the eye, that our beasts of burden had not journeyed more than eight days through this desert, when we saw them in some manner exult and double their pace at the sight of the trees that appeared at a distance. This was chiefly observable when the day's journey had been rather long. This scarcity of wood in the western regions, so much at variance with what is seen in other parts of North America, proceeds from two principal causes. In the plains on this side of Platte river, from the custom which the Indians who live here have adopted, to fire their prairies towards the end of autumn, in order to have better pasture at the return of spring; but in the Far West, where the Indians do not follow this practice, (because they fear to drive away the animals that are necessary for their subsistence, or to expose themselves to be discovered by the strolling parties of their enemies,) it proceeds from the nature of the soil, which being a mixture of sand and light earth, is every where so very barren that with the exception of the absynth that covers the plains, and the gloomy verdure that shades the mountains, vegetation is confined to the vicinity of rivers,—a circumstance which renders a journey through the Far West extremely long and tedious.

At considerable distances, chiefly between the Kants and the Platte rivers, are found blocks of granite of different sizes and colors. The reddish is the most common. In some of the stony parts of the Black Hills are also seen numberless quantities of small pebbles of all shades. I have seen some that were united into solid masses. If these were well polished they would present the appearance of fine mosaics. The columns of the House of Representatives in Washington are deemed very handsome, and are made of similar concretions.

On the feast of St. Peter a remarkable occurrence took place. We discovered an equally curious quarry, which, at first, we took for white marble, but we soon found it something more valuable. Astonished at the facility with which we could fashion this kind of stone into any shape, most of the travellers made calmuts of it. I had several made myself, with the intention of offering them as presents to the Indians, so that for the space of forty-eight hours our camp was filled with lapidaries. But the greater number of these calmuts could not withstand the action of the fire, and broke. It was alabaster.

The first rock which we saw, and which truly deserves the name, was the famous Rock Independence. It is of the same nature as the Rocky Mountains. At first I was led to believe that it had received this pompous name from its isolated situation and the solidity of its basis; but I was afterwards told that it was called so because the first travellers who thought of giving it a name, arrived at it on the very day when the people of the United States celebrate the anniversary of their emancipation from Great Britain. We reached this spot on the day that immediately succeeds this celebration. We had in our company a young Englishman, as jealous of the honor of his nation as the Americans; hence we had a double reason not to cry hurra for Independence. Still, on the following day, lest it might be said that we passed this lofty monument of the desert with indifference, we cut our names on the south side of the rock, under initials (I. H. S.) which we would wish to see engraved on every spot. On account of all these names, and of the dates that accompany them, as well as of the hieroglyphics of Indian warriors, I have surnamed this Rock "the Great Record of the Desert." I shall add a few remarks about the mounds that are seen in the vicinity of the Platte river. The most remarkable of all, at least that which is best known to the generality of travellers, is the mound to which they have given the name of "chimney." It is called so on account of its extraordinary form; but instead of applying to it an appellation which is rather unworthy this wonder of nature, just because it bears some resemblance to the object after which it is named, it would have been more proper to call it "the inverted funnel," as there is no object which it resembles more. Its whole height, including the base, body and column, is scarce less than four or five hundred feet; the column or chimney is only about one hundred and thirty feet high, so that there is nothing striking in the loftiness of its dimensions. But what excites our astonishment, is the manner in which this remnant of a mountain, composed of sand and clay, has been so shaped, and how it has for such a length of time preserved this form, in spite of the winds that are so violent in these parts. It is true that this mound, and all those that are found near it, is composed of a successive num-

CHIMNEY.

ber of horizontal and perpendicular strata, and has about the middle a zone or belt, consisting of a vine of petrified clay. If from these two facts it would be inferred that at a certain height the substance of which the horizontal and perpendicular strata are formed, is susceptible of being hardened so as to approach the nature of stone, then we might perhaps account in some manner for the wonderful formation of this curious ornament. Yet the main difficulty would still remain, and we would at last be compelled to have recourse to the system of occult qualities. The existence of the chimney is therefore a problem, and if any scientific person should wish to solve it, I would advise him to repair to this monument without delay, as a cleft which is seen at the top, and which in all probability will soon extend to the base, threatens to leave nothing of it but the remembrance of its existence.

The chimney is not the only remarkable mound to be met with in this vast solitude. There are many others of various forms. One is called " the House," another " the Castle," a third " the Fort," &c. And, in fact, if a traveller was not convinced that he journeys through a desert, where no other dwellings exist but the tents put up at night and removed in the morning, he would be induced to believe them so many ancient fortresses or Gothic castles and with a little imagination, based upon some historical knowledge, he might think himself transported amid the ancient mansions of Knight errantry. On one side are seen large ditches, and high walls; on the other, avenues, gardens and orchards; farther on, parks, ponds, and lofty trees. Sometimes the fancy presents a castle of the middle ages, and even conjures up the lord of the manor; but instead of all these magnificent remains of antiquity, we find only barren mounds on all sides, filled with cliffs formed by the falling of the waters, and serving as dens to an infinite number of rattle snakes and other venomous reptiles.

After the Missouri, which in the Far West is what the Mississippi is in the North, the finest rivers are the Kanzas, the Platte, and the Eau Sucree. The first of these falls into the Missouri, and receives the waters of a great number of tributary streams. Of these tributaries we counted as many as eighteen before we reached the Platte. Hence we may infer that the country abounds in springs, and that the soil is compact and covered with verdure. The reverse may be said of the neighborhood of the Platte, where springs and verdure are seldom seen. Even on the mounds that run parallel to its banks, the waters that fall from the clouds, upon a sandy and porous soil, run down into the vallies. But the prairies that receive the overflowing waters of the river are extremely fertile, and appear beautiful in spring, being enamelled with a great variety of flowers. The sight of the river itself is still more pleasing; though in spite of all its beauties, it has, like the most remarkable of its mounds, received a vulgar name. This proceeds from the custom which some travellers have of applying to objects the names of things with which they are well acquainted. They have called it *Platte* or Flat river, on account of its width and shallowness; the former often extending six thousand feet, whilst its depth is but from three to five feet, and sometimes less. This want of proportion destroys its utility. Canoes cannot be used to ascend it, and if barges sometimes come down from Fort La Ramee to the mouth, it is because they are so constructed that they may be converted into sledges and pushed on by the hands of men. The author of Astoria has properly defined it "the most magnificent and most useless of rivers." Abstraction made of its defects, nothing can be more pleasing than the perspective which it presents to the eye; though besides the prairie flowers and the ranunculus, its banks bear only the eglantine and the wild vine; for on account of the fires made in the autumn the lofty vegetation is entirely confined to the islands that stud its surface. These islands are so numerous that they have the appearance of a labyrinth of groves floating on the waters. Their extraordinary position gives an air of youth and beauty to the whole scene. If to this be added the undulations of the river, the waving of the verdure, the alternations of light and shade, the succession of these islands varying in form and beauty, and the purity of the atmosphere, some idea may be formed of the pleasing sensations which the traveller experiences on beholding a scene that seems to have started into existence fresh from the hands of the creator. Fine weather is common in this temperate climate. However, it happens sometimes, though but seldom, that the clouds floating with great rapidity open currents of air so violent, as suddenly to chill the atmosphere and produce the most destructive hail storms. I have seen some hailstones of the size of an egg. It is dangerous to be abroad during these storms. A Sheyenne Indian was lately struck by a hailstone, and remained senseless for an hour. Once as the storm was raging near us, we witnessed a sublime sight. A spiral abyss seemed to be suddenly formed in the air. The clouds followed each other into it with such velocity, that they attracted all objects around them, whilst such clouds as were too large and too far distant to feel its influence turned in an opposite direction. The noise we heard in the air was like that of a tempest. On beholding the conflict we fancied that all the winds had been let loose from the four points of the compass. It is very probable that if it had approached much nearer, the whole caravan would have made an ascension into the clouds, but the Power that confines the sea to its boundaries and said—"Hitherto shalt thou come," watched over our preservation. The spiral column moved majestically towards the North, and ght ed on the surface of the Platte. Then, another scene was exhibited to our view. The waters, agitated by its powerful action, began to turn round with frightful noise, and were suddenly drawn up to the clouds in a spiral form. The column appeared to measure a mile in height; and such was the violence of the winds which came down in a perpendicular direction, that in the twinkling of an eye the trees were torn and uprooted, and their boughs scattered in every direction. But what is violent does not last. After a few minutes, the frightful visitation ceased. The column, not being able to sustain the weight at its base was dissolved almost as quickly as it had been formed. Soon after the sun re-appeared: all was calm and we pursued our journey. In proportion as we proceeded towards the sources of this wonderful river, the shades of vegetation became more gloomy, and the brows of the mountains more cragged. Every thing seemed to wear the aspect, not of decay, but of age, or rather of venerable antiquity. Our joy was extatic as we sung the following Ode composed for the occasion:

> Non ce n'est plus une ombre vaine,
> Mes yeux ont vu, j'en suis certain,
> Dans l'azur d'un brilliant lointain,
> Des Monts Rocheux la haute chaine, &c.

> O! no—it is no shadow vain,
> That greets my sight—yon lofty chain
> That pierces the ethereal blue;
> The Rocky Mounts appear in view.

> I've seen the spotless, virgin snow,
> Glist'ning like gems upon their brow—

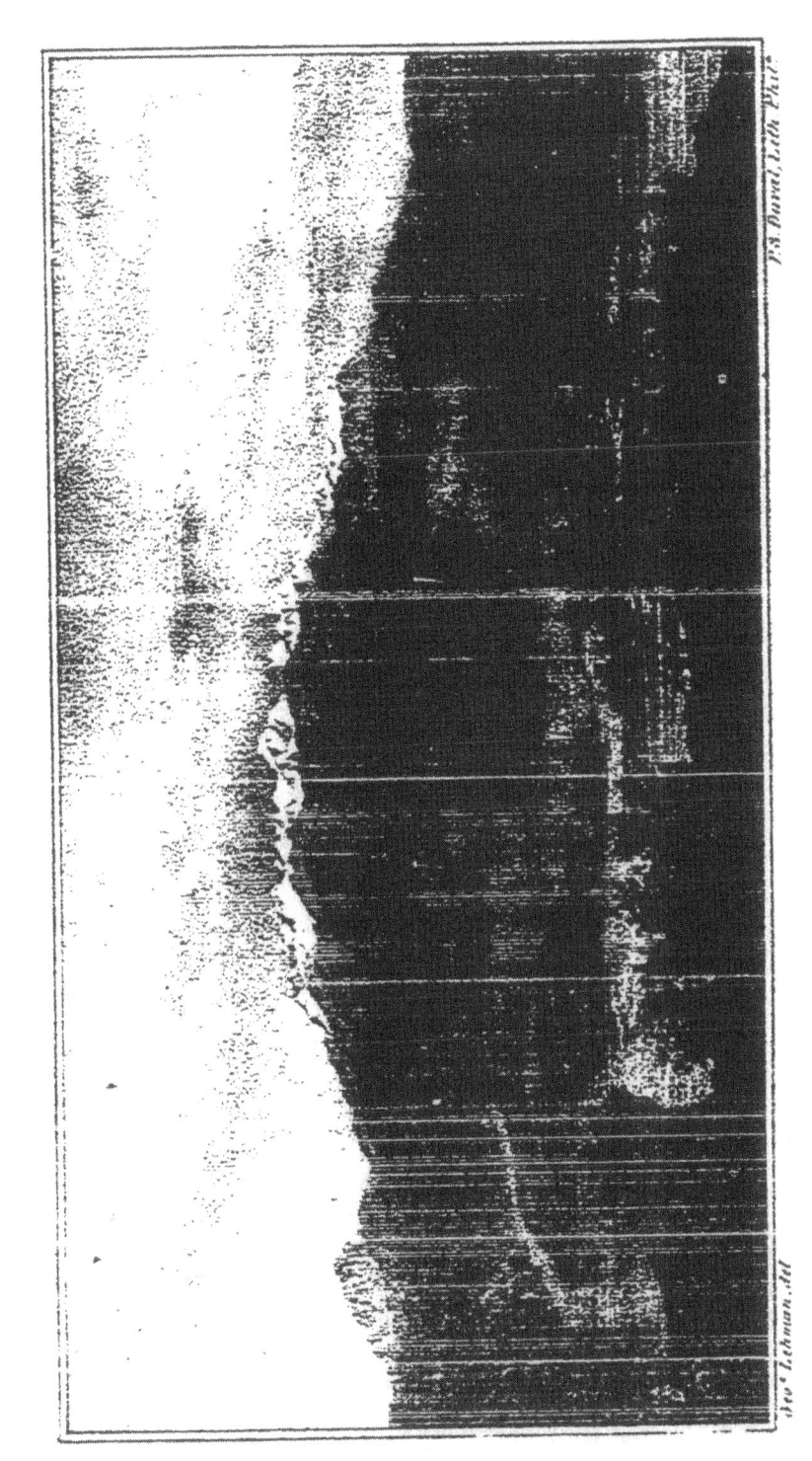

A VIEW OF THE ROCKY MOUNTAINS.

Ode.

And o'er yon giant peak now streams
The golden light of day's first beams.

How from their ice-clad summits, steep,
The living waters joyous leap!
And gently on thro' vallies gay,
Sweeter than honey wend their way.

It is because on yon proud height,
The standard floats of life and light:
It is, that there th' Omnipotent
Hath pitched His everlasting tent—
The God whose love no tongue can tell,
Among his children deigns to dwell.

All hail! majestic Rock—the home
Where many a wand'rer yet shall come;
Where God himself, from His own heart,
Shall health and peace and joy impart.

Sorrow adieu—farewell to fear,—
The sweet-voiced hymn of peace I hear;
Its tone hath touched the red-man's soul:
Lo! o'er his dark breast tear-drops roll.

O! soon the silent wilderness
Shall echo with his song of praise;
And infant lips, from morn till ev'n,
Shall chaunt thy love—great King of heav'n.

Father and God! how far above
All human thought, Thy wondrous love!
How strange the path by which Thy hand
Would lead the Tribes of this bleak land,
From darkness, crime and misery,
To live and reign in bliss with Thee!

As I have been speaking of rivers I shall give (you) a short geographical description of the Missouri, which I am inclined to call my river, as I have so often ascended and descended it during the last four years, travelled along its banks, and crossed almost all its tributaries from the mouth of the Yellow Stone to the place where the mighty river mingles its turbid stream with that of the peaceful Mississippi. I have drunk the limpid waters of its sources, and the muddy waters at its mouth, distant more than three thousand miles from each other. The prodigious length of its course, the wildness and impetuosity of its current have induced the Scioux to call it " the *furious*." Whenever I crossed this magnificent river the sensations which I experienced bordered on the sublime, and my imagination transported me through the world of prairies which it fertilises, to the colossal mountains whence it issues. It is in the heart of the Rocky Mountains that the Missouri takes its rise, together with many other magnificent streams; such as " the Father of Waters," into whose bosom it flows, after having fertilised its own borders to a vast extent,—the Arkansas, and the Red river, both, like itself, majestic tributaries; the Columbia, which becomes the reservoir of all the waters of the Oregon territory, and the Rio Colorado which after winding its course through a gloomy and rocky desert, invigorates the most beautiful part of California. The Missouri, properly so called, is formed by three considerable forks that unite their waters at the entrance of one of the passes of the Rocky mountains. The North fork is called " the Jefferson," the South " the Gallatin," and the one between them " the Madison." Each one of these is subdivided into several small arms that flow from the mountains, and almost mingle their waters with those of the upper forks of the Columbia on the western side. I have drunk of both, distant only about fifty yards from each other; for the same field of snow supplies both the Atlantic and Pacific oceans. After the junction of the forks, the Missouri for a considerable distance, becomes an impetuous and foaming torrent. Below this, its bed is more spacious, and its course more tranquil. Steep rocks of a black hue jut and rise above its current to a height of nearly a thousand feet. The mountains, along whose base it runs, are shaded by pines, cedars, fir and turpentine trees. Some of these mountains present a solitary aspect, and wear a look of unspeakable grandeur. The river, for the space of seventeen miles, is seen raging and foaming, rolling from cataract to cataract with a roaring noise that is repeated by all the neighboring echoes. The first of these cataracts measures ninety-eight feet in height; the second, nineteen; the third, forty-seven, and the fourth, twenty-six. Below the Falls, the beautiful river of Mary, flowing from the North, adds its peaceful waters to those of the rapid and impetuous stream. Still lower, but on the opposite side, the Dearborn and the Fancy disembogue themselves through mouths respectively 150 feet in width. After many other rivers of considerable width and extent, we come to the Yellow Stone, the largest but one of all the tributaries of the Missouri, and resembling the latter in many respects. This river too has its source in the Rocky Mountains, and is 850 yards wide at its mouth; its bed is spacious, its current rapid; its length is about 1600 miles, and at its confluence with the Missouri it appears to be the larger of the two. For a considerable distance above the mouth its banks are well wooded, and its bottom lands are extensive and very fertile. The grey and black bear, the big horn, the antelope, the stag and the common deer frequent these regions, whilst coal and iron mines are in such abundance that for 50 years they might supply fuel and materials to a countless number of steam engines.

After the Missouri has received the Yellow Stone river, its bottom lands become more extensive; yet as little or no wood is found on them, it may be long before attempts will be made to cultivate them. The White Earth river coming from the North, and the Goose river from the South, are not very considerable. The width of each at the mouth is 300 yards. The Little Missouri, though shallow, has a rapid current, and has its sources in the South, as also the following streams: Cane river, near the village of the Mandans; Cannon Ball river, Winnipenhu, Sewarzena and Sheyenne river, which is navigable for 400 miles; a rapid and muddy stream, 400 yards at the mouth; Peton river and White river, so called on account of the color of its waters, which are unwholesome. It is navigable for 300 miles, has a rapid current, and measures about 300 yards at its mouth. The lands which it waters in the upper country are barren, and abound in animal and vegetable petrifactions, whilst its banks have every where a fantastic appearance. Next and on the same side we meet the Poncas and Running Water river, the latter of which has a fine current. Medicine and Jacques rivers enter the Missouri from the opposite side; the latter is also called the rendezvous of the beaver hunters and runs nearly parallel with the Missouri. After the White Stone and the Vermillion, we find the Big Sioux river, on which is found the fine red stone quarry explored by the Indians to make their calumets. The Floyd and the Roger, the Maringoin, the Nishnebatlana and the Nedowa fall into the Missouri on the Northern side. Its chief tributary, the Platte, rises like itself in the Rocky Mountains and extends its course nearly two thousand miles. Though it be a mile wide at the mouth yet it is shallow, as its name indicates, and is not navigable the two Newahas flow from the South and the Little

Platte from the North. The Kanzas, on the South side, is about a thousand miles long, and is navigable to a great distance. Grand river, from the North, is a wide, deep and navigable stream. The two Charetons are found on the same side, whilst the Osage and Gasconade rivers enter from the South. The former is an important stream, navigable for 600 miles, and having its sources near the waters of the Arkansas; whilst the latter, though navigable only for 66 miles, is equally important, on account of the fine large pine forests that supply St. Louis and the adjacent country with lumber. I shall say nothing of the many other less remarkable tributaries of the Missouri, such as the Blue Water, the Mine, the Bonne Femme, the Manitoo, the Muddy, the Loutre, the Cedar, the Buffalo, the St. Johns, the Wood river, the Charette Bonhomme, Femme, Osage, &c. The length of the Missouri, from its sources to the Yellow Stone, is 880 miles, from the Yellow Stone to its junction with the Mississippi, is about 2200. I subjoin a list of the Forks of its great tributaries which I have seen and crossed.

Beaver Head, Big Hole Fork, Stinking Water, Forks of the Jefferson, Powder River, Tongue River, Rose-bud River, Big Horn River, Clarke River, Rocky River, Traverse River, Loutre River, 25 Yard River, Gallatin River, Wind River, Forks of the Yellow Stone. Horn River, Wolf River, Bigwood River, North Fork River, South Fork River, Cabin Pole River, Horse River, La Ramee, Eau Sucree, Forks of the Platte. Grande Sableuse, Horse Shoe River, St. Peter's River, Red River, Kennion River, Deer River, The Torrent, Branches of the North Fork of the Platte. Soldier's River, Ouaggerehoosse River, Vermillion River, Black Vermillion River, Sick River, Knife River, Blue Waters, Forks of the Kanzas. Mary's River,

Big Bone, Yungar River, Potatoes River, Grand Fork, Forks of the Osage.

I left off my narrative on Sugar River, otherwise called Eau Sucree; I must interrupt it to listen to the good tidings that are brought from the mountains.

I remain, Rev. and Dear Father,
Your dutiful Son in Christ,
P. J. De Smet, S. J.

LETTER V.

Fort Hall, August 16th, 1841.

Rev. and Dear Father Provincial:

It was on the eve of the beautiful festival of the assumption that we met the vanguard of the Flat Heads. We met under the happiest auspices, and our joy was proportionate. The joy of the savage is not openly manifested—that of our dear neophytes was tranquil; but from the beaming serenity of their looks, and the feeling manner in which they pressed our hands, it was easy to perceive that, like the joy which has its source in virtue, theirs was heartfelt and profound. What had they not done to obtain a mission of "Black Gowns?" For twenty years they had not ceased to supplicate the Father of mercies; for twenty years, in compliance with the counsels of the poor Iroquois, who had established themselves in their tribe, they had conformed, as nearly as they could, to our creed, our manners, and even to our religious practices. In what Catholic parish was the Sunday, for example, ever more religiously observed?— During the ten years just elapsed, four deputations, each starting from the banks of the Bitter Root, on which they usually assembled, had courageously ventured to St. Louis, over a space of 3000 miles,—over mountains and vallies, infested by Black Feet and other hostile tribes.

Of the first deputation, which started in 1831, three died of diseases produced by the change of climate. The second embassy reached its destination; but owing to the great want of missionaries in the Diocess of St. Louis, received nothing but promises. The third, which set out in 1837, consisted of five members, all of whom were unmercifully massacred by the Sioux. All these crosses, however, were insufficient to abate their zeal. In 1839, they sent two Iroquois deputies, one of whom was named Peter, and the other " Young Ignatius," to distinguish him from another called " Old Ignatius." These they earnestly advised to make still more pressing entreaties to obtain the long sought blessing, a " Black Gown, to conduct them to heaven." Their prayers were, at length, heard, even beyond their hopes. One Black Gown was granted, together with a promise of more, if necessary for their greater good. While Peter returned in haste to the tribe to acquaint them with the complete success of their mission, Ignatius remained at Westport, to accompany the promised missionary. I had the happiness to be that missionary; I visited the nation, and became acquainted, in person, with their wants, their dispositions, and the necessities of the neighboring tribes. After an absence of a year, I was now returning to them no longer alone, but with two Fathers, three brothers, laborers and all that was essential to the success of the expedition. They themselves had travelled upwards of 800 miles to meet us, and now, that we were together, both parties were full of vigor and hope. What joy must not these good Indians, at that moment, have experienced? Being unable, however, to express their happiness, they were silent: their silence surely could not be ascribed to a deficiency of intelligence or a want of sentiment, for the Flat Heads are full of feeling, and many are truly intelligent. These, too, were the *elite* of the nation. Judge of it by what follows.

The chief of this little embassy pourtrayed himself in the following address to his companions, a few days subsequently, on viewing the plan of the first hamlet: " My dear children," said he, " I am but an ignorant and wicked man, yet I thank the Great Spirit for the favors which he has conferred on us,—(and entering here into an admirable detail, he concluded thus :) Yes, my dear friends, my heart has found content; notwithstanding my wickedness I despair not of the goodness of God. Henceforth, I wish to live only that I may pray ; I will never abandon prayer; (religion) I will pray until the end of my life, and when I die I will commit myself into the hands of the Author of life ; if he condemn me, I shall submit to his will, for I have deserved punishment; if he save me, I shall bless him forever. Once more, then, my heart has found content.— What shall we do to evince the love we bear our fathers?" Here he made practical resolutions, but I must hasten to commemorate the zeal of each of those who formed the embassy.

Simon, who had been baptised the preceding year, was the oldest of the nation, and was so burdened with the weight of years, that even when seated, he needed a stick for his support. Yet, he had no sooner ascertained that we were on our route to join the tribe, than mounting his horse and mingling with the young warriors who were prepared to go forth to meet us, he said: " My children, I shall accompany you; if I die on the way, our Fathers, at least, will know the cause of my death." During the course of the journey, he repeatedly exhorted his companions: " courage, my children," he would say, " remember that we are going to the presence of our Fathers;" and urging his steed forward, whip in hand, he led on his youthful followers, at the rate of fifty miles per day.

Francis, a boy from six to seven years old, grand son of Simon, was an orphan from the very cradle. Having served at the altar, the preceding year, he would not be refused permission to accompany his grandfather: his heart told him that he was about to recover father and mother, and enjoy all the happiness that loving parents can bestow.

Ignatius, who had advised the fourth deputation, and had been a member of it,—who had succeeded in his mission, and introduced the first Black Gown into the tribe,— who had just recently exposed himself to new dangers, in order to introduce others, had crowned his zealous exertions by running for days without eating or drinking, solely that he might reach us the sooner.

Pilchimo, his companion and brother to one of the martyrs of the third deputation, was a young warrior, already reputed brave among the brave. The preceding year, his presence of mind and his courage had saved seventy of his brethren in arms from the fury of nearly nineteen hundred Black Feet.

Francis Xavier was the son of old Ignatius, who had been the leader of the second and third deputation, and had fallen a victim to his devotion to the cause of religion and of his brethren. Francis Xavier had gone to St. Louis at the age of ten, in the company of his courageous father, solely that he might have the happiness of receiving baptism. He had finally attached himself without reserve to the service of the mission, and supplied our table with a daily mess of fis`..

Gabriel, who was of mixed blood, but an adopted child of the nation, was interpreter for the missionaries. Being the first to join us on the banks of the Green river, he merited the title of precursor of the Flat Heads. His bravery and zeal had four times induced him to travel, for our sakes, over a space of 400 miles, which separated us from the great camp.

Such were they who now greeted us. Let them tell their own story.

They had prayed daily to obtain for me a happy journey and a speedy return. Their brethren continued in the same good disposition; almost all, even children and old men, knew by heart the prayers which I had taught them the preceding year. Twice on every week day, and three times on each Sunday, the assembled tribe recited prayers in common. Whenever they moved their camp, they carried with them, as an ark of safety, the box of ornaments left in their custody. Five or six children, whom I had baptised went to heaven during my absence; the very morrow of my departure, a young warrior whom I had baptised the day previous, died in consequence of a wound received from the Black Feet about three months before.— Another, who had accompanied me as far as the fort of the Crows, and was as yet but a catechumen, died of sickness in returning to the tribe, but in such happy dispositions that his mother was perfectly consoled for his loss by the conviction that his soul was in heaven. A girl, about twelve years of age, seeing herself on the point of dying, had solicited baptism with such earnestness that she was baptised by Peter the Iroquois, and received the name of Mary.—After having sung a canticle in a stronger voice than usual, she died, saying: "Oh how beautiful! I see Mary, my mother." So many favors from heaven were calculated to instigate the malice of hell. The enemies of salvation had accordingly attempted to sow the cockle among the good grain, by suggesting to the chiefs of the tribe that my conduct would be like that of so many others, who, "once gone, had never returned." But the great chief had invariably replied: "You wrong our father; he is not double-tongued, like so many others. He has said: 'I will return,' and he will return, I am sure." The interpreter added that it was this conviction which had impelled the venerable old man, notwithstanding his advanced age, to place himself at the head of the detachment bound for Green river; that they had arrived at the rendezvous on the 1st of July, which was the appointed day; that they had remained there till the 16th, and would have continued to occupy the same position, had not the scarcity of provisions obliged them to depart. He stated also that the whole tribe had determined to fix upon some spot as a site for a permanent village; that, with this view, they had already chosen two places which they believed to be suitable; that nothing but our presence was required to confirm their determination, and they relied with such implicit confidence on our speedy arrival, that the great chief, on starting from Green river, had left there three men to await us, advising them to hold that position until no longer tenable.

Here, I have much to relate that is not less edifying than serious; but before I enter upon the chapter of noble actions, I must conclude what I had commenced in my preceding letter. But I feel bound, before all, to pay Mr. Ermatinger, the captain of Fort Hall, the tribute of gratitude which we owe him.

Although a protestant by birth, this noble Englishman gave us a most friendly reception. Not only did he repeatedly invite us to his table, and sell us, at first cost, or at one-third of its value, in a country so remote, whatever we required; but he also added, as pure gifts, many articles which he believed would be particularly acceptable. He did more: he promised to recommend us to the good will of the Governor of the honorable English Company, who was already prepossessed in our favor; and, what is still more deserving of praise, he assured us that he would second our ministry among the populous nation of the Snakes, with whom he has frequent intercourse. So much zeal and generosity give him a claim to our esteem and gratitude. May heaven return to him a hundred fold the benefits he has conferred on us. It was at Fort Hall that we took our final leave of the American Colony, with which we had, till then, pursued the same route. It was previously to this, while we were yet at Green river, that those who came to that wild region, merely for information or pleasure, had turned back, with some fewer illusions than when they started out upon the journey. They were five or six in number. Among them was a young Englishman, who had been our messmate from St. Louis. In taking leave of us, this young man, who was in many respects estimable, assured us that, if providence should ever again throw us together, the meeting would give him the highest satisfaction, and that he would always be happy to do us all the service in his power. He was of a good English family, and like most of his countrymen, fond of travel: he had already seen the four quarters of the globe; but *qui multum peregrinantur.* ..... He cherished so many prejudices, however, against the Catholic religion, that, despite all our good wishes, we were of no service to him in the most essential relation. We recommended him to our friends. I have treasured up one of his beautiful reflections: "We must travel in the desert to witness the watchful care of Providence over the wants of man."

They who had started, purely with the design of seeking their fortune in California, and were pursuing their enterprise with the constancy which is characteristic of Americans, had left us, but a few days before our arrival at the fort, in the vicinity of the boiling springs which empty into Bear river. There now remained with us but a few of the party, who had come to the fort in order to revictual. Among the latter were the leader of the Colony and a reputed deacon of the Methodist sect. Both were of a peaceable disposition, and manifested for us the highest regard; but the former, like so many others, being very indifferent as to religious matters, held as a maxim, " that it was best to have no religion, or else to adopt that of the country in which we live;" and wishing to display his great Bible erudition, he in proof of his paradox, cited as a text of St. Paul the ancient proverb: *Si fueris Romæ, Romano vivite more.* The minister was of the same opinion, but yet he wished some religion, it being well understood that his was the best. I say *his*, because he was neither *a* Methodist, *a* Protestant nor *a* Catholic—not even a Christian; he maintained that a Jew, a Turk, or an Idolatar may be as agreeable as any other in the sight of God. For the proof of his doctrine, he relied (strange to say) on the authority of St. Paul, and particularly on this text: *Unus Dominus una fides.* In fact, these were the very words with which he greeted us, the first time we saw him, and which formed the subject of a long valedictory discourse that he delivered in one of the meeting houses of Westport, previous to his departure for his western mission. By whom was he sent? We have never ascertained. His zeal frequently induced him to dispute with us; it was not difficult to show him that his ideas, with the exception of one, were vague and fluctuating. He acknowledged it himself; but after having wandered from point to point, he always returned to his favorite tenet, which, according to him, was the fundamental principle of all true belief: " that the love of God is the first of duties, and that to inculcate it we must be tolerant." This was his strongest point of support, the foundation of all his reasoning, and the stimulus of his zeal. The term Catholic, according to him, was but another word for " love and philanthropy." He carried his absurdities and contradictions so far, that he excited the hilarity of the whole camp. His ingenuous simplicity was even greater than his tolerance. For example, he once said to me: " Yesterday one of the members of my persuasion returned to me a book which I had lent him, stating that it contained an exposition of the Roman creed." When I asked him his opinion of it, he replied, " that the book was full of errors;" yet it was an exposition of Methodist principles that I had given him. " Witness," said he, with emphasis, " the blinding influence of prejudice."

I had daily conversations with some one of the caravan, and frequently with several. And although Americans are slow to change their creed, we had the consolation to relieve our travelling companions of a heavy load of prejudice against our holy religion. They parted from us, exhibiting signs of respect and veneration; nay, even of preference for Catholicity. These controversies so com-

DEVIL'S GATE.

pletely engrossed my mind, my heart and my senses, that I arrived almost unconsciously on the banks of Snake river. Here a great danger and a profitable lesson awaited us; but before speaking of the adventures of our journey, I shall conclude what remains to be related of the country we traversed.

We halted with our narrative upon the shore of the Sweet-water. This stream is one of the most beautiful tributaries of the Platte. It owes its name, indeed, to the purity of its waters. It is distinguished from its fellow tributaries by the numerous wanderings of its current—a proof that the fall of its bed is but slight. But suddenly changing its course, we see or rather hear it rushing impetuously through a long cleft in a chain of mountains. These mountains, which harmonize well with the torrent, exhibit the most picturesque scenes; travellers have named this spot the Devil's Entrance. In my opinion, they should have rather called it Heaven's Avenue, for if it resembles hell on account of the frightful disorder which frowns around it, it is still a mere passage, and it should rather be compared to the way of heaven on account of the scene to which it leads. Imagine, in short, two rows of rocks, rising perpendicularly to a wonderful height, and, at the foot of these shapeless walls, a winding bed, broken, encumbered with trunks of trees, with rubbish, and with timber of all dimensions; while, in the midst of this chaos of obstacles, the roaring waves force a passage, now rushing with fury, then swelling with majesty, and anon spreading with gentleness, accordingly as they find in their course a wider or more straitened passage. Above these moving and noisy scenes, the eye discerns masses of shadow, here relieved by a glance of day, there deepening in their gloom by the foliage of a cedar or pine, till finally, as the sight travels through the long vista of lofty galleries, it is greeted by a distant perspective of such mild beauty, that a sentiment of placid happiness steals upon the mind. Such is the spectacle we admired at the distance of nine or ten miles from the Rock Independence, on the morning of 6th July. I doubt whether the solitude of the Carthusian monastery, called La Grande Chartreuse, of which so many wonders are related, can, at least at first sight, offer greater attractions to him whom divine grace has called to a contemplative life. As for me, who am not called to such a state, at least exclusively, after an hour of raptures, I began to understand the expression of the Carthusian friar, *pulchrum transeuntibus;* and I hastened to proceed.

Hence we directed our course more and more towards the heights of the Far West, ascending, some times clambering, until we reached the summit, from which we discovered another world. On the 7th of July we were in sight of the immense Oregon Territory. I will not presume to add to the many pompous descriptions which have been given of the spectacle now before us. I shall say nothing either of the height, the number, or the variety of those peaks, covered with eternal snows, which rear their heads, with menacing aspect, to the heavens. Nor will I speak of the many streams descending from them and changing their course, with unexpected suddenness; nor of the extreme rarification of the air with the consequent effect upon objects susceptible of contraction, at so great an elevation. All this is common; but to the glory of the Lord, I must commemorate the imperious necessity I experienced, of tracing his holy name upon a rock, which towered pre-eminent amid the grandeur around. May that ever adorable name be to travellers a monument of our gratitude, and a pledge of salvation. Henceforth we descended towards the Pacific—first, by following, then by crossing the Little and the Great Sandy Rivers. In the vicinity of the latter, as the Captain had mistaken one road for another, the caravan wandered for three days at random. I, myself, on a fine evening, strayed from the rest. I thought myself entirely lost; how was I to act? I did what every sincere believer would have done in the same circumstances, I prayed; and then urging on my horse, I travelled several miles, when it struck me that it would be prudent to retrace my steps. I did so instantly, and it was fortunate, for the caravan was far behind. I found it encamped; still ignorant however of its position, and on a soil so arid that our jaded beasts were necessitated to fast for the night. Days follow, but resemble not each other; two days subsequently, we were surrounded with abundance, filled with joy, all once more united, and on the banks of a river not less celebrated among the hunters of the west, than the shores of the Platte. This river loses itself not far below, in clefts of rocks said to be no less than two hundred miles in extent, among which there are countless swarms of beavers, although the trapper has never ventured to hunt them, on account of the extreme peril of the enterprise. At a certain period of the year, both trappers and Indians flock to this spot, for the purpose of bartering all kinds of merchandise. It was here, but eight years ago, the wagons that first undertook to cross the Rocky Mountains, found the Pillars of Hercules, and it was here too that we found the messenger of the Flat Heads, to whom I have already alluded. This river is the Rio Colorado of the West. . . . We rested two days upon its banks, with the company of Captain F., who had just returned from California. What they told us concerning that distant country dissipated many illusions, and caused some of our companions, who travelled for amusement, to return.

On the 20th of July we seriously thought of continuing our journey. To a company like ours, it was not an easy matter. ' The remembrance of the expedition of Bonneville was still fresh in the minds of all; but our object was not the same; we had no articles but such as were necessary.— They could be transported conveniently only by wagons. We placed all our confidence in God. We soon crossed the river, and our equippage was seen coming in all directions, over vallies and mountains. We were compelled to clear a passage, some times in the middle of a ravine, some times on the declivity of a rock, and frequently through bushes. We travelled in this manner for ten days, to reach Bear river, which flows through a wide and beautiful valley, surrounded by lofty mountains and often intersected by inaccessible rocks. We continued our march through it during eight successive days. The river resembles in its course the form of a horse shoe, and falls into the great Salt lake, which has no communication with the sea. On our way, we met several families of Soshonees or Snake Indians, and Soshocos or Uprooters. They speak the same language, and are both friends to the whites. The only difference we could observe between them, was that the latter were by far the poorer. They formed a grotesque group, such as is not to be seen in any other part of the Indian territory. Represent to yourself a band of wretched horses, disproportionate in all their outlines, loaded with bags and boxes to a height equal to their own, and these surmounted by rational beings young and old, male and female, in a variety of figures and costumes, to which the pencil of a Hogarth or a Breugel could scarcely do justice, and you will have an idea of the scene we witnessed. One

SODA SPRINGS.

of these animals, scarcely four feet high, had for its load four large sacks of dried meat, two on each side, above which were tied several other objects, terminating in a kind of platform on the back of the living beast; and, on the summit of the whole construction, at a very high elevation, was seated cross-legged on a bear skin a very old person smoking his calmut. At his side, on another Rosinante, was mounted an old Goody, probably his wife, seated in the same manner on the top of sacks and bags, that contained all sorts of roots, dried beans and fruits, grains and berries; in short, all such comestibles as the barren mountains and the beautiful vallies afford. These they carried to their winter encampment. Some times we have seen a whole family on the same animal, each according to his age, the children in front, the women next, and the men behind. On two occasions I saw thus mounted, five persons, of whom two at least had the appearance of being as able to carry the poor horse as the horse was to support the weight of these two Soshocos gentlemen.

Some places on the Bear river exhibit great natural curiosities. A square plain of a few acres in extent presents an even surface of fuller's earth of pure whiteness, like that of marble, and resembling a field covered with dazzling snow. Situated near this plain are a great many springs, differing in size and temperature. Several of them have a slight taste of soda, and the temperature of these, is cold. The others are of a milk warm temperature, and must be wholesome; perhaps they are not inferior to the celebrated waters of the Spa, or of the lime springs in Belgium. I am inclined to believe so, though I am not firm in the opinion; at all events, they are surrounded by the mountains over which our wagons found it so difficult to pass. I therefore invite neither sick nor sound to test them. In the same locality there is a hole in the ground, out of which air and water escape alternately. The earth for some distance around resounds like an immense vault, and is apt to frighten the solitary traveller as he passes along.

It was here that we left Bear River. On the 14th of August our wagons having proceeded ten hours without intermission, arrived at the outlet of a defile which seemed to us the end of the world. On our right and left were frightful mountains; in our rear a road which we were by no means tempted to retrace; in front a passage through which rushed a torrent; but so small that the torrent itself seemed with difficulty, to force its way. Our beasts of burthen were, for the first time, exhausted. Murmurs arose against the captain, who, however, was imperturbable, and as he never shrunk from difficulties, advanced to reconnoitre the ground. In a few moments he made us a sign to approach; one hour after we had surmounted every obstacle, for we had traversed the highest chain of the Rocky Mountains and were nearly in sight of Fort Hall. On the evening previous to the departure of the camp from the Soda Springs, I directed my course towards the fort, to make a few necessary arrangements. The young F. Xavier was my only companion. We were soon involved in a labyrinth of mountains, and about midnight, we were on the summit of the highest chain. My poor guide, being able to see nothing through the darkness but frightful precipices, was so pitifully embarrassed that after veering about for a while, like a weather-cock, he confessed himself lost. That was not a place, nor was it a time, to wander at random; I, therefore, took, what I considered, the only alternative, that of waiting for the morning sun to extricate us from our embarrassment. Wrapped up in my blanket and with my saddle for a pillow, I stretched myself upon the rock, and immediately fell into a sound sleep. Early the next morning, we descended by a small cleft in the rocks, which the obscurity of the night had concealed and arrived on a plain watered by the New Port, one of the tributaries of Snake River. We trotted or gallopped over fifty miles in the course of the day. The whole way presented evident remains of volcanic eruptions; piles and veins of lava were visible in all directions, and the rocks bore marks of having been in a state of fusion. The river, in its whole length, exhibits a succession of beaver ponds, emptying into each other by a narrow opening in each dike, thus forming a fall of between three and six feet. All these dikes are of stone, evidently the work of the water and of the same character and substance as the stalactites found in some caverns.

We arrived late in the evening, within half a mile of the Fort, but being unable to see our way in the darkness, and not knowing where we were, we encamped for the night among the bushes, near the margin of a small brook.

I have the honor to be
    Rev. Father Provincial,
        Your most humble and obedient servant and son,
            P. J. DE SMET, S. J.

LETTER VI.

Camp of the Big-Face, 1st Sept. 1841.
Rev. and Dear Father Provincial:

NEARLY four months had elapsed since our departure from Westport, when we met the main body of the nation to which we had been sent. Here we found the principal chiefs, four of whom had advanced a day's journey to welcome us. They met us at one of the sources of the Missouri called Beaver-Head, where we had encamped. Having crossed the small river under the direction of these new guides we came to an extensive plain, at the western part of which the Flat Heads lay encamped. This was on the 30th of August, and it was only towards night that we could distinctly discern the camp. A number of runners who rapidly succeeded each other, informed us that the camp was not far distant. Contentment and joy were depicted on their countenances. Long before the Flat Head warrior, who is surnamed the Bravest of the Brave, sent me his finest horse to Fort Hall, having strongly recommended that no one should mount him before he was presented to me. Soon after the warrior himself appeared, distinguished by his superior skill in horsemanship, and by a large red scarf, which he wore after the fashion of the Marshals of France. He is the handsomest Indian warrior of my acquaintance. He came with a numerous retinue. We proceeded at a brisk trot, and were now but two or three miles from the camp, when at a distance we descried a warrior of lofty stature. A number of voices shouted Paul! Paul! and indeed it was Paul, the great chief, who had just arrived after a long absence, as if by special permission of God, to afford him the satisfaction of introducing me personally to his people. After mutual and very cordial demonstrations of friendship, the good old chief insisted upon returning to announce our arrival. In less than half an hour all hearts were united and moved by the same sentiments. The tribe had the appearance of a flock crowding with eagerness around their shepherd. The mothers offered us their little children, and so moving was the scene that we could scarcely refrain from tears. This evening was certainly one of the happiest of our lives. We could truly say that we had reached the peaceful goal. All previous dangers, toils and trials, were at an end and forgotten. The hopeful thought that we would soon behold the happy days of the primitive Christians revive among these Indians, filled our minds, and the main subject of our conversations became the question: " What shall we do to comply with the requisitions of our signal vocation?"

I engaged Father Point, who is skilled in drawing and architecture, to trace the plan of the Missionary Stations. In my mind, and still more in my heart, the material was essentially connected with the moral and religious plan. Nothing appeared to us more beautiful than the *Narrative of Muratori*. We had made it our Vade Mecum. It is chiefly to these subjects that we shall devote our attention for the future, bidding farewell to all fine perspectives, animals, trees and flowers. or favoring them only with an occasional and hasty glance.

From Fort Hall we ascended the Snake River, also called Lewis' Fork, as far as the mouth of Henry's Fork. This is unquestionably the most barren of all the mountain deserts. It abounds in absynth, cactus, and all such plants and herbs as are chiefly found on arid lands. We had to resort to fishing for the support of life, and our beasts of burden were compelled to fast and pine; for scarcely a mouthful of grass could be found during the eight days which it took us to traverse this wilderness. At a distance we beheld the colossal summits of the Rocky Mountains. The three Tetons were about fifty miles to our right, and to the left we had the three mounds at a distance of thirty miles.

From the mouth of Henry's Fork we steered our course towards the mountains over a sandy plain furrowed by deep ravines, and covered with blocks of granite. We spent a day and night without water. On the following day we came to a small brook, but so arid is this porous soil, that its waters are soon lost in the sand. On the third day of this truly fatiguing journey we entered into a beautiful defile, where the verdure was both pleasing and abundant, as it is watered by a copious rivulet. We gave to this passage the name of "the Father's Defile," and to the rivulet that of St. Francis Xavier. From the Father's Defile, to the place of our destination, the country is well watered, for it abounds with small lakes and rivulets, and is surrounded by mountains, at whose base are found numberless springs. In no part of the world is the water more limpid or pure, for whatever may be the depth of the rivers, the bottom is seen as if there were nothing to intercept the view. The most remarkable spring which we have seen in the mountains, is called the Deer's lodge. It is found on the bank of the main Fork of the Bitter Root or St. Mary's River; to this Fork I have given the name of St. Ignatius. This spring is situated on the top of a mound thirty feet high, in the middle of a marsh. It is accessible on one side only. The water bubbles up, and escapes through a number of openings at the base of the mound, the circumference of which appears to be about sity feet. The waters at the base are of different temperatures: hot, lukewarm and cold, though but a few steps distant from each other. Some are indeed so hot that meat may be boiled in them. We actually tried the experiment.

I remain, Rev. Father Provincial,
    Yours, &c.
        P. J. DE SMET, S. J.

LETTER VII.

St. Ignatius' River, 10th Sept. 1841.

Rev. and Dear Father Provincial:

I INFORMED your Reverence that flowers are found in abundance near the rock called the Chimney. Whilst we were there Father Point culled one flower of every kind, and made a fine nosegay in honor of the Sacred heart of Jesus, on the day of the Feast. As we proceeded towards the Black Hills, the flowers diminished in number, but now and then we found some which we had not seen any where. I have taken notice of many of them, for the amusement of amateurs. Among such as are double, the most common and those that are chiefly characterised by the soil on which they grow, are to be found on this side the Platte River. The rose-colored lupine flourishes in the plain contiguous to the Platte, as far as the Chimney. Beyond it grows a medicinal plant, bearing a yellow flower with five petals, called the prairie epinette; and still farther on, where the soil is extremely barren, are seen three kinds of the prickly-pear; the flowers of these are beautiful, and known among Botanists by the name of *Cactus Americana*. They have already been naturalized in the flower gardens of Europe. The colors of the handsomest roses are less pure and lively than the carnation of this beautiful flower. The exterior of the chalice is adorned with all the shades of red and green. The petals are evasated like those of the lily. It is better adapted than the rose to serve as an emblem of the vain pleasures of this nether world, for the thorns that surround it are more numerous, and it almost touches the ground. Among the Simples, the most elegant is the blue-bell of our gardens, which however, far surpasses it by the beauty of its form, and the nicety of its shades, varying from the white to the deepest azure. Adam's Needle, found only on the most barren elevation, is the finest of all pyramidals. About the middle of its stem, which is generally about three feet high, begins a pyramid of flowers, growing close to each other, highly shaded with red, and diminishing in size as they approach the summit, which terminates in a point. Its foot is protected by a number of hard, oblong, ribbed, and sharp leaves, which have given it the name of Adam's Needle. The root is commonly of the thickness of a man's arm, its color white, and its form resembling that of the carrot. The Indians eat it occasionally and the Mexicans use it to manufacture soap. There are many other varieties of flowers some of them very remarkable and rare even in America, which are still without a name even among travellers. To one of the principal, distinguished by having its bronzed leaves disposed in such a manner as to imitate the chapter of a Corinthian column, we have given the name of Corinthian. Another, a kind of straw color, by the form of its stem, and its division into twelve branches, brought to our minds the famous dream of the Patriarch Joseph, and we have called it the Josephine. A third, the handsomest of all the daisies *(Reines Marguerites)* that I have ever seen, having a yellow disk, with black and red shades, and seven or eight rays, any of which would form a fine flower, has been named by us the Dominical, not only because it appeared like the Lady and Mistress of all the flowers around, but also because we discovered it on Sunday.

Shrubs. The shrubs that bear fruit are few. The most common are the currant and gooseberry of various sizes and colors, the hawthorn, the rasberry, the wild cherry and the service-berry. Currants, white, red, black and yellow, grow every where along the mountains. The best are found on the plains, where they are exposed to be ripened by the sun. I have classed the wild cherry and the service-berry among shrubs, because they are generally of low growth and do not deserve the name of trees. The service-berry *(cornier)* grows on a real shrub, and is a delicious fruit, called by travellers the mountain pear, though it bears no resemblance to the pear, its size being that of a common cherry. The mountain cherry differs much from the European cherry. The fruit hangs in clusters around the branches, and is smaller than the wild cherry, whilst its taste and color, and the form of the leaves are nearly the same as those of the latter. Cherries and service-berries constitute a great portion of the Indians' food whilst the season lasts, and they are dried by them to serve for food in the winter. I may perhaps mention other fruits, plants and roots, that grow spontaneously in different parts of the Far West, and are used as food by the Indians for want of better sustenance.

Flax is very common in the valleys between the mountains. What must appear singular is that the root of it is so fruitful that it will produce new stems for a number of years—we examined one of them, and found attached to it about 30 stems, which had sprung from it in former years. Hemp is also found, but in very small quantities.

Trees. There are but few species of trees in the regions which we lately passed. Scarcely any forests are found on the banks of rivers, for which I have already assigned a reason. On the plains we find bushes, and now and then the willow, the alder, the wax tree, the cotton tree, or white poplar whose bark is used for horse feed in winter, and the aspen whose leaves are always trembling. Some Canadians have conceived a very superstitious idea of this tree. They say that of its wood the Cross was made on which our Saviour was nailed, and that since the time of the crucifixion, its leaves have not ceased to tremble! The only lofty trees found on the mountains are the pine and the cedar which is either white or red. The latter is chiefly used for furniture, as it is the most resistible wood of the West. There are several species of the pine: the Norwegian, the resinous, the white, and the elastic, so called because the Indians use it to make bows.

So great is the violence of the winds in the vicinity of the Black Hills, that the cotton wood, which is almost the only tree that grows there, displays the most fantastic shapes. I have seen some whose branches had been so violently twisted that they became incorporated with the trunk, and after this, grew in such strange forms and directions that at a distance it was impossible to distinguish what part of the tree was immediately connected with the roots.

BIRDS. I shall say but little of the birds. They are various in form, color and size; from the pelican and the swan to the wren and the humming bird. Muratori, speaking of the last, compares him to the nightingale, and is astonished that such shrill and loud sounds should proceed from so small a body. The celebrated author must have been mistaken, unless the humming bird of South America be different from that of the Rocky Mountains. The latter does not sing but makes a humming noise with his wings as he flies from flower to flower.

REPTILES. With respect to reptiles, they have been frequently described, and I mention them only to give thanks to God, by whose Providence we have been delivered from all such as are venomous, chiefly from the rattle snake. Neither men nor beasts belonging to our caravan have suffered from them, though they were so numerous in places that our wagoners killed as many as twelve in one day.

Insects abound in these regions. The ant has often attracted the notice of naturalists. Some have seemed to doubt whether the wheat stored up by this little insect serves for winter provisions or for the construction of its dwelling. No wheat grows in this country. Yet the ant stores up small pebbles of the size and form of grains of wheat, which inclines me to believe that they use both for the construction of their cells. In either case the paternal Providence of God is manifest. They display as much foresight in providing dwellings that are out of the reach of humidity and inundations, as in laying up food for future wants. It is probable, however, that here they find food of another kind, and this might easily be ascertained. Fleas are not known in the mountains, but there is another sort of vermin nearly allied to it, to which I have alluded in one of my former letters. And what shall I say of musquitoes? I have suffered so much from them, that I cannot leave them unnoticed. In the heart of the prairie they do not trouble the traveller, if he keep aloof from the shade, and walk in the burning sun. But at nightfall they light on him, and hang on him till morning, like leeches sucking his blood. There is no defence against their darts, but to hide under a buffalo skin, or wrap oneself up in some stuff which they cannot pierce, and run the risk of being smothered.— When green or rotten wood can be procured, they may be driven away by smoke, but in such case the traveller himself is smoked, and in spite of all he can do, his eyes are filled with tears. As soon as the smoke ceases, they return to the charge till other wood is provided and thrown on the fire, so that the traveller's sleep is frequently interrupted, which proves very annoying after the fatigue of a troublesome journey. Another species of insects, called brulots, are found by myriads in the desert, and are not less troublesome than the musquito. They are so small that they are scarcely perceptible, and light on any part of the body that is uncovered, penetrating even into the eyes, ears and nostrils. To guard against them, the traveller, even in the warmest weather, wears gloves, ties a handkerchief over his forehead, neck and ears, and smokes a short pipe or a cigar to drive them from his eyes and nostrils. The fire-fly is a harmless insect. When they are seen in great numbers, darting their phosphoric light through the darkness, it is a sure sign that rain is at hand. The light which they emit is very brilliant, and appears as if it proceeded from wandering meteors. It is a favorite amusement with the Indians to catch these insects, and after rubbing the phosphoric matter over their faces, to walk around the camp, for the purpose of frightening children and exciting mirth.

As our hunters were scarcely ever disappointed in finding game, we have seldom had recourse to fishing; hence our acquaintance with the finny race is rather limited.— On some occasions, when provisions were becoming scarce, the line had to supply the place of the gun. The fish which we generally caught were the mullet, two kinds of trout, and a species of carps. Once, whilst we lay encamped on the banks of Snake river, I caught more than a hundred of these carps in the space of an hour. The anchovy, the sturgeon, and the salmon, abound in the rivers of the Oregon Territory. There are six species of salmon. They come up the rivers towards the end of April, and after spawning, never return; but the young ones go down to the sea in September, and it is supposed that they re-enter the rivers the fourth year after they have left them.

QUADRUPEDS. The Beaver seems to have chosen this country for his own. Every one knows how they work, and what use they make of their teeth and tail. What we were told by the trappers is probably unknown to many.—When they are about constructing a dam, they examine all the trees on the bank, and chose the one that is most bent over the water on the side where they want to erect their fort. If they find no tree of this kind they repair to another place, or patiently wait till a violent wind gives the requisite inclination to some of the trees. Some of the Indian tribes believe that the beavers are a degraded race of human beings, whose vices and crimes have induced the Great Spirit to punish them by changing them into their present form; and they think, after the lapse of a number of years, their punishment will cease, and they will be restored to their original shape. They even believe that these animals use a kind of language to communicate their thoughts to each other, to consult, deliberate, pass sentence on delinquents, &c. The Trappers assured us that such beavers as are unwilling to work, are unanimously pro-scribed, and exiled from the Republic, and that they are obliged to seek some abandoned hole, at a distance from the rest, where they spend the winter in a state of starva-tion. These are esily caught, but their skin is far inferior to that of the more industrious neighbors, whose foresight and perseverance have procured them abundant provi-sions, and a shelter against the severity of the winter sea-son. The flesh of the beaver is fat and savory. The feet are deemed the most dainty parts. The tail affords a sub-stitute for butter. The skin is sold for nine or ten dollars' worth of provisions or merchandise, the value of which does not amount to a single silver dollar. For a gill of whiskey, which has not cost the trader more than three or four cents, is sometimes sold for three or four dollars, though the chief virtue which it possesses is to kill the body and soul of the buyer. We need not wonder then when we see that wholesale dealers in this poisonous article realize large fortunes in a very short time, and that the retailers, of whom some received as much as eight hundred dollars per annum, often present a most miserable appearance before the year expires. The Honorable Hudson Bay Company does not belong to this class of traders. By them the sale of all sorts of liquors is strictly forbidden.

The Otter is an inhabitant of the mountain rivers. His color is dark brown or black. Like the beaver, he is incessantly pursued by the hunters, and the number of both these animals is yearly diminished. Among other amphibious animals we find two species of the frog. One does not differ from the European, but the other offers scarcely any resemblance. It has a tail and horns and is only found on the most arid soil. By some of our travellers it was called the Salamander.

Opossums are common here. They are generally found near marshes and ponds that abound in small clawfish, of which they are extremely fond. To catch them he places himself on the bank, and lets his long hairless tail hang down in the water. The crawfish are allured by the bait, and as soon as they put their claws to it, the opossum throws them up, seizes them sideways between his teeth, and carries them to some distance from the water, where he greedily but cautiously devours his prey.

The Badger inhabits the whole extent of the desert; he is seldom seen, as he retires to his hole at the least approach of danger. Some naturalists refer this animal to the genuine Ursus. Its size is that of the Dormouse; its color silver grey; its paws are short, and its strength prodigious. A Canadian having seized one as he entered the hole, he required the assistance of another man to pull him out.

The Prairie Dog, in shape, color and agility, more resembles the squirrel than the animal from which it has taken its name. They live together in separate lodges, to the number of several thousands. The earth which they throw up to construct their lodges, forms a kind of slope which prevents the rain from entering the holes. At the approach of man, this little animal runs into its lodge, uttering a piercing cry, which puts the whole tribe on their guard. After some minutes, the boldest show a part of their heads, as if to spy the enemy, and this is the moment which the hunter chooses to kill them. The Indians informed us that they sometimes issue in a body, apparently to hold a council, and that wisdom presides over their deliberations. They admit to their dwellings the bird of Minerva, the striped squirrel, and the rattlesnake, and it is impossible to determine what is the cause of this wonderful sympathy. It is said too that they live only on the dew of the grass root, a remark founded upon the position of their village, which is always found where the ground is waterless and barren.

The Polecat or Memphitis Americana, is a beautifully speckled animal. When pursued, it raises its tail, and discharges a large quantity of fluid, which nature has intended for its defence. It repeats these discharges in proportion as the pursuer comes near it. So strong is the fœtid odor of this liquid that neither man nor beast can bear it. It happened once that Rev. Father Van Quickenborne saw two of these cats. He took them for young cubs, and pleased with the discovery, he alighted from his horse, and wished to catch them. He approached them cautiously, and was just ready to put his large hat over one of them, when all at once a discharge was made that covered him all over. It was impossible to go near him—all around him was infected. His clothes could no longer be used, and the poor man, though rather late, resolved never again to attempt to catch young bears!

The Cabri (Antelope) resembles the deer in form and size, the antlers are smaller and have but two branches; the color of the animal resembles that of the stag; the eyes are large and piercing; and its gait in the wilderness is a kind of elegant gallop. Sometimes the Antelope stops short and rears his head to observe his pursuer; this is the most favorable moment to kill him. When started or shot at and missed, he darts forward with incredible swiftness, but curiosity induces him to halt and look back. The hunter tries to amuse his curiosity, by holding up and waving some bright colored object: the animal approaches, and curiosity becomes the cause of his death. The flesh is wholesome, and easily digested, but it is used only where deer and buffalo meat are wanting. The Antelope hunt is a favorite sport with the Indians. They choose a spot of ground from fifty to eighty feet square, and enclose it with posts and boughs, leaving a small opening or entrance, two or three feet wide. From this entrance they construct two wings or hedges, which they extend for several miles.—After this they form a large semicircle, and drive the Antelopes before them till they enter between the hedges, where they press so hard upon them that they force them into the square enclosure, in which they kill them with clubs. I have been told that the number of Antelopes thus driven into the enclosure, often amounts to more than two hundred. The meat of the buffalo cow is the most wholesome and the most common in the west. It may be called the *daily bread* of the traveller, for he never loses his relish for it.— It is more easily procured than any other, and it is good throughout. Though some prefer the tongue, others the hump, or some other favorite piece, all the parts are excellent food. To preserve the meat it is cut in slices, thin enough to be dried in the sun; sometimes a kind of hash is made of it, and this is mixed with the marrow taken from the largest bones. This kind of mixture is called Bull or Cheese, and is generally served up and eaten raw, but when boiled or baked it is of more easy digestion, and has a more savory taste to a civilized palate. The form and size of the buffalo are sufficiently known. It is a gregarious animal, and is seldom seen alone. Several hundreds herd together, the males on one side, the females on the other, except at a certain season of the year. In the month of June we saw an immense herd of them on the Platte.— The chase of this animal is very interesting. The hunters are all mounted; at the signal given, they fall upon the herd, which is soon dispersed; each one choses his own animal: for he who slays the first is looked upon as the king of the chase—his aim must be sure and mortal, for the animal, when wounded, becomes furious, turns upon his hunter and pursues him in his turn. We once witnessed a scene of this kind. A young American had the imprudence to swim over a river and pursue a wounded buffalo with no other weapon but his knife. The animal turned back upon him, and had it not been for the young Englishman, whom I have already mentioned, his imprudence would have cost him his life. The greatest feat of a hunter is to drive the wounded animal to any place he thinks proper. We had a hunter named John Gray, reputed one of the best marksmen of the mountains; he had frequently given proofs of extraordinary courage and dexterity, especially when on one occasion he dared to attack five bears at once. Wishing to give us another sample of his valor, he drove an enormous buffalo he had wounded, into the midst of the caravan. The animal had stood about fifty shots, and been pierced by more than twenty balls; three times he had fallen, but fury increasing his strength, he had risen, after each fall, and with his horns threatened all who dared to approach him. At last the hunter took a decisive aim, and the buffalo fell to rise no more.

The small chase is carried on without horses. An experienced hunter, though on foot, may attack a whole herd of buffalos; but he must be skilful and cautious. He must approach them against the wind, for fear of starting the game, for so acute is the scent of the buffalo that he smells his enemy at a very considerable distance. Next, he must approach them as much as possible without being seen or suspected. If he cannot avoid being seen, he draws a skin over his head, or a kind of hood, surmounted by a pair of horns, and thus deceives the herd. When within gun shot, he must hide himself behind a bank or any other object. There he waits till he can take sure aim. The report of the gun, and the noise made by the fall of the wounded buffalo, astound, but do not drive away the rest. In the meantime, the hunter re-loads his gun, and shoots again, repeating the manœuvre, till five or six, and sometime more buffalos have fallen, before he finds it necessary to abandon his place of concealment.— The Indians say that the buffalos live together as the bees, under the direction of a queen, and that when the queen is wounded, all the others surround and deplore her.

If this were the case, the hunter who had the good fortune to kill the queen, would have fine sport in despatching the rest. After death, the animal is dressed, that is, he is stripped of his robe, quartered and divided; the best pieces are chosen and carried off by the hunter, who, when the chase has been successful, is sometimes satisfied with the tongue alone. The rest is left for the wolves. These voracious prowlers soon come to the banquet, except when the scene of slaughter is near the camp. In such cases they remain at bay till night, when all is still. Then they come to the charge, and set up such howling that they frighten the inexperienced traveller. But their yells and howlings, however frightful, have little or no effect upon those whose ears have become accustomed to such music. These sleep with as little concern as if there were not a wolf in the country.

Of wolves we have seen four varieties, the grey, the white, the black, and the bluish. The grey seems to be the most common, as they are the most frequently seen.— The black wolves are large and ferocious animals. They sometimes mingle with a herd of buffalos, and at first appear quite harmless, but when they find a young calf strayed from its dam, or an old cow on the brink of a precipice, they are sure to attack and kill the former, and to harass the latter till they succeed in pushing it down the precipice. The wolves are very numerous in these regions—the plains are full of holes, which are generally deep, and into which they retire when hunger does not compel them to prowl about, or when they are pursued by the huntsman. There is a small sized wolf, called the medicine wolf, regarded by the Indians as a sort of Manitou. They watch its yelpings during the night, and the superstitious conjurers pretend to understand and interpret them. According to the loudness, frequency, and other modifications of these yelpings, they interpret that either friends or foes approach the camp, &c., and if it happens that on some other occasion they conjecture right, the prediction is never forgotten, and the conjurers take care to mention it on every emergency.

There are also four kinds of bears, distinguished by the colors: white, black, brown and grey. The white and grey bears are what the lion is in Asia, the kings of the mountains: they are scarcely inferior to the lion in form and courage. I have sometimes joined in the chase of this animal, but I was in good company—safe from danger.— Four Indian hunters ran around the bear and stunned him with their cries—they soon despatched him. In less than a quarter of an hour after this, another fell beneath their blows. This chase is perhaps the most dangerous; for the bear, when wounded, becomes furious, and unless he be disabled, as was the case in the two instances mentioned, he attacks and not unfrequently kills his pursuers. Messrs. Lewis and Clarke, in their expedition to the sources of the Missouri, adduce a striking proof of the physical strength of this animal, which shows that he is a most formidable enemy. One evening, the men who were in the hindmost canoe, discovered a bear, crouched in the prairie, at a distance of about three hundred yards from the river. Six of them, all skilful hunters, left the canoe, and advanced to attack him. Protected by a little eminence, they approached without being perceived, till they were but forty steps from the animal. Four of the men discharged their guns, and each one lodged a ball in his body—two of the balls had pierced the lungs. The bear, frantic with rage, starts up and rushes upon his enemies, with wide extended jaws. As he approached, the two hunters who had kept their fire, inflicted two wounds on him; one of the balls broke his shoulder, which for a few moments retarded his progress, but before they could re-load their guns, he was so close upon them that they had to run with the greatest speed to the river. Here he was at the point of seizing them—two of the men threw themselves into the canoe, the four others scattered and hid themselves among the willows, where they loaded and fired with the greatest expedition. They wounded him several times, which only served to increase his fury; at last he pursued two of them so closely, that they were compelled to provide for their safety by leaping into the river from a perpendicular bank nearly twenty feet high. The bear followed them, and was but a few feet from them, when one of the hunters who had come from his lurking place, sent a ball through his head and killed him. They dragged him to the shore, and there ascertained that not less than eight balls passed through his body.

I remain, Rev. and dear Father Provincial,

Yours, &c.

P. J. De Smet, S. J.

LETTER VIII.

Hell Gate, 21st Sept. 1841.

Rev. and Dear Father Provincial:

It is on a journey through the desert that we see how attentive Providence is to the wants of man. I repeat with pleasure this remark of my young Protestant friend, because the truth of it appears through the narrative which I have commenced, and will appear still more evidently in what is to follow. Were I to speak of rivers, the account would be long and tedious, for in five days we crossed as many as eighteen, and crossed one of them five times in the space of a few hours. I shall only mention the most dangerous among them. The first, which we found it very difficult to cross, was the South Fork of the Platte. But as we had been long apprised of the difficulty, we took our precautions before hand, and some of our Canadians had explored it with so much care, that we forded it, not without great difficulty, but without any serious accident. The greatest distress was felt by the dogs of the caravan. Left on the bank, when all had crossed, nothing but fidelity towards their masters could have induced them to swim over a river but little less than a mile wide, and having so rapid a current that it would have carried away wagons and carts, had they not been supported on all sides, while the mules exerted all their strength to pull them onward. The poor dogs did not attempt to cross till they found that there was no medium left between encountering the danger and losing their masters. The passage over these rivers is generally effected by means of a bull boat, the name given to a kind of boat, constructed on the spot with buffalo hides. They are indispensable when the current is impetuous, and no ford can be found. Thanks to our Canadians, we wanted them neither on this nor any other occasion.

The second difficult passage was over the North Fork, which is less wide, but deeper and more rapid than the Southern. We had crossed the latter in carts. Having mustered a little more courage, we determined to cross the North Fork on horseback. We were induced to do so, on seeing our hunter drive before him a horse on which his wife was mounted, whilst at the same time he was pulling a colt that carried a little girl but one year old. To hold back under such circumstances would have been a disgrace for Indian Missionaries. We therefore resolved to go forward. It is said that we were observed to grow pale, and I am inclined to believe we did; yet, after our horses had for some time battled against the current, we reached the opposite shore in safety, though our clothes were dripping wet. Here we witnessed a scene, which, had it been less serious, might have excited laughter. The largest wagon was carried off by the force of the current, in spite of all the efforts, shouts and cries of the men, who did all they could to keep themselves from being drowned. Another wagon was literally turned over. One of the mules showed only his four feet on the surface of the water, and the others went adrift entangled in the gears. On one side appeared the American captain, with extended arms, crying for help. On the other, a young German traveller was seen diving with his beast, and soon after both appearing above water at a distance from each other. Here a horse reached the shore without a rider; further on, two

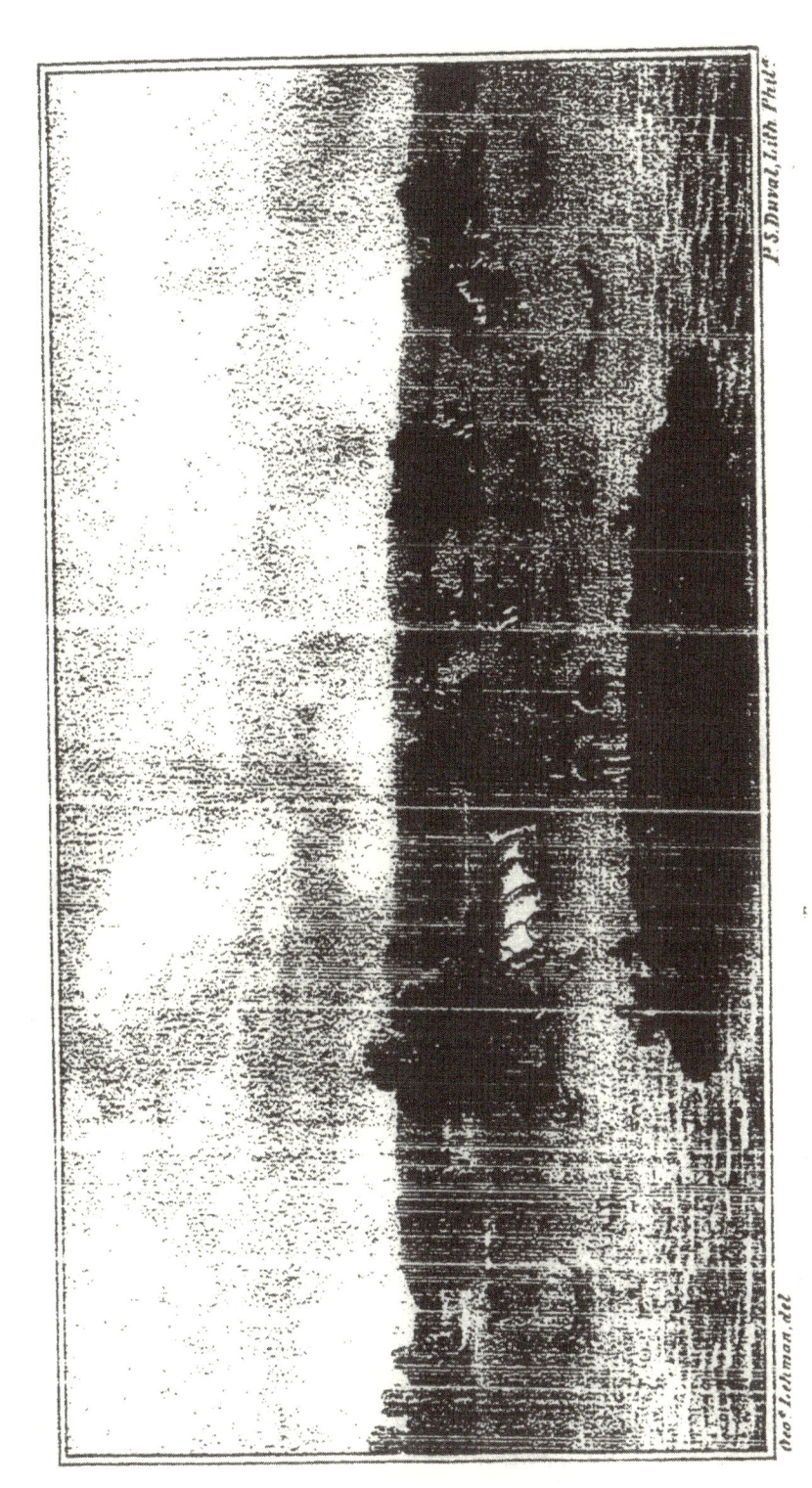

FORDING THE RIVER PLATTE.

riders appeared on the same horse; finally, the good brother Joseph dancing up and down with his horse, and Father Mengarrini clinging to the neck of his, and looking as if he formed an indivisible part of the animal. After all our difficulties, we found that only one of the mules was drowned. As the mule belonged to a man who had been the foremost in endeavoring to save both men and horses, the members of the caravan agreed to make him a present of a horse, as a reward for his services. We offered thanks to God for our escape from danger. I mentioned before that great dangers awaited us on Snake river. This stream being much less deep and wide than the other two, and having such limpid waters that the bottom can every where be seen, could only be dangerous to incautious persons. It sufficed to keep our eyes open, for any obstacle could easily be distinguished and avoided. But whether it were owing to want of thought or attention, or to the stubborn disposition of the team, Brother Charles Huet found himself all at once on the border of a deep precipice, too far advanced to return. Down went mules, driver and vehicle, and so deep was the place, that there scarcely appeared any chance to save them. Our hunter, at the risk of his life, threw himself into the river, to dive after the poor brother, whom he had to pull out of the carriage. All the Flat Heads who were with us, tried to save the vehicle, the mules and the baggage. The baggage, with the exception of a few articles, was saved; the carriage was raised by the united efforts of all the Indians, and set afloat; but after this operation it was held by but one of them, he found that his strength was inadequate to the task, and crying that he was being drowned, let go his hold. The hunter plunged in after him, and was himself at the point of losing his life, on account of the efforts which the Indian made to save his own. Finally, after prodigies of valor, exhibited by all the Flat Heads, men, women and children, who all strove to give us a proof of their attachment, we lost what we considered the most safe, the team of the carriage. The gears had been cut to enable the mules to reach the shore, but it is said that these animals always perish when once they have had their ears under water. Thus we lost our three finest mules. This loss was to us very considerable, and would have been irreparable, had it not been for the kindness of Captain Ermatinger. Whilst the people of the caravan were drying our baggage, I returned to the Fort, where the generous Captain repaired our loss for a sum truly inconsiderable, when compared with what must be paid on such occasions to those who wish to avail themselves of the misfortunes of others. We had escaped the danger, and were besides taught a very useful lesson, for it was remarked that it was the first day since we began our journey, on which, by reason of the bustle occasioned by our departure from the Fort, we had omitted to say the prayers of the itinerary.

We had dangers of another description to encounter, from which we were also delivered by the aid of God's grace. Once as we travelled along the banks of the Platte, several members of the caravan separated from the main body, contrary to the express orders of the Captain, who, together with Father Point and myself, had started a little ahead to look out for a place of encampment. We succeeded in finding a proper site, and we had already unsaddled our horses, when all at once we heard the alarm cry: *the Indians! the Indians!* And in fact, a body of Indians, appearing much larger than it really was, was seen in the distance, first assembling together, and then coming full

CHEYENNE WARRIORS.

gallop towards our camp. In the mean time a young American, unhorsed and unarmed, makes his appearance, complaining of the loss he had sustained, and indignant at the blows he had received. He seizes the loaded rifle of one of his friends, and rushes forward to take signal vengeance on the offender. The whole camp is roused; the American youth is determined to fight; the Colonel orders the wagons to be drawn up in double file, and places between them whatever may be exposed to plunder. All preparations are made for a regular defence. On the other hand, the Indian squadron, much increased, advances and presents a formidable front. They manœuvre as if they intend to hem in our phalanx, but at sight of our firm position, and of the assurance of the Captain, who advanced towards them, they checked their march, finally halted, and came to a parley, of which the result was that they should return to the American whatever they had taken from him, but that the blows which he had received should not be returned. After this, both parties united in smoking the calumet. This band consisted of 80 Sheyenne warriors, armed for battle. The Sheyennes are looked upon as the bravest Indians in the prairie. They followed our camp for two or three days. As the chiefs were admitted to our meals, both parties separated with mutual satisfaction.

On another occasion we were in company with the vanguard of the Flat Heads, and had penetrated into an impassible defile between the mountains, so that after having travelled the whole day, we were forced to retrace our steps At night the rumor was spread that a party of Banac Indians lay encamped in the neighborhood. The Banacs had this very year killed several white men; but it soon appeared that they were more frightened than ourselves, for before day break they had removed from the place.

Without being aware of it, we had escaped a much greater danger on the banks of Green River. We did not know the particulars of this danger till after we had arrived at Fort Hall. There we heard that almost immediately after our separation from the travellers who were on their way to California, and with whom we had till then lived as brothers, they divided themselves into two bands, and each band again subdivided into two parties, one to attend to the chase, the other to guard the horses. The hunter's camp was guarded only by five or six men and some women, who had also to keep watch over the horses and baggage of the others. A booty so rich and so much exposed could not but tempt the Indians who roamed in the neighborhood, and waited, as is their custom, till a seasonable opportunity should offer to commence the attack. When least expected, they fell first upon the horses, and then upon the tents, and though the guardians made a courageous defence, and sold their lives dearly, yet they burned and pillaged the camp, taking away whatever might be serviceable to them; thus giving a terrible lesson to such as expose themselves to lose all, by not remaining united to withstand the common enemy.*

But a few days after we had received this sad intelligence we ourselves were much alarmed. We apprehended lest we should have to defend our lives against a large body of Black Feet Indians, whose warriors continually infest the country through which we were then travelling. It was reported that they were behind the mountain, and soon

---

* The massacre of these travellers gave rise to several vague reports. As we had started together it was supposed by many that we had not yet separated when this unfortunate accident took place. Hence it was circulated in the United States, and even in some parts of Europe, that the Catholic Missionaries had all been killed by the Indians.

after that they were in sight. But our brave Indians, glowing with the desire to introduce us to their tribe, were undaunted, and would have attacked them, had they been a hundred times more numerous. Pilchimo, brandishing his musket in the air, started off with the greatest rapidity, and was followed by three or four others. They crossed the mountain and disappeared, and the whole camp made ready to repel the assailants. The horses were hitched and the men under arms, when we saw our brave Indians return over the mountain, followed by a dozen others. The latter were Banacs, who had united rather with a mind to fly than to attack us. Among them was a chief, who showed the most favorable dispositions. I had a long conference with him on the subject of religion, and he promised that he would use all his endeavors to engage his men to adopt religious sentiments. Both he and his retinue left us the day after the arrival of the Flat Heads, who came to wish us joy for the happy issue of our long journey. We here remarked how the power of reason acts upon the heart of the savage. The Banac chief was brother to an Indian of the tribe who had been killed by one of the Flat Head chiefs present on this occasion. They saluted each other in our presence and separated as truly Christian warriors would have done, who show enmity to each other only on the field of battle. Yet as the Flat Heads had more than once, been basely betrayed by the Banacs, the former did not offer to smoke the calmut. I hope that we shall have no difficulty to bring on a reconciliation. The Flat Heads will undoubtedly follow the advice we shall give them, and I feel confident that the Banacs will be satisfied with the conditions.

I have the honor to be
 Rev. and dear Father Provincial,
  Your devoted servant and son,
   P. J. De Smet, S. J.

LETTER IX.

St. Mary's, 18th October, 1841.

Rev. and Dear Father:

AFTER a journey of four months and a half on horseback through the desert, and in spite of our actual want of bread, wine, sugar, fruit, and all such things as are called the conveniences of life, we find our strength and courage increased, and are better prepared than ever to work at the conversion of the souls that Providence entrusts to our care. Next to the Author of all good things, we returned thanks to her whom the church reveres as the Mother of her Divine Spouse, since it has pleased the Divine goodness to send us the greatest consolations on several days consecrated to her honor. On the feast of her glorious Assumption we met the vanguard of our dear neophytes. On the Sunday within the Octave, we, for the first time since my return, celebrated the Holy Mysteries among them. On the following Sunday our good Indians placed themselves and their children under the Immaculate Heart of Mary, of which we then celebrated the feast. This act of devotion was renewed by the great chief in the name of his whole tribe, on the feast of her Holy Name. On the 24th of September, the feast of our Lady of Mercy, we arrived at the river called Bitter Root, on the banks of which we have chosen the site for our principal missionary station. On the first Sunday of October, feast of the Rosary, we took possession of the promised land, by planting a cross on the spot which we had chosen for our first residence. What motives of encouragement does not the Gospel of the present Sunday add to all these mentioned before. To-day too we celebrate the Divine Maternity, and what may we not expect from the Virgin Mother who brought forth her Son for the salvation of the world. On the feast of her Patronage we shall offer by her mediation to her Divine Son, twenty-five young Indians, who are to be baptized on that day. So many favors have induced us unanimously to proclaim Mary the protectress of our mission, and give her name to our new residence.

These remarks may appear silly to such as attribute every thing to chance or necessity, but to such as believe in the wise dispensations of the Providence of God, by which all things are governed and directed, all these circumstances, together with the wonderful manner in which we have been called, sent and led to this new mission; and still more the good dispositions manifested by the Indians, will appear very proper motives to inspire us with fresh courage, and with the hope of establishing here, on a small scale, the order and regularity which once distinguished our missions in Paraguay. This hope is not founded on imagination, for whilst I am writing these lines, I hear the joyful voices of the carpenters, re-echoing to the blows on the smith's anvil, and I see them engaged in raising the *house of prayer*. Besides, three Indians, belonging to the tribe called Pointed Hearts, having been informed of our arrival among the Flat Heads, have just come to entreat us to have pity on them. "Father," said one of them to me, "we are truly deserving your pity. We wish to serve the Great Spirit, but we know not how. We want some one to teach us. For this reason we make application to you." O had some of my brethren, now so far distant from us, been present here last Sunday, when towards night we raised the august sign of salvation, the standard of the cross, in this small but zealous tribe; how their hearts would have been moved on seeing the pious joy of these children of the forest! What sentiments of faith and love did they exhibit on this occasion, when headed by their chief, they came to kiss the foot of the cross, and then prostrate on their knees, made a sacred promise, rather to suffer death a thousand times, than to forsake the religion of Jesus Christ! Who knows how many of this chosen band may be destined to become apostles and martyrs of our holy religion! Were we more numerous, I feel confident that many other tribes would become members of the kingdom of God; perhaps more than two hundred thousand might be converted to Christ. The Flat Heads and the Pointed Hearts, it is true are not numerous tribes, but they are surrounded by many others who evince the best dispositions. The Ponderas or Pends-d'oreilles are very numerous, and live at a distance of four or five days journey from our present establishment. The chief who governed them last year and who has been baptized and called Peter, is a true apostle. In my first visit to them I baptized two hundred and fifty of their children. Many other tribes have the same origin, and though differing in name, their languages are nearly allied. Next to these are found the Spokans, who would soon follow the example of the neighboring tribes; the Pierced Noses, who are disgusted at the conduct of the Protestant ministers that have settled among them; the Snakes, the Crows and the Banacs whose chief we have seen. Last year I visited the Sheyennes, whom I twice met on the banks of the Platte; the numerous nation of the Scioux, and the three allied tribes called Mandans, Arickarees and Minatarees, who all have given me so many proofs of respect and friendship; the Omahas, with whom I have had so many conferences on the subject of religion, and many others who seem inclined to embrace the truth.

The Black Feet are the only Indians of whose salvation we would have reason to despair, if the ways of God were the same as those of man, for they are murderers, thieves, traitors, and all that is wicked. But were not the Chiquitos, the Chiriquans, the Hurons, and the Iroquois equally wicked before their conversion, which required much time and great help from above? And is it not to the last, that, under God, the Flat Heads owe their desire of becoming members of his church, and the first germs of the copious fruit that has been produced among them? What is more, the Black Feet are not hostile to Black Gowns. We have been assured by other Indians that we would have nothing to fear, if we presented ourselves amongst them as ministers of religion. When last year I fell into the hands of one of their divisions, and it was ascertained that I was an interpreter of the Great Spirit, they carried me in triumph on a buffalo robe to their village, and invited me to a banquet, at which all the great men of the tribe assisted. It was on this occasion, that, whilst I said grace, I was astonished to see that they struck the earth with one hand and raised the other towards heaven, to signify that the earth produces nothing but evil, whilst all that is good comes from above. From all this you will easily conclude that the harvest is great, whilst the laborers are few.

It is the opinion of the Missionaries who accompany me, and of the travellers I have seen in the Far West, in short, of all those who have become acquainted with the Flat Heads, that they are characterised by the greatest simplicity, docility and uprightness. Yet, to the simplicity of children is joined the courage of heroes. They never begin the attack, but wo to such as provoke them or treat them unjustly. A handful of their warriors will not shrink from an enemy twenty times more numerous than they; they will stand and repel the assault, and at last put them to flight, and make them repent their rashness. Not long before my first arrival among them, seventy men of the tribe, finding themselves forced to come to an engagement with a thousand Black Feet warriors, determined to sustain the attack, and rather to die than retreat. Before the engagement they prostrated themselves and addressed such prayers as they had learned to the Great Spirit. They rose full of courage, sustained the first shock, and soon rendered the victory doubtful. The fight, with several interruptions, was continued five successive days, till at last the Black Feet, astounded at the boldness of their antagonists, were panic struck, and retreated from the scene of action, leaving many killed and wounded on the field of battle, whilst not one warrior of the Flat Heads was killed. But one died of the wounds he had received, and his death happened several months after the engagement, on the day succeeding his baptism—(though the point of an arrow had pierced his skull.) It was on the same occasion that Pilchimo, whom I have already mentioned, gave remarkable proofs of valor and attachment to his fellow warriors. All the horses were on the point of falling into the enemy's hand. Pilchimo was on foot. Not far off was a squaw on horseback; to see the danger, to take the sqraw from her horse and mount it himself, to gallop to the other horses, and bring them together, and drive them into the camp, was the affair of a few minutes. Another warrior, named Sechelmeld, saw a Black Foot separated from his company, and armed with a musket. The Black Foot, taking the warrior for one of his own tribe, asked the Flat Head to let him mount behind him. The latter wishing to make himself master of the musket, agreed to the proposal. They advance on the plain, till Sechelmed seeing that the place favored his design, seizes his fellow rider's weapon, exclaiming; "Black Foot! I am a Flat Head, let go your musket." He wrests it from his hands, despatches him, remounts the horse, and gallops off in pursuit of the enemy.

The following feat equally deserves to be recorded: A Black Foot warrior was taken and wounded whilst in the act of stealing a horse. The night was dark and the wound had rendered him furious. He held his loaded gun, and threatened death to any one that should approach him. Peter, one of the chiefs already mentioned, though diminutive in size, and far advanced in years, felt his courage revived; he runs up to the enemy, and with one blow fells him to the ground. This done he throws himself on his knees, and raising his eyes towards heaven, he is reported to have said: "Great Spirit! thou knowest that I did not kill this Black Foot from a desire of revenge, but because I was forced to it; be merciful to him in the other world. I forgive him from the bottom of my heart all the evils which he has wished to inflict upon us, and to prove the sincerity of my words I will cover him with my garment." This Peter was baptized last year, and became the apostle of his tribe. Even before baptism, his simplicity and sincerity prompted him to give this testimony of himself: "If ever I have done evil it was through ignorance, for I have always done what I considered good." It would be tedious to give an account of his zealous endeavors. Every morning, at an early hour, he rides through the whole village, stops at every hut, speaks a few words of encouragement and reproof, as circumstances require, and exhorts all to be faithful in the performance of their religious and social duties.

I have spoken of the simplicity and the courage of the Flat Heads; I shall make some other remarks concerning their character. They little resemble the majority of the Indians, who are, generally speaking, uncouth, importunate, improvident, insolent, stubborn and cruel.— The Flat Heads are disinterested, generous, devoted to their brethren and friends; irreproachable, and even exemplary, as regards probity and morality. Among them, dissensions, quarrels, injuries and enemities are unknown. During my stay in the tribe last year, I have never remarked any thing that was contrary to modesty and decorum in the manners and conversation of the men and women. It is true that the children, whilst very young, are entirely without covering, but this is a general custom among the Indians, and seems to have no bad effect upon them; we are determined, however, to abolish this custom as soon as we shall be able to do it. With respect to religion, the Flat Heads are distinguished by the firmness of their faith, and the ardor of their zeal. Not a vestige of their former superstitions can be discovered. Their confidence in us is unlimited. They believe without any difficulty the most profound mysteries of our holy religion, as soon as they are proposed to them, and they do not even suspect that we might be deceived, or even could wish to deceive them. I have already mentioned what exertions they have made to obtain Black-gowns for their tribe; the journeys, undertakings, the dangers incurred, the misfortunes suffered to attain their object. Their conduct during my absence from them has been truly regular and edifying. They attend divine service with the greatest punctuality, and pay the most serious attention to the explanation of the Catechism. What modesty and fervent piety do they not exhibit in their prayers, and with what humble simplicity they speak of their former blindness, and of such things as tend to reflect honor upon their present conduct. On this last subject their simplicity is truly admirable: "Father," some will say, with down cast eyes, "what I tell you now I have never mentioned to any one, nor shall I ever mention it to others; and if I speak of it to you, it is because you wish and have a right to know it."

The chiefs, who might be more properly called the fathers of the tribe, having only to express their will, and are obeyed, are always listened to, and are not less remarkable for their docility in our regard than for the ascendancy they possess over their people. The most influential among them, surnamed "The Little Chief," from the smallness of his stature, whether considered as a christian or a warrior, might stand a comparison with the most renowned character of ancient chivalry. On one occasion, he sustained the assaults of a whole village, which, contrary to all justice, attacked his people. On another occasion, when the Banacs had been guilty of the blackest treason, he marched against them with a party of warriors not one-tenth the number of their aggressors. But, under such a leader, his little band believed themselves invincible, and invoking the protection of heaven, rushed upon the enemy, and took signal vengeance of the traitors, killing nine of their number. More would have been killed, had not the voice of Little Chief arrested them in the very heat of the pursuit, announcing that it was the Sabbath, and the hour of prayer. Upon this signal, they gave over the pursuit, and returned to their camp. Arrived there, they immediately, without thinking of dressing their wounds, fell upon their knees in the dust, to render to the Lord of Hosts the honor of the victory. Little Chief had received a ball through the right hand, which had entirely deprived him of its use; but seeing two of his comrades more severely wounded than himself, he with his other hand rendered them every succor in his power, remaining the whole night in attendance upon them. On several other occasions, he acted with equal courage, prudence and humanity, so that his reputation became widely spread. The Nez-perces, a nation far more numerous than the Flat Heads, came to offer him the dignity of being their Great Chief. He might have accepted it without detriment to the rights of any one, as every Indian is free to leave his chief, and place himself under any other head he may think proper, and, of course, to accept any higher grade that may be offered to him. But Little Chief, content with the post assigned him by Providence, refused the offer, however honorable to him, with this simple remark, "By the will of the Great Master of life I was born among the Flat Heads, and if such be His will, among the Flat Heads I am determined to die;"—a patriotic feeling, highly honorable to him. As a warrior, still more honorable to his character are the mildness and humility manifested by him. He said to me, once: "Till we came to know the true God, alas, how blinded were we! We prayed, it is true— but to whom did we address our prayers? In truth, I know not how the Great Spirit could have borne with us so long." At present his zeal is most exemplary; not content with being the foremost in all the offices at chapel, he is always the first and last at the family prayers, and even before break of day he is heard singing the praises of his Maker. His characteristic trait is mildness; and yet he can assume due firmness, not to say severity of manner, when he sees it necessary to exercise more rigorous discipline. Some days before our arrival, one of the young women had absented herself from prayer, without a sufficient reason. He sent for her, and after reading her a lecture before all the household, enforced his motives for greater attention in future, by a smart application of the cane. And how did the young offender receive the correction? With the most humble and praiseworthy submission.

The Flat Heads are fond of praying. After the regular evening prayer, they will assemble in their tents to pray or sing canticles. These pious exercises will frequently be prolonged till a late hour; and if any wake during the night, they begin to pray. Before making his prayer, the good old Simeon gets up and rakes out the live coals upon his hearth, and when his prayer is done, which is always preceded and followed by the sign of the cross, he smokes his calmut and then turns in again. This he will do three or four times during the night. There was a time, also, when these more watchful spirits of the household, not content with praying themselves, would awaken the sleepers, anxious to make them partakers of the good work.— These pious excesses had sprung from a little piece of advice I had given them on my first visit, that " on waking at night it was commendable to raise the heart to God." It has since been explained to them how they are to understand the advice. This night, between the 25th and 26th, the prayers and canticles have not ceased. Yesterday, a young woman having died who had received baptism four days previously, we recommended them to pray for the repose of her soul. Her remains were deposited at the foot of the Calvary, erected in the midst of the camp. On the cross upon her grave might confidently be inscribed the words: *In spem Resurrectionis*—In hope of a glorious Resurrection. We shall shortly have to celebrate the commemoration of the faithful departed; this will afford us an opportunity of establishing the very christian and standing custom of praying for the dead in their place of interment.

On Sundays, the exercises of devotion are longer and more numerous, and yet they are never fatigued with the pious duty. They feel that the happiness of the little and of the humble is to speak with their Heavenly Father, and that no house presents so many attractions as the house of the Lord. Indeed, so religiously is the Sunday observed here, that on this day of rest, even before our coming, the most timorous deer might wander unmolested in the midst of the tribe, even though they were reduced by want of provisions to the most rigorous fast. For, in the eyes of this people, to use the bow and arrow on this day, would not have appeared less culpable than did the gathering of wood to the scrupulous fidelity of the people of God.— Since they have conceived a juster idea of the law of grace, they are less slaves to " the letter that killeth ;" but still desirous to be faithful to the very letter, they are studious to do their best, and when any doubt arises, they hasten to be enlightened thereon, soliciting in a spirit of faith and humility that permission of which they may think themselves to stand in need.

The principal chief is named "Big Face," on account of the somewhat elongated form of his visage; he might more nobly and more appropriately be named The Nestor of the Desert, for as well in years as in stature and sagacity he has all the essentials of greatness. From his earliest infancy, nay, even before he could know his parents, he had been the child of distress. Being left a helpless orphan, by the death of his mother, with no one to protect him, it was proposed to bury him with her in the same grave—a circumstance that may serve to give some idea of the ignorance and brutality of his tribe. But the Almighty, who had other purposes in his regard, moved the heart of a young woman to compassionate his helpless condition, and offer to become a mother to him. Her humanity was abundantly recompensed by seeing her adopted son distinguished above all his fellows by intelligence, gentleness, and every good disposition. He was grateful, docile, charitable, and naturally so disposed to piety, that, from a want of knowing the true God, he more than once was led to place his trust in that which was but the work of his own hands.— Being one day lost in a forest, and reduced to extremity, he began to embrace the trunk of a fallen tree, and to conjure it to have pity upon him. Nor is it above two months since a serious loss befel him; indeed one of the most serious that could happen to an Indian—the loss of three calmuts at the same time. He spent no time in retracing his steps, and to interest heaven in his favor, he put up the following prayer: "Oh Great Spirit, you who see all things and undo all things, grant, I entreat you, that I may find what I am looking for; and yet let thy will be done." This prayer should have been addressed to God. He did not find the calmuts, but in their place he received what was of more incomparable value—simplicity, piety, wisdom, patience, courage, and cool intrepidity in the hour of danger. More favored in one respect than Moses, this new guide of another people to God, after a longer sojournment in the wilderness, was at length successful in introducing his children into the land of promise. He was the first of his tribe who received baptism, and took the name of Paul, and like his patron, the great Apostle, he has labored assiduously to gain over his numerous children to the friendship and love of his Lord and Master.

I remain, Rev. Father Provincial,
Yours, &c.
P. J. DE SMET, S. J.

LETTER X.

St. Mary's, Rocky Mountains, 26th Oct. 1842.
Rev. and Dear Father Provincial:

This last letter will contain the practical conclusions of what has been stated in the preceding. I am confident that these conclusions will be very agreeable and consoling to all persons who feel interested in the progress of our holy religion, and who very prudently refuse to form a decided opinion, unless they can found it on well attested facts.

From what has hitherto been said, we may draw this conclusion, that the nation of the Flat Heads appear to be a chosen people—" the elect of God;" that it would be easy to make this tribe a model for other tribes,—the seed of two hundred thousand christians, who would be as fervent as were the converted Indians of Paraguay; and that the conversion of the former would be effected with more facility than that of the latter. The Flat Heads have no communication with corrupt tribes; they hold all sects in aversion; they have a horror of idolatry; they cherish much sympathy for the whites, but chiefly for the Black Gowns, (Catholic Priests) a name, which, in consequence of the prepossessions and favorable impressions, which they have received from the Iroquois, is synonymous with goodness, learning, and Catholicity. Their position is central.— Their territory sufficiently extensive to contain several missions; the land is fertile, the country surrounded by high mountains. They are independent of all authority except that of God, and those who represent him. They have no tribute to pay but that of prayer; they have already acquired practical experience of the advantages of a civilized over a barbarous state of life; and in fine, they are fully convinced and firmly persuaded that without the religion that is announced to them, they can be happy neither in this world nor in the next.

From all these considerations, we may again draw the conclusions, that the best end which we can propose to ourselves is that which our Fathers of Paraguay had in view when they commenced their missionary labors; and that the means to attain this end should be the same, chiefly because these means have been approved by the most respectable authorities, crowned with perfect success, and admired even by the enemies of our religion.

The principle being admitted, it only remains to form a correct idea of the method employed by our Fathers in Paraguay to improve the minds, and hearts of their Neophytes, and to bring them to that degree of perfection of which they conceived them susceptible. After having seriously reflected on what Muratori relates of the establishments in Paraguay, we have concluded that the following points should be laid down, as rules to direct the conduct of our converts.

1. *With regard to God.*—Simple, firm, and lively faith with respect to all the truths of religion, and chiefly such as are to be believed as Theologians express it, *necessitate medii et necessitate præcepti.* Profound respect for the only true religion; perfect submission to the church of God, in all that regards faith and morality, discipline, &c. Tender and solid piety towards the Blessed Virgin

and the Saints. Desire of the conversion of others. Courage and fortitude of the Martyrs.

2. *With regard to our neighbor.*—Respect for those in authority, for parents, the aged, &c. Justice, charity, and generosity towards all.

3. *With regard to one's self.*—Humility, modesty, meekness, discretion, temperance, irreproachable behavior, industry or love of labor, &c.

We shall strenuously recommend the desire of the conversion of others, because Providence seems to have great designs with respect to our small tribe. In one of our instructions given in a little chapel, constructed of boughs, not less than twenty-four nations were represented, including ourselves. Next, the courage and fortitude of the Martyrs, because in the neighborhood of the Black Feet there is continual danger of losing either the life of the soul, or that of the body. Also, industry or the love of labor, because idleness is the predominant vice of Indians; and even the Flat Heads, if they are not addicted to idleness, at least, manifest a striking inaptitude to manual labor, and it will be absolutely necessary to conquer this.— To ensure success, much time and patience will be required. Finally and chiefly, profound respect for the true religion, to counteract the manœuvres of various sectaries, who, desirous as it would seem, to wipe away the reproach formerly made by Muratori, and in our days by the celebrated Dr. Wiseman, use all their efforts to make proselytes, and to appear disinterested, and even zealous in the propagation of their errors.

4. *With regard to the means.*—Flight from all contaminating influence; not only from the corruption of the age, but from what the gospel calls the world. Caution against

all immediate intercourse with the whites, even with the workmen, whom necessity compels us to employ, for though these are not wicked, still they are far from possessing the qualities necessary to serve as models to men who are humble enough to think they are more or less perfect, in proportion as their conduct corresponds with that of the whites. We shall confine them to the knowledge of their own language, erect schools among them, and teach them reading, writing, arithmetic and singing. Should any exception be made to this general rule, it will be in favor of a small number, and only when their good dispositions will induce us to hope that we may employ them as auxiliaries in religion. A more extensive course of instruction would undoubtedly prove prejudicial to these good Indians, whose simplicity is such that they might easily be imposed upon, if they were to come in contact with error, whilst it is the source of all truth and virtue when enlightened by the flambeau of faith. La Harpe himself, speaking of the Apostolic laborers of our society, says that the perfection of our ministry consists in illumining by faith the ignorance of the savage.

To facilitate the attainment of the end in view, we have chosen the place of the first missionary station, formed the plan of the village, made a division of the lands, determined the form of the various buildings, &c. The buildings deemed most necessary and useful at present are, a church, schools, work houses, store houses, &c. Next, we have made regulations respecting public worship, religious exercises, instructions, catechisms, confraternities, the administration of the Sacraments, singing, music, &c. All this is to be executed in conformity with the plan formerly adopted in the Missions of Paraguay.

Such are the resolutions which we have adopted, and

which we submit to be approved, amended or modified, by those who have the greater glory of God at heart, and who, by their position and the graces of their state of life are designed by the Most High to communicate to us the true spirit of our Society.

Believe me to be,
>Rev. and dear Father Provincial,
>>Your devoted son in Christ,
>>>P. J. DE SMET, S. J.

LETTER XI.

St. Mary's, December —, 1841.

Reverend Father:

I shall here give you the remarks and observations I have made, and the information I have gathered, during this last journey, concerning some customs and practices of the savages.

In speaking of the animals, I inquired of seven Flat Heads, who were present, how many cows they had killed between them in their last hunt? The number amounted to one hundred and eighty-nine—one alone had killed fifty-nine. One of the Flat Heads told me of three remarkable *hits* which had distinguished him in that chase. He pursued a cow, armed merely with a stone, and killed her by striking her while running, between the horns; he afterwards killed a second with his knife; and finished his exploits by spearing and strangling a large ox. The young warriors frequently exercise themselves in this manner, to show their agility, dexterity and strength. He who spoke looked like a Hercules. They then, (a rare favor, for they are not boasters,) kindly showed me the scars left by the balls and arrows of the Black Feet in their different encounters. One of them bore the scars of four balls which had pierced his thigh; the only consequence of which was a little stiffness of the leg, scarcely perceptible. Another had his arm and breast pierced by a ball. A third, beside some wounds from a knife and spear, had an arrow, five inches deep, in his belly. A fourth had still two balls in his body. One among them, a cripple, had his leg broken by a ball sent by an enemy concealed in a hole; leaping on one leg he fell upon the Black Foot, and the hiding place of the foe became his grave. "These Black Feet," I remarked, " are terrible people." The Indian who last spoke replied in the sense of the words of Napoleon's grenadier, " Oui, mais ils meurent vite apres." I expressed a desire to know the medicines which they used in such cases; they, much surprised at my question, replied, laughing, " we apply nothing to our wounds, they close of themselves." This recalled to me the reply of Captain Bridger in the past year. He had had, within four years, two quivers-full of arrows in his body. Being asked if the wounds had been long suppurating, he answered in a comical manner, " among the mountains nothing corrupts."

The Indians who live on Clarke river are of the middle size. The women are very filthy. Their faces, hands and feet are black and stiff with dirt. They rub them every morning with a composition of red and brown earth mixed up with fish oil. Their hair, always long and dishevelled, serves them for a towel to wipe their hands on. Their garment is generally tattered, and stiff and shining with dust and grease. They seem to be less subjected to slavish labor than the squaws that live East of the Mountains, still they have to toil hard, and to do whatever is most difficult. They are obliged to carry all the household furniture or to row the canoe when they move from one place to another; at home, they fetch the wood and the water, clean the fish, prepare the meals, gather the roots and fruits of the season, and when any leisure time is left, they spend it in making mats, baskets and hats of bull-rushes. What must appear rather singular is, that the men more frequently handle the needle than the squaws. Their chief occupations, however, are fishing and hunting. These Indians suffer much from opthalmic affections. Scarcely a cabin is to be found on Clarke river, in which there is not a blind or one eyed person, or some one laboring under some disease of the eye. This probably proceeds from two causes—first, because they are frequently on the water and exposed from morning till night to the direct and reflected rays of the sun, and next, because living in low cabins made of bull-rushes, the large fire they make in the centre fills it with smoke, which must gradually injure their eyes.

Conjurers are found here as well as in some parts of Europe. They are a kind of physicians. Whatever may be the complaint of the patient these gentlemen have him stretched out on his back, and his friends and relatives are ordered to stand round him, each one armed with two sticks of unequal length. The doctor or conjurer neither feels the pulse nor looks at the tongue, but with a solemn countenance commences to sing some mournful strain, whilst those present accompany him with their voices and beat time with the sticks. During the singing the doctor operates on the patient, he kneels before him, and placing his closed fists on the stomach, leans on him with all his might. Excessive pain makes the patient roar, but his roarings are lost in the noise, for the doctor and the bystanders raise their voices higher in proportion as the sick man gives utterance to his sufferings. At the end of each stanza the doctor joins his hands, applies them to the patient's lips, and blows with all his strength. This operation is repeated till at last the doctor takes from the patient's mouth, either a little white stone, or the claw of some bird or animal, which he exhibits to the bystanders, protesting that he has removed the cause of the disease, and that the patient will soon recover. But whether he recover or die, the quack is here as elsewhere rewarded for his exertions. *Mundus vult decipi*, is the watchword of quacks, jugglers and mountebanks; and it seems that the Indian conjurers are not unacquainted with it. I received this description of their method of curing diseases from a clerk of the Hudson Bay Company. I shall subjoin another anecdote concerning the religious ideas entertained by the Tehenooks. All men, they say, were created by a divinity called *Etalapasse*, but they were created imperfect or unfinished. Their mouths were not cleft, their eyes were closed, and their hands and feet were immoveable; so that they were rather living lumps of flesh than men. Another divinity, whom they call *Ecannum*, (resembling the *Nanaboojoo* of the Potowattamies,) less powerful, but more benevolent than the former, seeing the imperfect state of these men, took a sharp stone and with it opened their mouths and eyes. He also gave motion to their hands and feet. This merciful divinity did not rest satisfied with conferring these first favors on the human race. He taught them to make canoes and paddles, nets and all the implements now used by the Indians. He threw large rocks into the rivers to obstruct their courses, and confine the fish in order that the Indians might catch them in larger quantities.

When I speak of the Indian character, I do not mean to include the Indians that live in the neighborhood of civilized man, and have intercourse with him. It is acknowledged in the United States, that the whites who trade with those Indians, not only demoralize them by the sale of spirituous liquors, but communicate to them their own vices, of which some are shocking and revolting to nature. The Indian left to himself, is circumspect and discreet in his words and actions. He seldom gives way to passion; except against the hereditary enemies of his nation. When there is question of them, his words breathe hatred and vengeance. He seeks revenge, because he firmly believes that it is the only means by which he can retrieve his honor when he has been insulted or defeated; because he thinks that only low and vulgar minds can forget an injury, and he fosters rancor decause he deems it a virtue. With respect to others, the Indian is cool and dispassionate, checking the least violent emotion of his heart. Thus should he know that one of his friends is in danger of being attacked by an enemy lying in wait for him, he will not openly tell him so, (for he would deem this an act of fear,) but will ask him where he intends to go that day, and after having received an answer, will add with the same indifference, that a wild beast lies hidden on the way. This figurative remark will render his friend as cautious as if he were acquainted with all the designs and movements of the enemy. Thus again, if an Indian has been hunting without success, he will go to the cabin of one of his friends, taking care not to show the least sign of disappointment or impatience, nor to speak of the hunger which he suffers. He will sit down and smoke the calmut with as much indifference as if he had been successful in the chase. He acts in the same manner when he is among strangers. To give signs of disappointment or impatience, is looked upon by the Indians as a mark of cowardice, and would earn for them the appellation of " old woman," which is the most injurious and degrading epithet that can be applied to an Indian. If an Indian be told that his children have distinguished themselves in battle,—that they have taken several scalps, and have carried off many enemies and horses, without giving the least sign of joy, he will answer: "They have done well." If he be informed that they have been killed or made prisoners, he will utter no complaint, but will simply say: "It is unfortunate." He will make no inquiries into the circumstances; several days must elapse before he asks for further information.

The Indian is endowed with extraordinary sagacity, and easily learns whatever demands attention. Experience and observation render him conversant with things that are unknown to the civilized man. Thus, he will traverse a plain or forest one or two hundred miles in extent, and will arrive at a particular place with as much precision as the mariner by the aid of the compass. Unless prevented by obstacles, he, without any material deviation, always travels in a straight line, regardless of path or road. In the same manner he will point out the exact place of the sun, when it is hidden by mists or clouds. Thus, too, he follows with the greatest accuracy, the traces of men or animals, though these should have passed over the leaves or the grass, and nothing be perceptible to the eye of the white man. He acquires this knowledge from a constant application of the intellectual faculties, and much time and experience are required to perfect this perceptive quality. Generally speaking, he has an excellent memory.— He recollects all the articles that have been concluded upon in their councils and treaties, and the exact time when such councils were held or such treaties ratified.

Some writers have supposed that the Indians are guided by instinct, and have even ventured to assert that their children would find their way through the forests as well as those further advanced in age. I have consulted some of the most intelligent Indians on this subject, and they have uniformly told me that they acquire this practical knowledge by long and close attention to the growth of plants and trees, and to the sun and stars. It is known that the north side of a tree is covered with a greater quantity of moss than any other, and that the boughs and foliage on the south side are more abundant and luxuriant. Similar observations tend to direct them, and I have more than once found their reflections useful to myself in the excursions I have made through the forests. Parents teach their children to remark such things, and these in their turn sometimes add new discoveries to those of their fathers. They measure distances by a day's journey. When an Indian travels alone, his day's journey will be about 50 or 60 English miles, but only 15 or 20 when he moves with the camp. They divide their journeys, as we do the hours, into halves and quarters; and when in their councils they decide on war or on distant excursions, they lay off these journeys with astonishing accuracy on a kind of map, which they trace on bark or skins. Though they have no knowledge of geography, nor of any science that relates to it, yet they form with sufficient accuracy maps of the countries which they know; nothing but the degrees of longitude and latitude are wanting in some to make them exact.

I remember to have read in Fr. Charlevoix' journal that the Indians are remarkably superstitious with respect to dreams. This is still the case, though they interpret them in various ways. Some maintain that during sleep the rational part of the soul travels about, whilst the sensitive continues to animate the body. Others say that the good Manitoo or familiar spirit gives salutary advice concerning the future, whilst others hold that in sleep the soul visits the objects about which she dreams. But all look upon dreams as sacred, and as the ordinary channels through which the Great Spirit and the Manitoos communicate their designs to man. Impressed with this idea, the Indian is at a loss to conceive why we disregard them. As they look upon dreams as representations of the desires of some unearthly genius, or of the commands of the Great Spirit, they deem themselves bound to observe and obey them. Charlevoix tells us somewhere, and I have seen instances of a similar kind, that an Indian who had dreamed that he had cut off his finger, actually cut it, and prepared himself for the act by a fast. Another having dreamed that he was a prisoner among a hostile nation, not knowing how to act, consulted the jugglers, and according to their decision, had himself bound to a stake, and fire applied to several parts of his body. I doubt whether the quotation is correct, as I have not the work of Charlevoix to consult, but I know that I have described a superstitious belief which is generally held by the Indians of the present day.

When the Pottowatomies or any of the northern nations make or renew a treaty of peace, they present a wampum, sash or collar. The wampum is made of a shell called baceinum, and shaped into small beads in the form of pearls. When they conclude an alliance, offensive or defensive, with other tribes, they send them a wampum, sash and tomahawk dipped in blood, inviting them to come and drink of the blood of their enemies. This figurative expression often becomes a reality. Among the nations of the West the calumet is looked upon with equal reverence, whether in peace or war. They smoke the calumet to confirm their treaties and alliances. This smoking is considered a solemn engagement, and he who should violate it, would be deemed unworthy of confidence, infamous, and an object of divine vengeance. In time of war, the calumet and all its ornaments are red. Sometimes it is partly red, and partly of some other color. By the color and the manner of disposing the feathers, a person acquainted with their practices, knows at first sight what are the designs or intentions of the nation that presents the calumet.

The smoking of the calumet forms a part of all their religious ceremonies. It is a kind of sacred rite which they perform when they prepare themselves to invoke the Great Spirit, and take the sun and moon, the earth and the water as witnesses of the sincerity of their intentions, and the fidelity with which they promise to comply with their engagements. However ridiculous this custom of smoking may appear to some, it has a good effect among the Indians. Experience has taught them that the smoke of the calumet dispels the vapors of the brain, aids them to think and judge with greater accuracy and precision, and excites their courage. This seems to be the principal reason why they have introduced it into their councils, where it is looked upon as the seal of their decisions. It is also sent as a pledge of fidelity to those whom they wish to consult, or with whom they desire to form an alliance. I know that the opinions of the Indians concerning the beneficial effects of smoking the calumet will be sanctioned by few persons, because it is demonstrated from experience that the smoke of tobacco acts as a powerful narcotic upon the nervous system, and produces suporfic and debilitating effects; but it should be remembered that such effects are not produced when the smoke is inhaled into the lungs, as is the universal practice of the Indians.

The funeral ceremonies of the Calkobins, who inhabit New Caledonia, west of the mountains, are fantastic and revolting. Mr. Cox, in his journal, tells us that the body of the deceased is exposed in his lodge for nine days, and on the tenth is burned. They choose for this purpose an elevated place, and there erect a funeral pile.—

In the meanwhile, they invite their neighbors from all sides, entreating them to repair to the ceremony. All the preparations being completed, the corpse is placed on the pile, which they light, while the spectators manifest the greatest joy. All that the deceased possessed is placed around the body; and if he be a person of distinction, his friends purchase for him a cloak, a shirt, and a pair of breeches: these are laid beside him. The medicine man must be present, and, for the last time, has recourse to his enchantments, to recall the departed to life. Not succeeding, he covers the dead body—that is, he makes a present of a piece of cloth, or leather, and thus appeases the anger of the relatives, and escapes the vengeance they have a right to inflict upon him. During the nine days on which the corpse is exposed, the widow is obliged to remain near it from the rising to the setting of the sun; and, notwithstanding the excessive heats of summer, no relaxation is allowed from this barbarous custom. While the doctor is occupied in his last operation, the widow must lie down beside the corpse, until he orders her to withdraw from the pile; and this order is not given until the unfortunate being is covered with blisters. She then is made to pass and repass her hands through the flames, to collect the fat, which flows from the body: with this she rubs her person. When the friends of the deceased observe that the sinews of the legs and arms begin to contract, they force the miserable widow to return to the pile, and straighten the limbs.

If, during the lifetime of the husband, the woman had been unfaithful to him, or had neglected to provide for his wants, his relations then revenge themselves upon her; they throw her upon the pile, from whence she is dragged by her own relations. She is again cast upon it, and again withdrawn, until she falls into a state of insensibility.

The body being consumed, the widow gathers together the largest bones; these she encloses in a birch box, which she is forced to carry for many years. She is looked upon while in this state as a slave; the hardest and most laborious work falls to her lot; she must obey every order of the women, and even of the children; and the least disobedience or repugnance draws down upon her severe chastisement. The ashes of her husband are deposited in a tomb, and it is her duty to remove from thence the weeds. These unhappy women frequently destroy themselves to avoid so many cruelties. At the end of three or four years the relatives agree to put an end to her mourning. They prepare a great feast for this occasion, and invite all the neighbors. The widow is then introduced, still carrying the bones of the husband; these are taken from her, and shut up in a coffin, which is fastened at the end by a stake about twelve feet long. All the guests extol her painful widowhood; one of whom pours upon her head a vessel of oil, whilst another covers her with down. It is only after this ceremony that the widow can marry again; but, as may be readily supposed, the number of those who hazard a second marriage is very small.

I have the honor to be
 Rev. and dear Father Provincial,
  Your devoted servant and son,
   P. J. DE SMET, S. J.

LETTER XII.

St. Marie, Dec. 30th, 1841.

Reverend Father:

I HAVE given you the happy and consoling result of my journey in November. Before the close of the year I have yet to make you acquainted with what has passed during my absence, and since my return, among the Flat Heads; all goes to prove what I have advanced in my preceding letters.

The Rev. Fathers Mengarini and Point were not idle during my absence. The following will give you some idea of the state of affairs on my return, both in regard to material and spiritual matters, as well as the practices and usages established, which could not but tend to strengthen, more and more, our good neophytes.

The plan mentioned in my letters, and unanimously approved, and which we were urged to carry into execution, was, to commence with what appeared to be the most urgent. We enclosed the field destined to become God's portion of the settlement. We started the buildings intended to be hereafter dependencies of the farm, but serving temporarily for a church and residence, on account of the approach of winter, and our wish to unite the whole colony. These works were indispensable, and were carried on with such spirit that in the space of a month the new buildings could shelter from four to five hundred souls.

The Flat Heads, assisting us with their whole heart and

strength, had, in a short time, cut from two to three thousand stakes; and the three brothers, with no other tools than the axe, saw and auger, constructed a chapel with pediment, colonade and gallery, balustrade, choir, seats, &c. by St. Martin's day; when they assembled in the little chapel all the catechumens, and continued the instructions which were to end on the third of December, the day fixed for their baptism. In the interval between these two remarkable epochs, there was, on each day, one instruction more than usual. This last instruction, intended chiefly for grown persons, was given at 8 o'clock in the evening, and lasted about an hour and a quarter. These good savages, whose ears and hearts are alike open when the word of God is addressed to them, appeared still better disposed in the evening; the silence being unbroken by the cries of infants or children. Our heavenly Father so graciously heard their prayers, that on St. Francis Xavier's day the good Fathers had the consolation of baptising two hundred and two adults.

So many souls wrested from the demons was more than enough to excite their rage,—seeds of distrust, hindrances occasioned by the best intentioned, the sickness of the interpreter and sexton, at the very moment their assistance was most required; a kind of hurricane, which took place the evening before the baptism, and which overturned three lodges in the camp, the trees torn from their roots, and every thing in appearance about to be uprooted, even to the foundations of the church—the organ unintentionally broken by the savages, on the eve of being applied to so beautiful a purpose—all seemed to conspire against them; but the day for baptism arrives, and every cloud disappears.

The Fathers had intended to solemnize the marriages of
14*

the husbands and wives on the same day as their baptism. They had even announced that the ceremony would take place after baptism; but the sacred rite having occupied a much longer time than they supposed, on account of the necessity of interpreting all that was said, they were obliged to defer this sacrament until the next day, trusting to God and the new Christians, for the preservation of their baptismal innocence.

As our former Missionaries have left nothing in writing on the conduct we should observe with regard to marriage, it may, perhaps, be useful to relate here what has been our course, in order that our conduct may be rectified if it has not been judicious.

We hold the principle, that, generally speaking, there are no valid marriages among the savages of these countries; and for this reason; we have not found one, even among the best disposed, who, after marriage had been contracted in their own fashion, did not believe himself justified in sending away his first wife, whenever he thought fit, and taking another. Many even have several wives in the same lodge. It is, however, true, that many when entering the marriage state, promise that nothing but death will ever separate them; that they will never give their hand to another. But what impassioned man or woman has not said as much? Can we infer from this that the contract is valid, when it is universally received, that even after such promises they have not the less right to do as they please, when they become disgusted with each other? We are then agreed on this principle, that among them, even to the present time, there has been no marriage, because they have never known well in what its essence and obligation consisted. To adopt an opposite view would be to involve oneself in a labyrinth of difficulties, from which it would be very difficult to escape. This was, if I am not mistaken, the conduct of St. Francis Xavier in the Indies, since it is said in his Life, that he praised before the married those whom he supposed to be dearest to them, that they might be more easily induced to keep to one alone. Secondly, supposing then that there were material faults in their marriages, the necessity of a renewal was not spoken of but for the time which followed baptism, and this took place the day following that happy occasion.

After the Fathers had gained the necessary information respecting the degrees of relationship, and had given the necessary dispensations, the marriage ceremony, preceded by a short instruction, was performed, and contributed greatly to give the people a high idea of our holy religion.

The twenty-four marriages then contracted presented that mixture of simplicity, of respectful affection, and profound joy, which are the sure indications of a good conscience. There were among the couples, good old men and women; but their presence only rendered the ceremony more respectable in the eyes of those assembled; for among the Flat Heads all that relates to religion is sacred; unhappy he who would so express himself before them, as to lead them to believe that he thought otherwise. They left the chapel, their hearts filled with sentiments purified by that grace which constitutes the charm of every state of life, and especially of those in wedlock.

The only thing that appeared strange to them was, when the Fathers spoke of taking the names of witnesses; but when they were told that this was only done because the church so ordained, to give more authority and dignity to the marriage contract, they no longer saw in it any thing but what was reasonable, and the question was, who should be witness for the others?

The same astonishment was manifested with regard to god-fathers. The interpreter had translated the word god-father, a term which is not in their language, by second father. The poor savages not knowing what this meant, or what consequences this title would imply, were not eager to make a choice. To be a god-father moreover offered no great attraction. As soon as we made them understand it, their difficulties vanished, and the more easily; for not to multiply spiritual affinities, a god-father only was given to the men, and a god-mother to the women; and as to the obligations attached to the honour of being sponsors, they were much less here than elsewhere, the Black Gowns promising to take upon themselves the greatest part of the burden. For the first baptisms our choice of sponsors was very limited; only thirteen grown persons were qualified to act in this capacity,—but the most aged persons being baptised before the others, they, without laying aside the lighted candle, (the symbol of faith) were chosen for the second division; and so in like manner with the rest.

The day preceding the baptism, the Fathers, on account of their labors, were only able to collect the colony twice; besides, F. Mengarini was indisposed. In the evening, however, he assembled the people, and great was their astonishment on beholding the decorations of the chapel. Some days previously the Fathers had engaged all who were willing, to make matts of rushes or straws. All the women, girls and children, assembled eagerly for this good work, so that they had enough to cover the floor and ceiling, and hang round the walls. These matts, ornamented with festoons of green, made a pretty drapery around the altar. On a canopy was inscribed the holy name of Jesus. Among the ornaments they placed a picture of the Blessed Virgin over the tabernacle; on the door of the tabernacle a representation of the heart of Jesus. The pictures of the way of the Cross, in red frames; the lights, the silence of night, the approach of the important day, the calm after the hurricane, which had burst on them only a few moments before—all these circumstances united, had, with the grace of God, so well disposed the minds and hearts of our Indians, that it would have been scarcely possible to find on earth an assembly of savages more resembling a company of saints. This was the beautiful bouquet which the Fathers were permitted to present to Saint Francis Xavier. The next day they were engaged from eight o'clock in the morning until half past ten at night, in the church, excepting only one hour and a half, which they gave to repose. The following was the order followed. First, they baptized the chiefs and married men. These were chosen as godfathers for the young men and little boys; then the married women, whose husbands were living with them; afterwards the widows and wives who had been cast off; and, lastly, the young women and girls.

It was gratifying to hear with what intelligence these good savages replied to all the questions addressed to them, and to see them praying at the moment of receiving baptism. At the end, each received a taper whose blended light beautifully illuminated our humble chapel.

But let us come to something still more edifying. I shall not speak of their assiduous attendance at the instructions,—of their eagerness to hear our words,—of the evident profit they received from them; all this is common in the course of a mission; but rarely do we witness the heroic sacrifices which these Indians have made. Many, who had two wives, have retained her whose children were most numerous, and with all possible respect dismissed the other. One evening, a savage came to seek the

Fathers at the lodge, which was filled with Indians, and unabashed by any merely human consideration, asked what he should do in his present circumstances? On the instant he acted according to the instructions given him; he dismissed his youngest wife, giving her what he would have wished another to give to his sister, if in the same situation, and was re-united to his first wife, whom he had forsaken. After an instruction, a young woman, asking to speak, said that "she desired very much to receive baptism, but that she had been so wicked she dared not make the request." Each one would have made a public confession. A great number of young mothers, married according to the mode of the savages, but abandoned by their husbands, who were of some other tribe, renounced them most willingly, to have the happiness of being baptised.

The ordinary regulations observed in the village are as follows: when the *Angelus* rings, the Indians rise from sleep; half an hour after, the morning prayers are said in common; all assist at Mass and at the instruction. A second instruction is given at evening, towards sun set, and lasts about an hour and a quarter. At two o'clock in the afternoon we have the regular catechism for the children, at which grown persons may assist if they think proper. The children are formed into two divisions: the first is composed exclusively of those who know the first prayers; the second of the smaller children. One of the Fathers each morning visits the sick, to furnish them with medicines, and give them such assistance as their wants may require.

We have adopted the system of instruction and bestowing rewards, in usage in the schools of the brothers of the christian doctrine. During catechism, which lasts about an hour, we have recitations and explanations, intermingled with canticles. Every day, for each good answer, tickets of approbation are given; one or more, according to the difficulty of the question proposed. Experience has proved that these tickets given at once, are less embarrassing than when we mark their names on a list; the former plan takes less time, and interests the children more, rendering them, besides, more assiduous and careful. These tickets serve, at the same time, as certificates of attendance at catechism, and as tokens of intelligence and good will, they please the parent not less than their children. The former are incited to make their children repeat what has been said at catechism, to render them capable of answering better the following day; and also with a desire of improving themselves. The wish to see their children distinguish themselves, has attracted almost the whole colony to catechism; none of the chiefs who have children fail to be there; and there is not less emulation among the parents than among the children themselves. A still greater value is attached to the tickets, from the exactitude and justice with which the deserving are rewarded. They who have obtained good tickets during the week, are rewarded on Sunday with crosses, medals, or ribbons, publicly distributed. On the first Sunday of every month they distribute to those who have received the most good tickets in the course of the month, medals or pictures, which become their private property. These pictures, preserved with care, are great stimulants, not only to the study of their catechism but also to the practice of piety. They are monuments of victory, examples of virtue, exhortations to piety, and models of perfection. Their rarity, and the efforts necessary to obtain them, also enhance their worth. As we desire to inspire the savages, who are naturally inclined to idleness, with a love for work, it has been judged suitable to reward their little efforts in the same manner as we recompense their improvement in, and knowledge of their catechism.

To maintain order, and promote emulation among them, the catechism children are divided into seven or eight sections, of six each; the boys on one side, the girls on the other. At the head of each section there is a chief, who must assist the children placed under him to learn their catechism; that thus every child may indulge the hope of meriting a reward at the end of the week or month. They are so divided that the competitors, to the number of five or six in each section, may be of nearly equal capacity.

Father Point, who was, immediately after Christmas, to accompany the assembled camps of Flat Heads, Pends-d'oreilles, Nez-perces, &c. prepared for his new campaign by a retreat of eight days. Twenty-four marriages, as I have already said, had been celebrated during my absence, and two hundred and two adults, with little boys and girls from eight to fourteen years of age, had been baptised. There were still, thirty-four couples, who awaited my return, to receive the sacraments of baptism and marriage, or to renew their marriage vows. The Nez-perces had not yet presented their children for baptism. There was an old chief of the Black Feet nation, in the camp, with his son and his little family, five in all, who had been hitherto very assiduous in their attendance at prayers and catechism. The day succeeding my arrival I commenced giving three instructions daily, besides the catechism, which was taught by the other Fathers. They profited so well, that with the grace of God, a hundred and fifteen Flat Heads, with three chiefs at their head, thirty Nez-perces with their chief and the Black Foot chief and his family, presented themselves at the baptismal font on Christmas day. I began my Masses at seven o'clock in the morning; at five o'clock, P. M. I still found myself in the chapel: The heart can conceive, but the tongue cannot express the emotions which such a consoling spectacle may well awaken. The following day I celebrated a solemn Mass of Thanksgiving for the signal favours with which our Lord had deigned to visit his people. From six to seven hundred new Christians, with bands of little children, baptised in the past year,—all assembled in a poor little chapel, covered with rushes—in the midst of a desert, where but lately, the name of God was scarcely known; offering to the Creator their regenerated hearts, protesting that they would persevere in His holy service even to death, was an offering, without doubt, most agreeable to God, and which, we trust, will draw down the dews of heaven upon the Flat Head nation and the neighbouring tribes.

On the 29th the large camp, accompanied by the Fathers, left us for the great buffalo hunt, and joined the Pendsd'oreilles, who awaited them at two day's journey hence; there will be above two hundred lodges. I am filled with hope for the success and fresh victories, with which, I trust, God will deign to reward the zeal of his servant. In the mean time we occupy ourselves (Father Mengarini and myself) in translating the cathechism into the Flat Head tongue; and in preparing one hundred and fifty persons for their first communion.

Our good brothers and the Canadians are engaged at the same time in erecting around our establishment a strong pallisade, fortified with bastions, to shelter us from the incursions of the Black Feet, whom we daily expect to visit us. Our confidence in God is not weakened; we take the precautions which prudence dictates, and remain without fear at our post.

A young Sinpoil has just arrived in our camp, and these

are his words: "I am a Sinpoil, my nation is compassionate. I have been sent to hear your words, and learn the prayer you teach the Flat Heads. The Sinpoils desire also to know it, and to imitate their example." This young man proposes to pass the winter in our camp, and return in the spring to his own nation, to sow among them the seeds of the gospel.

The whole Flat Head nation converted—four hundred Kalispels baptised—eighty Nez-perces, several Cœurs-d'aliene, many Kocetenays, Black Feet, Serpents and Banacs,—the Sinpoils, the Chaudieres, who open their arms to us, and eagerly ask for Fathers to instruct them; the earnest demands from Fort Vancouver on the part of the Governor, and of the Rev. Mr. Blanchette, assuring us of the good desires and dispositions of a great number of nations, ready to receive the gospel,—in a word, a vast country, which only awaits the arrival of true ministers of God, to rally round the standard of the Cross—behold the beautiful bouquet, Rev. Father, which we have the happiness of presenting you at the close of 1841. It is at the foot of the crucifix that you are accustomed to ask counsel of heaven for the welfare of the nations entrusted to your children. Our number is very far from sufficient for the pressing and real wants of this people. The Protestants are on the *qui vive*. Send us then some Fathers and Brothers to assist us, and thousands of souls will bless you at the throne of God for all eternity.

Recommending myself to your holy prayers,
I have the honour to be, with the most profound respect and esteem,
Rev. Father, Yours, &c.
P. J. DE SMET, S. J.

BOOK II.

INDIAN MODE OF TRAVELLING.

NARRATIVE

OF

A Year's Residence among the Indian Tribes

OF THE

ROCKY MOUNTAINS.

Madison Forks, 15th August, 1842.

Rev. and dear Father:

AFTER a journey of four months and a half across an ocean of prairies and mountains, where we met many an obstacle, we arrived this day a year ago, under the auspices of the Queen of Heaven, at one of the Forts of the honorable company of Hudson Bay, called Fort Hall. Mr. Ermantiger, the estimable commander of this Fort, received us in the most friendly manner, and loaded us with favours. At this place we found the vanguard of our dear neophytes awaiting us. How joyful and happy was this meeting. What had they not done to obtain Black Gowns to visit them? Four times had their deputations crossed the Western desert—eight of their people had perished on the road, three from sickness, and five fell victims to the Scioux tribe. Twice from the Bitter Root river almost all their people had transported themselves to the Green river, a distance of more than five hundred miles from their usual encampment. In fine, those who then joined us had at the first news of our approach again traversed the half of that space to meet us; nor could they, on first seeing us, express their feelings but by their silence. Very soon, however, they gave vent to the grateful sentiments of their hearts, in such a manner as to astonish us. "I am very ignorant and wicked," exclaimed the chief Wistelpo to his companions, "nevertheless I am grateful to the Great Spirit for all he has done for us." Detailing all the benefits he had received he terminated his discourse in the following manner: "Yes, my dear friends, my heart is filled with contentment, notwithstanding its wickedness. I do not despair of the goodness of God, I only wish for life to employ it in prayer; never will I give up praying; I will continue to pray until my death, and when that hour comes I will throw myself into the arms of the Master of Life. If it be His will that I should be lost I will submit to his decree. Should he wish to save me I will bless him forever. Once more I repeat, my heart is happy. What can we do to prove to our Fathers that we love them."— Here the chief made some practical reflections.

They informed us that since I left them in 1840 their brothers had always remained in the same dispositions; that according to the plan I had laid out for them, all the people met twice every day, and three times on Sundays, to recite in common the prayers I had taught them. They also told us that the chest containing the sacred ornaments and vases, which we had left in their charge, was carried about as the ark of salvation, wherever they went; that five or six children, dying after having received the sacrament of baptism, had taken their flight to heaven; that a young warrior, the day after his baptism, had died from the effects of a wound, which, without the aid of a miracle, would have carried him off long before; and finally, that a young child, finding herself at the point of death, solicited baptism with the greatest earnestness, and after having received this favour from the hands of Peter, an Iroquois, she repeated three times to the witnesses of her happiness: "pray for me—pray for me—pray for me;" then she prayed herself and sang canticles with a stronger voice than any of the others, and upon drawing her last breath, she exclaimed, pointing towards heaven: " Oh! what a beautiful sight! I behold Mary, my mother, happiness does not belong to earth, in heaven alone must you seek it. Listen to what the Black Gowns tell you, because they profess the truth ;" and immediately afterwards expired.

We left Fort Hall on the 19th of the month, conducted by our new guides, who were not long in giving us striking proof of their devotion towards us. At the crossing of a very rapid river, called the Lewis' Fork or Snake River, from the savages who people its borders, one of our brothers, not being able to guide the mules of his cart, was dragged into a place so deep that his whole equipage was plunged under the water; immediately the good savages threw themselves into the river, raised the cart out of the water, employed their hands and feet so usefully, that only three mules were drowned and some bags of provisions lost.

The 29th we met near the source of the Missouri, called the Beaver Head, a detachment of Flat Heads, having as their leader Ensyla, called the Little Chief, who has since received in baptism the name of Michael, on account of his fidelity and courage. A few days previous, a party of Indians having been discovered on the adjacent heights, a cry was raised of "the Black Feet! the Black Feet!" Instantly the little camp put itself on the defensive. Two of the bravest Flat Heads, lifting up their muskets in the air, started off at full gallop to reconnoitre the enemy. Already they had disappeared from our view, leaving us somewhat anxious, but they soon returned, at the head of about ten strangers. They were not the Black Feet, but a party of the Banac tribe, a species of men half inimical and half friendly to the Flat Heads, who for that very reason, as we shall see later, were more to be feared than open enemies. When Michael joined us, the camp of these people was already united with ours. Their chief and Michael knew each other but too well, from having once been engaged in an affair in which Michael, finding himself shamefully betrayed and attacked by a whole Banac village, had only been able to save himself and six men, who accompanied him, by killing the brother of the Banac chief, with eight of his people. They nevertheless shook hands with each other, and separated the next day, without appearing to entertain any unpleasant recollections. I had a conversation with the Banac chief on the subject of prayer. He listened attentively to what I told him, and promised to do amongst his people what the Flat Heads did amongst theirs. The 30th, after having wound through a mountain pass, to which we gave the name of the Fathers' Defile, we advanced as far as a large plain, on the western verge of which the Flat Heads were encamped. As we drew near, runners approached us constantly. Already, Stiettiet Loodzo, surnamed the bravest of the brave, and distinguished from the others by a large red ribbon, had presented himself. Soon after, we perceived at a distance another savage, of tall stature, hastening towards us with rapid strides. At the same time, many cried out—"Paul," "Paul;" and indeed it was Paul, surnamed "Big Face," the great chief of the nation; Paul, who, owing to his virtue and his great age, had been baptized the preceding year—Paul, whom they thought absent, but who had just arrived, as though by God's special permission, that he might have the satisfaction of presenting us himself to his people. At sun-set we were in the midst of a most affecting scene. The Missonaries were surrounded by their neophytes—men, women, young people, and children in their mothers' arms, all anxious to be among the first to shake hands with us. Every heart was moved. That evening was certainly beautiful. On the feast of the holy name of Mary, the whole camp renewed the consecration of themselves to their future Patroness, which had been previously made by the vanguard of the first settlement.

About the time the Church celebrates the feast of Mary's pure heart, it seemed as though the God of the Christians wished to give to *her* new children the consolation of seeing the principal eras in their lives coincide, and in some manner become identified with those happy days consecrated especially to her honor. It was on the feast which the Church celebrates in memory of her triumph, that we first met with the Flat Heads; it will be on the 24th of September, also one of the festivals, that we shall arrive on the borders of our little Paraguay, and on the feast of the Holy Rosary we shall select a beautiful spot for our first settlement, and call it by the holy name of Mary. It is again remarkable that the nomination took place on another feast called the Patrocinium, or Patronage of the Blessed Virgin; and thus, Mary, chosen patroness of the settlement, was hailed for the first time on this spot with the angelical salutation, accompanied by the ringing of bells. It was a great consolation for us to speak of her goodness, in the presence of the representatives of twenty-six different nations. I forgot to mention that on the day we took possession of the Blessed Mary's new demesne, we set up a large cross in the middle of the camp, a circumstance rendered more striking, from having, as they assured me, been predicted by the young girl, called Mary, of whom I spoke to you before. How much I wished that all those who take a sincere interest in the progress of our holy religion, could have been present. How their hearts would have glowed within them on beholding all the good Flat Heads, from the great chief to the smallest child, piously coming up to press their lips to the wood which was the instrument of the world's salvation, and on their bended knees taking the solemn promise of dying a thousand times rather than abandon prayer, (religion.) I started the 28th October for Fort Colville, which is situated on the Columbia river, to procure provisions. Ours had become so scanty, and we entertained such slight hopes of obtaining them, that we had already thought of converting into fishermen the carpenters of our settlement. In case of their not being successful, and thereby unable to supply our wants, we intended accompanying the savages on their hunting expeditions. Our only building as yet was a wooden house, without a roof, and the winter had already set in. We began by recommending our wants to God, and with God's assistance we found ourselves, on St. Martin's day, in possession of a temporary chapel, large enough to contain all the colony, with about one hundred of the Pierced Nose tribe, whom curiosity had attracted to the neighborhood. Since that period they have been so careful in avoiding sin, so exact in attending our instructions, and the fruit of the divine word has been so visible in our settlement, that on the 3d of December two hundred and two catechumens were ranged in our chapel, waiting for baptism. This was too beautiful an offering to St. Francis Xavier, apostle of the Indians, not to excite the fury of man's great enemy.— Accordingly, for a few days previously we encountered multiplied trials. To speak only of the most visible, the prefect, interpreter and sexton fell sick. The very eve of the great day the environs were laid waste by a sort of hurricane—the church windows were broken, large trees were rooted up, and three huts were thrown down; but these obstacles, far from prejudicing the triumph of religion, served only to render it still more striking.

The catechumens having assembled in the chapel, which had been adorned with its most beautiful ornaments, and where they had been conducted for the more immediate preparations of their hearts prior to receiving the great sacrament of baptism, were so struck by the imposing appearance of the chapel, and the melodious sounds of the organ, now heard for the first time in the wilderness, that they were not able to express their admiration. The next day, with the exception of the time the Fathers took for their dinner, they were in church from eight o'clock in the morning until half past ten in the evening. How delightful it was to listen to the intelligent answers of the good savages to all the questions proposed to them. Never will those who were present forget the pious spirit of their replies. The rehabilitations of their marriages succeeded baptism, but not without great sacrifices on their part, because, until that time, the poor Indians had been ignorant of the unity and indissolubility of the conjugal tie. We could not help admiring the mighty effects of the sacrament of baptism in their souls. One poor husband hesitated as to which of his wives he should select. The oldest of them, perceiving his irresolution, said to him: "You know how much I love you, and I am also certain that you love me, but you cherish another more; she is younger than I am. Well, remain with her; leave me our children, and in that manner we can all be baptized." I could cite many such traits.

I will here begin the narrative of my journey to Colville. On the eve of my departure I informed the Flat Heads of my intentions. I requested them to procure some horses, and a small escort, in case I should meet with any of their enemies, the Black Feet. They brought to me seventeen horses, the number I had asked them; and ten young and brave warriors, who had already been often pierced with balls and arrows in different skirmishes, presented themselves to accompany me on my journey. With pleasure I bear testimony to their devotedness, their child-like simplicity and docility, politeness, complaisance and rare hilarity; but, above all, to their exemplary piety.

These good Flat Heads endeavored in every manner to divine and anticipate all my wants. On the afternoon of the 28th October, as I have already said, we commenced our march, and encamped at a distance of ten miles from St. Mary's. That day we met no one but a solitary hunter, who was carrying a buck, the half of which he offered to us, with great eagerness. This furnished us with an excellent supper, and a good breakfast for the next morning. The 29th, snow fell in large flakes, notwithstanding which we continued our march. We crossed, in the course of the day, a fine stream, without a name—the same one which the famous travellers, Lewis and Clarke, ascended in 1806, on their way to the section of country occupied by the tribe of the Pierced Noses, (or Sapetans.) I will call it the river of St. Francis Borgia. Six miles further south we crossed the beautiful river of St. Ignatius. It enters the plain of the Bitter Root,—which we shall henceforward call St. Mary's,—by a beautiful defile, commonly called, by the mountaineers or Canadian hunters, the Devil's Gate; for what reason, however, I know not. These gentlemen have frequently on their lips the words devil and hell; and it is perhaps on this account that we heard so often these appellations. Be not then alarmed when I tell you that I examined the Devil's pass, went through the Devil's gate, rowed on Satan's stream, and jumped from the Devil's horns. The "rake," one of the passes, the horns, and the stream, really deserve names that express something horrible—all three are exceedingly dangerous. The first and second, on account of the innumerable snags which fill their beds, as there are entire forests swallowed up by the river. The third pass of which I spoke, adds to the difficulties of the others a current still stronger. A canoe launched into this torrent flies over it with the speed of an arrow, and the most experienced pilot trembles in spite of himself. Twice did the brave Iroquois, who conducted our light canoe, exclaim: "Father, we are lost;" but a loud cry of "courage—take courage, John, confide in God, keep steady to the oar," saved us in that dangerous stream, drew us out from between the horns and threatening teeth of this awful " rake." But let us return to our account of the journey to Colville. We spread our skins on the borders of a little river at the foot of a high mountain, which we were to cross the next day, having traversed St. Mary's valley, a distance of about forty miles. This valley is from four to seven miles wide, and above two hundred long. It has but one fine defile, already mentioned, and which serves as the entrance to, and issue from, the valley. The mountains which terminate it on both sides appear to be inaccessible; they are piles of jagged rocks, the base of which presents nothing but fragments of the same description, while the Norwegian pine grows on those that are covered with earth, giving them a very sombre appearance, particularly in the autumn, in which season the snow begins to fall. They abound in ducks, buffalos, and sheep, whose wool is as white as snow, and as fine as silk; also in all kinds of bears, wolves, panthers, carcasiux, tiger cats, wild cats, and whistlers, a species of mountain rat. The moose is found here, but is very seldom caught, on account of its extraordinary vigilance, for, on the slightest rustling of a branch it leaves off eating, and will not return to its food for a long time afterwards. The soil of the valley is, with some few exceptions, very light; it contains, however, some good pastures. The whole course of the river is well lined with trees; especially with the pine, the fir, cotton, and willow trees.

Amongst the most remarkable birds we distinguished the Nun's eagle, (so called by travellers on account of the color of its head, which is white, whilst the other parts of the body are black,) the black eagle, buzzard, waterfowl, heron, crane, pheasant and quail. On the 30th we ascended a gap in the mountrin. The two sides were very lofty, and studded with large pines, all the branches of which were covered with a black and very fine moss, that hung in festoons, or in the shape of mourning garlands, and added to the already funereal appearance of this pass. We here filed off by a little path, scarce worthy however of the name, for a distance of six miles. The road was filled with large blocks of stone and trunks of trees, placed as if it were on purpose to render the pass difficult and impracticable. The summit once attained, we proceeded to cross a smiling little plain, called the Camash Prairies, where the Flat Heads come every spring to dig up that nourishing root, which, together with the game they are able to procure, forms their chief nourishment. We very soon descended the mountain in a zigzag direction, and reached a beautiful plain, which is watered by two rivers, the St.

Aloysius and St. Stanislaus. They unite in this plain, whence they go to join the forks at Clark's, otherwise called the Flat Head river. This valley extends about ten miles. I perceived in this place one of those formidable Black Foot Indians in the act of hiding himself. I did not speak of it to my young companions, fearing that I might not be able to prevent a bloody struggle between them. I however took the precaution of having a good watch kept over our horses. The next day was Sunday, a day of rest. I celebrated the Holy Sacrifice of the Mass, and baptized three little children of the Pointed Hearts' tribe, whose parents had joined us on the road. The rest of the day was spent in prayer and instructions. The chief of our band twice addressed his companions, and spoke with much force and precision on the different portions of our religion, which he already had heard explained. The 1st of November—All Saints' Day—after having celebrated the Holy Sacrifice under a large poplar tree, we proceeded on our journey through a defile of about six miles. At the ford of the Great Clark's Fork, we met two encampments of the Kalispel tribe, who, having heard of our approach, had come thither to see us. Men, women and children, ran to meet us, and pressed our hands with every demonstration of sincere joy. The chief of the first camp was called Chalax. I baptized twenty-four children in his little village, and one young woman, a Koetenaise, who was dying. The chief of the second camp was named Hoytelps; his band occupied thirty huts. I spent the night amongst them; and, although they had never seen me before, they knew all the prayers that I had taught the Flat Heads on my first journey. The fact is, on hearing of my arrival in the mountains, they deputed an intelligent young man to meet me, and who was also gifted with a good memory. Having learned the prayers and canticles, and such points as were most essential for salvation, he repeated to the village all that he had heard and seen. He had acquitted himself of his commission so well, and with so much zeal, that he gave instructions to his people during the course of the winter. The same desire for information concerning religion, had communicated itself to the other small camps, and with the same cheering success. It was, as you can easily imagine, a great consolation for me to hear prayers addressed to the great God, and his praises sung in a desert of about three hundred miles extent, where a Catholic priest had never been before. They were overjoyed when they heard that I hoped before long to be able to leave a Missionary amongst them. I cannot pass over in silence, a beautiful custom that is observed by these good people: Every evening, after prayers, the chief instructs his people, or gives them some salutary advice, to which they all listen with most profound attention, respect and modesty. To see them at their devotions one would be more apt to mistake them for perfectly religious men than savages. The next day, before my departure, I baptised twenty-seven children of the tribe. On that evening we alighted amongst fifteen huts of the same nation, who received us with equal kindness. Their chief had come several miles to meet me. He acknowledged frankly that having become acquainted with some American ministers, in the course of the summer—he had been told by them that my prayer (religion) was not a good one. "My heart is divided," said he, "and I do not know what to adhere to." I had no trouble in making him understand the difference between those gentlemen and priests, and the cause of their calumnious attacks against the only true church of Christ, which their ancestors had abandoned. On the 3d of November, after prayers and instructions to the savages, we continued our march. We were on the borders of the Clarke Forks, to which we were obliged to keep close during eight days, whilst we descended the country bordering the stream. The river is at this place of a greenish blue, very transparent, caused probably by the deposit of a great quantity of oxigen of iron. Our path during a great part of the day was on the declivity of a lofty, rocky mountain; we were here obliged to climb a steep rough pass from 400 to 600 feet high. I had before seen landscapes of awful grandeur, but this one certainly surpassed all others in horror. My courage failed at the first sight; it was impossible to remain on horseback, and on foot my weight of two hundred and eleven pounds, was no trifle. This, therefore, was the expedient to which I resorted: My mule Lizette was sufficiently docile and kind to allow me to grasp her tail, to which I held on firmly: crying at one moment aloud, and at other times making use of the whip to excite her courage, until the good beast conducted me safely to the very top of the mountain.—There I breathed freely for awhile, and contemplated the magnificent prospect that presented itself to my sight.

The windings of the river with the scenery on its banks were before me, on one side hung over our heads, rocks piled on rocks in the most precipitous manner, and on the other stood lofty peaks crowned with snow and pine trees: mountains of every shape and feature reared their towering forms before us. It really was a fine view and one which was well worth the effort we had made. On descending from this elevation I had to take new precautions. I preceded the mule, holding her by the bridle, while she moved cautiously down to the foot of the "Bad Rock," (as it is called by the savages,) as though she feared stumbling and rolling with her master into the river which flowed beneath us. At this place Clarke's Fork runs through a narrow defile of rocky mountains; at times the soft murmurings of the waters charm the traveller, at others it spreads out and presents a calm surface clear as crystal. Wherever it is narrowed or intercepted by rocks it forms rapids, with falls and cascades; the noise of which, like that caused by a storm in the forest, is heard at a great distance. Nothing can be more diversified than this fine river. There is in this vicinity a great variety of trees, bushes and different species of the tamarisk tree. The lichnis, a medicinal plant mentioned by Charlevoix in his history of Canada, grows here abundantly. We met in the course of that day with only one family, and that was of the Kalispel tribe. Whilst the women were rowing up the river their light canoe, made of the fir tree bark, which contained their children and all the baggage, the men followed along the bank with their rifles or bows in their hands in pursuit of game.

On the 4th we entered a cedar and pine forest so dense that in its whole length we could scarcely see beyond the distance of twenty feet. Our beasts of burden suffered a great deal in it from the want of grass. We scarcely got through it after three day's march. It was a real labyrinth; from morning till night we did nothing but wind about to avoid thousands of trees, fallen either from fire, storms or age. On issuing from this forest we were charmed by an interesting prospect: Our view extended over the whole surface of the lake called "Pends-d'oreilles," studded with small islands covered with woods: over its inlets and the hills which overlook them, and which have for the most part their base on the borders of the lake and rise by gradual terraces or elevations until they reach the adjoining mountains, which are covered with perpetual snow. The lake is about 30 miles long and from 4 to 7 wide. At the head of it we traversed a forest, which is certainly a wonder of its kind; there is probably nothing similar to it in America. The savages speak of it as the finest in Oregon, and really every tree which it contains is enormous in its kind. The birch, elm and beech, generally small elsewhere, like the toad of La Fontaine, that aimed at being as large as the ox, swell out here to twice their size. They would fain rival the cedar, the Goliah of the forest, who, however, looking down with contempt upon his pitiful companions,

"Eleve aux cieux
Son frout audacieux."
"Rears to heaven his audacious head."

The birch and beech at its side, resemble large candelabras placed around a massive column. Cedars, of four and five fathoms in circumference, are here very common; we saw some six, and I measured one forty-two feet in circumference. A cedar of four fathoms, lying on the ground, measured more than two hundred feet in length. The delicate branches of these noble trees entwine themselves above the beech and elm; their fine, dense and ever-green foliage, forming an arch through which the sun's rays never penetrate; and this lofty vault, supported by thousands of columns, brought to the mind's eye, the idea of an immense, glorious temple, carpeted with the hardy ever-greens that live and flourish best in the shade.

Before entering the forest we crossed a high mountain by a wild winding path. Its sides are covered with fine cedars and pines, which are, however, of smaller dimensions than those in the forest. Several times whilst ascending the mountain I found myself on parapets of rocks, whence, thanks to my safe-footed mule, I retired in safety. Once I thought my career at an end. I had wandered from my companions, and following the path, I all at once came to a rocky projection which terminated in a point about two feet wide; before me was a perpendicular descent of three feet; on my left stood a rock as straight as a wall, and on my right yawned a precipice of about a thousand feet.— You can conceive that my situation was any thing but pleasant. The slightest false step would have plunged the mule and his rider into the abyss beneath. To descend was impossible, as on one side I was closed in by the rock, and suspended over a dreadful chasm on the other. My mule had stopped at the commencement of the descent, and not having any time to lose, I recommended myself to God, and as a last expedient sunk my spurs deeply into the sides of my poor beast; she made one bold leap and safely landed me on another parapet much larger than that I had left.

The history of the fine forest, and my leap from the dangerous rock, will be treated with incredulity by many of your acquaintance. If so, tell them that I invite them to visit both these places: "Venite et videte." I promise them before hand, that they will admire with me the wonders of nature. They will have, like me, their moments of admiration and of fear. I cannot pass over in silence the pleasant meeting I had in the depth of the forest. I discovered a little hut of rushes, situated on the banks of the river. Raising my voice to its highest pitch, I tried to make its inhabitants hear me, but received no answer. I felt an irresistible desire to visit it, and accordingly made my interpreter accompany me. We found it occupied by a poor old woman, who was blind, and very ill. I spoke to her of the Great Spirit, of the most essential dogmas of our faith, and of baptism. The example of the Apostle St.

Philip teaches us that there are cases when all the requisite dispositions may entirely consist in an act of faith, and in the sincere desire to enter Heaven by the right path. All the answers of the poor old woman were respectful, and breathing the love of God. "Yes," she would say, "I love the Great Spirit with my whole heart; all my life he has been very kind to me. Yes, I wish to be His child, I want to be His forever." And immediately she fell on her knees, and begged me to give her baptism. I named her Mary, and placed around her neck the miraculous medal of the Blessed Virgin. After leaving her, I overheard her thanking God for this fortunate adventure. I had scarcely regained the path, when I met her husband, almost bent to the earth by age and infirmity; he could hardly drag himself along. He had been setting a trap in the forest for the bucks. The Flat Heads who had preceded me, had told him of my arrival. As soon, therefore, as he perceived me, he began to cry out, with a trembling voice: "Oh how delighted I am to see our Father before I die. The Great Spirit is good—oh how happy my heart is." And the venerable old man pressed my hand most affectionately, repeating again and again the same expressions. Tears fell from my eyes on witnessing such affection. I told him that I had just left his hut, and had baptized his wife. "I heard," said he, "of your arrival in our mountains, and of your baptizing many of our people. I am poor and old; I had hardly dared to hope for the happiness of seeing you. Black-gown, make me as happy as you have made my wife. I wish also to belong to God, and we will always love Him." I conducted him to the borders of a stream that flowed near us, and after a brief instruction, I administered to him the Holy Sacrament of Baptism, naming him Simon. On seeing me depart, he repeated, impressively:

"Oh how good is the Great Spirit. I thank you, Skylax, (Black-gown) for the favor you have conferred on me. Oh how happy is my heart. Yes, I will always love the Great Spirit. Oh how good the Great Spirit is; how good He is." During that same journey, I discovered in a little hut of bulrushes, five old men, who appeared to be fourscore years old. Three of them were blind, and the other two had but one eye each; they were almost naked, and offered a real personification of human misery. I spoke to them for a considerable time on the means of salvation, and on the bliss of another world. Their answers edified me much, and affected me even to tears; they were replete with the love of God, a desire of doing right, and of dying well. You might have heard these good old men crying out from different parts of the hut, forming together a touching chorus, to which I sincerely wished that all the children of St. Ignatius could have listened. "Oh Great Spirit, what a happiness is coming to us in our old days! We will love you, O Great Spirit. *Le-mele Kaikolinzoeten; one le-mele eltelill.* We will love you, O Great Spirit. Yes, we will love you till death." When we explained to them the necessity of baptism, they demanded it earnestly, and knelt down to receive it. I have not found as yet amongst these Indians, I will not say opposition, but not even coldness or indifference. These little adventures are our great consolation. I would not have exchanged my situation, at that moment, for any other on earth. I was convinced that such incidents alone were worth a journey to the mountains. Ah, good and dear Fathers, who may read these lines, I conjure you, through the mercy of our Divine Redeemer, not to hesitate entering this vineyard; its harvest is ripe and abundant. Does not our Saviour tell us: "Ignem veni mittere in terram et quid volo nisi ut accendatur." It is amidst the poor tribes of these isolated mountains that the fire of divine grace burns with ardor. Superstitious practices have disappeared; nor have they amongst them the castes of East India. Speak to these Savages of heavenly things; at once their hearts are inflamed with divine love; and immediately they go seriously about the great affair of their salvation. Day and night they are at our sides, insatiable for the "Bread of Life." Often, on retiring, we hear them say, "Our sins, no doubt, rendered us so long unworthy to hear these consoling words." As to privations and dangers, the Oregon Missionaries must expect them, for they will certainly meet them, but in a good cause. Sometimes they will be obliged to fast, but a better appetite will be their reward. Their escapes from the many dangers of the road, or from enemies always on the alert, teach them to confide in God alone, and ever to keep their accounts in order. I here feel the full application of that consoling text of the Scripture: "My yoke is sweet, and my burden is light." At the last day it will be manifest that the holy name of Jesus has performed wonders amongst these poor people. Their eagerness to hear the glad tidings of salvation is certainly at its height. They came from all parts, and from great distances, to meet me on my way, and presented all their young children and dying relatives for baptism. Many followed me for whole days, with the sole desire of receiving instructions. Really our hearts bled at the sight of so many souls who are lost for the want of religion's divine and saving assistance. Here again may we cry out with the Scripture: "The harvest indeed is great, but the laborers are few." What Father is there in the Society whose zeal will not be enkindled on hearing these details? And where is the Christian who would refuse his mite to such a work as that of the "Propagation of the Faith?" that precious pearl of the Church, which procures salvation to so many souls, who otherwise would perish unaided and forever. During my journey, which lasted forty-two days, I baptized 190 persons, of whom 26 were adults, sick, or in extreme old age; I preached to more than two thousand Indians; who thus evidently conducted into my way by Providence, will not, I trust, tarry long in ranging themselves under the banner of Jesus Christ. With the assistance of my catechists, the Flat Heads, who were as yet but catechumens, the conversion of the Kalispel tribe was so far advanced that when the time came round for the winter's hunting, the Rev. Father Point enjoyed the consolation of seeing them join the Flat Head tribe, with the sole desire of profiting by the Missionary's presence. This gave him an opportunity to instruct and baptise a great number on the Purification and on the Feasts of the Canonization of St. Ignatius and St. Francis Xavier. On my return, the 8th of December, I continued instructing those of the Flat Heads who had not been baptized. On Christmas day I added 150 new baptisms to those of the 3d of December, and 32 rehabilitations of marriage; so that the Flat Heads, some sooner and others later, but all, with very few exceptions, had, in the space of three months, complied with every thing necessary to merit the glorious title of true children of God. Accordingly on Christmas eve, a few hours before the midnight Mass, the village of St. Mary was deemed worthy of a special mark of heaven's favour: The Blessed Virgin appeared to a little orphan boy named Paul, in the hut of an aged and truly pious woman.— The youth, piety and sincerity of this child, joined to the nature of the fact which he related, forbade us to doubt the truth of his statement. The following is what he recount-

APPARITION.

ed to me with his own innocent lips: "Upon entering John's hut, whither I had gone to learn my prayers, which I did not know, I saw some one who was very beautiful—her feet did not touch the earth, her garments were as white as snow; she had a star over her head, a serpent under her feet; and near the serpent was a fruit which I did not recognise. I could see her heart, from which rays of light burst forth and shone upon me. When I first beheld all this I was frightened, but afterwards my fear left me; my heart was warmed, my mind clear, and I do not know how it happened, but all at once I knew my prayers." (To be brief I omit several circumstances.) He ended his account by saying that several times the same person had appeared to him whilst he was sleeping; and that once she had told him she was pleased, that the first village of the Flat Heads should be called "St. Mary." The child had never seen or heard before any thing of the kind; he did not even know if the person was a man or woman, because the appearance of the dress which she wore was entirely unknown to him. Several persons having interrogated the child on this subject, have found him unvarying in his answers. He continues by his conduct to be the angel of his tribe.

On the 23d of December, Father Point, at the head of the inhabitants of forty lodges, started for the buffalo hunt.— On the road they met with huntsmen of five or six different tribes, some of whom followed him to the termination of the chase, from the desire of learning their prayers. The Flat Heads having prolonged their stay at St. Mary's as long as they possibly could, so as not to depart without receiving baptism, experienced such a famine, the first weeks of January, that their poor dogs, having not even a bone to gnaw, devoured the very straps of leather with which they tied their horses during the night. The cold moreover was so uninterruptedly severe that during the hunting season, which lasted three months, such a quantity of snow fell that many were attacked with a painful blindness, vulgarly called "snow disease." One day when the wind was very high, and the snow falling and freezing harder than usual, Father Point became suddenly very pale, and would no doubt have been frozen to death, in the midst of the plain, had not some travellers, perceiving the change in his countenance, kindled a large fire. But neither the wind, ice, or famine, prevented the zealous Flat Heads from performing on this journey all they were accustomed to do at St. Mary's. Every morning and evening they assembled around the Missionary's lodge, and more than three-fourths of them without any shelter than the sky, after having recited their prayers, listened to an instruction, preceded and followed by hymns. At day-break and sunset the bell was tolled three times for the Angelical Salutation. The Sunday was religiously kept; an observance which was so acceptable to God, that once especially it was recompensed in a very visible manner. The following is what I read in the Journal kept by Father Point during the winter's hunt.

Sixth February.—To-day, Sunday, a very high wind, the sky greyish, and the thermometer at the freezing point; no grass for the horses; the buffalos driven off by the Pierced Noses. The 7th, the cold more piercing—food for our horses still scarcer—the snow increasing; but yesterday was a time of perfect rest, and the fruits of it show themselves to-day in perfect resignation and confidence. At noon we reach the summit of a mountain, and what a change awaits us. The sun shines, the cold has lost its intensity; we have in view an immense plain, and in that plain good pasturages, which are clouded with buffalos. The encampment stops, the hunters assemble, and before sunset 155 buffalos have fallen by their arrows. One must confess that if this hunt were not miraculous, it bears a great resemblance to the draught of fishes made by Peter when casting his net at the word of the Lord, he drew up 153 fishes.—St. John, xxi. 11. The Flat Heads confided in the Lord, and were equally successful in killing 153 buffalos. What a fine draught of fishes! but what a glorious hunt of buffalos! Represent to yourself an immense amphitheatre of mountains, the least of which exceeds in height Mont Martre, and in the midst of this majestic enclosure a plain more extensive than that of Paris, and on this magnificent plain a multitude of animals, the least of which surpasses in size the largest ox in Europe. Such was the park in which our Indians hunted. Wishing to pursue them, continues Father Point, in his journal, I urged on my horse to a herd of fugitives, and as he was fresh, I had no difficulty in getting up to them. I even succeeded in compelling the foremost to abandon his post, but enraged, he stopped short, and presented such a terrible front, that I thought it more prudent to open a passage and let him escape. I acted wisely, as on the same day, one of these animals, in his fall, overturned a horse and his rider. Fortunately, however, the latter was more dexterous than I should have been in such a perilous situation; he aimed his blows so promptly and well, that of the three who were thrown, only two arose. On another occasion, a hunter who had been also dismounted, had no other means to avoid being torn to pieces than to seize hold of the animal by the horns just at the time he was about to trample him to death. A third hunter, fleeing at all speed, felt himself stopped by the plaited tail of his horse hooked on the buffalo's horn; but both fearing a trap, made every effort to disengage themselves. The buffalo hunt is attended with dangers, but the greatest of these does not consist in the mere pursuit of the animal, but proceeds rather from the bands of Black Feet who constantly lurk in these regions, especially when there is some prospect of meeting with the larger game, or stealing a number of horses. Of all the mountain savages the Black Feet are the most numerous, wicked, and the greatest thieves. Happily, however, from having been often beaten by the smaller tribes, they have become so dastardly, that unless they are twenty to one, they confine their attacks to the horses, which, thanks to the carelessness of their courageous enemies, they go about with so much dexterity and success, that this year, while our good Flat Heads were asleep, they discovered their animals as often as twenty times, and carried off more than one hundred of them. During the winter, about twenty of these gentlemen visited the Flat Heads in the day time, and without stealing any thing, but in this manner. There resided in the camp an old chief of the Black Feet tribe, who had been baptised on Christmas day, and named Nicholas; this good savage, knowing that the Missionary would willingly hold an interview with his brethren, undertook himself to harangue them during the night, and so well did he acquit himself, that upon the calumet's being planted on the limits of the camp, and the messenger being admitted to an audience, singing was heard in the neighboring mountains, and soon after a band of these brigands issued, armed as warriors, from the gloomy defile. They were received as friends, and four of the principals were ushered into the Missionary's lodge; they smoked the calumet and discussed the news of the day. The Missionary spoke of the necessity of prayer, to which subject they listened most attentively; nor did they manifest either surprise or repugnance. They told him that there had arrived

recently in one of their forests a man who was not married,
and who wore on his breast a large crucifix, read every day
in a big book, and made the sign of the cross before eating
any thing; and in fine, that he was dressed exactly like the
Black-gowns at St. Mary's. The Father did every thing
in his power to gain their good will—after which, they were
conducted to the best lodge in the encampment. It certainly would seem that such hosts were worthy of better
guests. However, towards the middle of the night, the explosion of fire arms was heard. It was soon discovered
that a Flat Head was firing at a Black Foot, just as the latter was leaving the camp, taking with him four horses.—
Fortunately, the robber was not one of the band that had
been received within the encampment, which, upon being
proved, far from creating any suspicion, on the contrary, had
the effect of their kindly offering them a grave for the unfortunate man. But whether they wished to appear to disapprove of the deed, or that they anticipated dangers from reprisals, they left the wolves to bury the body, and took their
departure. Good Nicholas, the orator, joined them, in
order to render the same services to the others that he had
to these. He went off, promising to return soon with the
evidences of his success. He has not been seen as
yet, but we are informed, he and his companions have
spoken so favorably of prayer, and the Black-gowns, that
already the Sunday is religiously observed in the camp
where Nicholas resides, and that a great chief, with the
people of sixty lodges, intend shortly to make our acquaintance, and attach themselves to the Flat Heads. In the
meanwhile, divine justice is punishing rigorously a number of their robbers. This year, the Pierced Noses caught
twelve of them in flagrant faults, and killed them. About
the time that the Black Foot above mentioned met his fate at

the hands of a Flat Head, thirty others were receiving the reward due to their crimes, from the Pends-d'oreilles tribe. A very remarkable fact in this last encounter is, that of the four who commenced, and the others who finished it, not one fell; although, in order to break in on the delinquents, who were retrenched behind a kind of rampart, they were obliged to expose themselves to a brisk fire. I saw the field of combat some time afterwards. Of the thirty robbers who had been slain, only five or six heads remained, and those so disfigured as to lead one to think that an age had already elapsed since their death.

Two years before, the same tribe, (Pends-d'oreilles) assisted by the Flat Heads, making in all a band of seventy men, stood an attack of fifteen hundred Black Feet, whom they defeated, killing in five days, during which time the battle lasted, fifty of their foes, without losing a single man on their side. They would not commence the attack until they had recited their prayers on their knees. A few days ago, the spot was pointed out to me where six Flat Heads withstood 160 Black Feet with so much resolution, that with a handful of their men who came to their aid, they gained the victory. The most perfidious nation, after the Black Feet, is the Banac tribe; they also bear the Flat Heads much ill will. It has happened more than once that at the very moment the Banac tribe were receiving the greatest proofs of friendship from the Flat Heads, the former were plotting their ruin. Of this you have already had one proof, but here is another. One day a detachment of two hundred Banacs visited the camp of the Flat Heads, and after smoking with them returned to their encampment. The small number of the Flat Heads had not, however, escaped their notice, and they determined to take advantage of their apparent weakness. Accordingly, they retraced their steps that very night to execute their base designs. But the chief, named Michael, having been advised of their intention, assembled in haste his twenty warriors, and after entreating them to confide in God, he rushed on these traitors so happily and vigorously, that at the first shock they were routed. Already nine of the fugitives had fallen, and most of the others would have shared the same fate if Michael, in the very heat of the pursuit, had not recollected that it was Sunday, and on that account stopped his brave companions, saying: "My friends, it is now the time for prayer; we must retire to our camp." It is by these and similar exploits, wherein the finger of God is visible, that the Flat Heads have acquired such a reputation for valor, that notwithstanding their inferior numbers, they are feared much more than they on their side dread their bitterest enemies. These victories however cannot but be fatal even to the conquerors; hence we will strive to inspire all with the love of peace, which may be accomplished if each party remains at home. For this purpose we must create among them a greater taste for agriculture than for hunting. But how can we compass this unless the same measures are employed for the missions of the Rocky Mountains that were so happily adopted for Paraguay. If the true friends of Religion only knew of what the Indians who surround us are capable when once converted, I can not doubt but that they would assist us in our efforts to accomplish so beautiful, so advantageous a project. It is, moreover, through the Iroquois of the North, whose cruelty formerly exceeded that of the Black Feet, that the knowledge of the true God came to the Flat Heads, and awakened amongst them the desire of possessing the Black-gowns. We have seen to what dangers the good Flat Heads exposed themselves to obtain Missionaries, and what sacrifices they have made to merit the title of children of God; and now what is their actual progress? In their village, enmities, quarrels and calumnies, are unknown; they are sincere and upright amongst themselves, and full of confidence in their Missionaries. They carry this to such a degree that they place implicit reliance on their veracity, and cannot suppose that they have any thing else in view but their happiness; they have no difficulty in believing the mysteries of our faith, or in approaching the tribunal of penance: difficulties which appear insurmountable to the pride and cowardice of many civilized christians. The first time they were asked if they believed firmly in all that was contained in the Apostles' creed, they answered, "Yes—very much." When they were spoken to about confession, some wished it to be public.— This will explain to you how it happened that before we resided three months amongst them we were enabled to baptize all the adults, and four months later to admit a large number to frequent communion. There are whole families who never let a Sunday go by without approaching the holy table. Often twenty confessions are heard consecutively without their being matter for absolution. This year we performed the devotion of the month of Mary, and I can flatter myself that the exercises were attended with as much piety and edification as in the most devout parishes of Europe. At the end of the month a statue was borne in triumph to the very place where our Blessed Mother designed to honor us with the aforementioned apparition.— Since that day a sort of pilgrimage has been established there, under the name of "Our Lady of Prayer." None pass the pious monument without stopping to pray on their knees; the more devout come regularly twice a day to speak to their Mother and her divine Son, and the children add to their prayers the most beautiful flowers they can cull in the prairies.

On the Feast of the Sacred Heart we made use of this monument, decorated with garlands of flowers, as a repository, and our people received for the first time, the benediction of the blessed sacrament; a happiness which they now enjoy every Sunday after vespers. Some of them already understand the nature of the devotion of the Sacred Heart. To propagate it we have laid the foundations of several societies, of which all the most virtuous men, women and young people have become members. Victor, the great chief, is prefect of one of these associations, and Agnes his wife is president of another. They were not elected through any deference for their dignity or birth, but solely on account of their great personal merits. A fact which proves that the *Flat Heads* regard merit more than rank, is, that the place of great chief becoming vacant by the death of Peter, they chose for his successor the chief of the men's society, and for no other reason did he obtain this high dignity than for the noble qualities, both of heart and head, which they all thought he possessed. Every night and morning, when all is quiet in the camp, he harangues the people; the subject of his discourse being principally a repetition of what the Black Gowns have said before. This good chief walks faithfully in the footsteps of his predecessor, which is no slight praise. This last, who was baptized at the age of 80, and admitted to communion in his 82d year, was the first to deserve this double favour, more on account of his virtue than his years. The day of his baptism he said to me, "If during my life I have committed faults they were those of ignorance; it appears to me that I never did any thing, knowing it to be wrong." At the time of his first communion, which preceded his death but a few days, having been asked if he had not some faults with which to reproach himself since his baptism—" Faults," he replied, with surprise, " how could I ever commit any, I whose duty it is to teach others how to do good?" He was buried in the red drapery he was accustomed to hang out on Sunday to announce that it was the day of the Lord. Alphonsus, in the prime of youth soon followed him. He said to me on the day of his baptism : " I dread so much offending again the Great Spirit, that I beg of him to grant me the grace to die soon." He fell sick a few days afterwards and expired with the most Christian dispositions, thanking God for having granted his prayerr In the hope of their glorious resurrection, their mortal remains have been deposited at the foot of the large cross.

Of twenty persons who died within the year, we have no reason to fear for the salvation of one.

Not having been able this year to obtain either provisions or sufficient clothes to supply the wants of our mission, I started for Fort Vancouver, the great mart of the honorable Hudson Bay Company, and distant about one thousand miles from our establishment. The continuation of this narrative will show you that this necessary journey was providential. I found myself during this trip a second time amongst the Kalispel tribe.

They continue with much fervour to assemble every morning and evening to recite prayers in common, and manifest the same attention and assiduity in listening to our instructions. The chiefs on their side are incessant in exhorting the people to the practice of every good work. The two principal obstacles that prevent a great number from receiving baptism, are—first, the plurality of wives; many have not the courage to separate themselves from those, by whom they have children. The second is their fondness for gambling, in which they risk every thing. I baptized 60 adults amongst them during this last journey.

Crossing a beautiful plain near the Clarke or Flat Head river, called the Horse prairie, I heard that there were 30 lodges of the Skalzy or Kœtenay tribe, at about two day's journey from us. I determined whilst awaiting the descent of the skiff, which could only start six days later, to pay them a visit, for they had never seen a priest in their lands before. Two half breeds served as my guides and escorts on this occasion. We gallopped and trotted all the day, travelling a distance of 60 miles. We spent a quiet night in a deep defile, stretched near a good fire, but in the open air. The next day, (April 14) after having traversed several mountains and valleys, where our horses were up to their knees in snow, we arrived about 3 o'clock in sight of the Kœtenay camp. They assembled immediately on my approach; when I was about twenty yards from them, the warriors presented their arms, which they had hidden until then under their buffalo robes. They fired a general salute which frightened my mule and made her rear and prance to the great amusement of the savages. They then defiled before me, giving their hands in token of friendship and congratulation. I observed that each one lifted his hand to his forehead after having presented it to me. I soon convoked the council in order to inform them of the object of my visit. They unanimously declared themselves in favour of my religion, and adopted the beautiful custom of their neighbours, the Flat Heads, to meet night and morning for prayers in common. I assembled them that very evening for this object and gave them a long instruction on the principal dogmas of our faith. The next day, I baptized all their little children and nine of their adults, previously instructed, amongst whom was the wife of an Iroquois, who had resided for thirty years with this tribe. The Iroquois and a Canadian occupy themselves in the absence of a priest in instructing them. My visit could not be long, I left the Kœtenay village about 12 o'clock, accompanied by twelve of these warriors and some half-blood Crees, whom I had baptized in 1840. They wished to escort me to the entrance of the large Flat Head lake, with the desire of giving me a farewell feast; a real banquet of all the good things their country produced. The warriors had gone on ahead and dispersed in every direction, some to hunt and others to fish. The latter only succeeded in catching a single trout. The warriors returned in the evening with a bear, goose and six swan's eggs. "Sed quid hoc inter tantos." The fish and goose were roasted before a good fire, and the whole mess was soon presented to me. Most of my companions preferring to fast, I expressed my regret at it, consoling them however by telling them that God would certainly reward their kindness to me. A moment after we heard the last hunter returning, whom we thought had gone back to the camp. Hope shone on every countenance. The warrior soon appeared laden with a large elk, and hunger that night was banished from the camp. Each one began to occupy himself; some cut up the animal, others heaped fuel on the fire, and prepared sticks and spits to roast the meat. The feast which had commenced under such poor auspices continued a great part of the night. The whole animal, excepting a small piece that was reserved for my breakfast, had disappeared before they retired to sleep. This is a sample of savage life. The Indian when he has nothing to eat does not complain, but in the midst of abundance he knows no moderation. The stomach of a savage has always been to me a riddle.

The plain that commands a view of the lake is one of the

most fertile in the mountainous regions. The Flat Head river runs through it and extends more than 200 miles to the North East. It is wide and deep, abounding with fish and lined with wood, principally with the cotton, aspen, pine and birch. There are beautiful sites for villages, but the vicinity of the Black Feet must delay for a long while the good work, as they are only at two day's march from the great district occupied by these brigands, from whence they often issue to pay their neighbours predatory visits. A second obstacle would be the great distance from any post of the Hudson Bay Company; consequently the difficulty of procuring what is strictly necessary. The lake is highly romantic, and is from 40 to 50 miles long. Mountainous and rocky islands of all sizes are scattered over its bosom, which present an enchanting prospect. These islands are filled with wild horses. Lofty mountains surround the lake and rise from its very brink.

On the 16th of April, after bidding adieu to my travelling companions, I started early in the morning, accompanied by two Canadians and two savages. That evening we encamped close to a delightful spring, which was warm and sulphurous; having travelled a distance of about fifty miles. When the savages reach this spring they generally bathe in it. They told me that after the fatigues of a long journey they find that bathing in this water greatly refreshes them. I found here ten lodges of the Kalispel tribe; the chief, who was by birth of the Pierced Nose tribe, invited me to spend the night in his wigwam, where he treated me most hospitably. This was the only small Kalispel camp that I had as yet met in my journeys. I here established, as I have done wherever I stopped, the custom of morning and evening prayers. During the evening the chief who had looked very gloomy, made a public exposition of his whole life. "Black Gown," said he, "you find yourself in the lodge of a most wicked and unhappy man; all the evil that a man could do on earth, I believe I have been guilty of: I have even assassinated several of my near relations; since then, there is nought in my heart but trouble, bitterness and remorse. Why does not the Great Spirit annihilate me? I still possess life, but there will be neither pardon nor mercy for me after death." These words and the feeling manner with which they were addressed to me drew tears of compassion from my eyes. "Poor, unfortunate man," I replied, "you are really to be pitied, but you increase your misery by thinking that you cannot obtain pardon. The devil, man's evil spirit, is the author of this bad thought. Do not listen to him, for he would wish to precipitate you into that bad place (hell). The Great Spirit who created you is a Father infinitely good and merciful. He does not desire the death of the sinner, but rather that he should be converted and live. He receives us into his favour and forgets our crimes, notwithstanding their number and enormity, the moment we return to Him contrite and repentant. He will also forgive you if you walk in the path which His only Son, Jesus Christ, came on earth to trace for us." I then recounted the instance of the good thief and the parable of the prodigal son. I made him sensible of the proof of God's goodness in sending me to him. I added that perhaps his life was drawing to a close, and that he might be in danger of falling into the bad place on account of his sins; that I would show him the right path, which if he followed he would certainly reach Heaven. These few words were as balm poured on his wounded spirit. He became calmer, and joy and hope appeared on his countenance. "Black Gown," said he, "your words re-animate me: I see, I understand better now, you have consoled me, you have relieved me from a burden that was crushing me with its weight, for I thought myself lost. I will follow your directions; I will learn how to pray. Yes, I feel convinced that the Great Spirit will have pity on me." There was fortunately in the camp a young man who knew all the prayers, and was willing to serve as his catechist. His baptism was deferred until the autumn or winter.

The results of my visit to the Pointed Hearts were very consoling. They form a small but interesting tribe, animated with much fervour.

As soon as they were certain of my visit, they deputed couriers in every direction to inform the savages of the approach of the Black-gown; and all, without exception, assembled at the outlet of the great lake which bears their name, and which was the place I had indicated. An ingenuous joy, joined to wonder and contentment, shone on every face when they saw me arrive in the midst of them. Every one hastened to greet me. It was the first visit of the kind they had received, and the following is the order they observed. Their chiefs and old men marched at the head; next came the young men and boys; then followed the women—mothers, young girls, and little children. I was conducted in triumph by this multitude to the lodge of the great chief. Here, as every where else in the Indian country, the everlasting calumet was first produced, which went round two or three times in the most profound silence. The chief then addressed me, saying: "Black-gown you are most welcome amongst us. We thank you for your charity towards us. For a long time we have wished to see you, and hear the words which will give us understanding. Our fathers invoked the sun and earth. I recollect very well when the knowledge of the true and one God came amongst them; since which time we have offered to Him our prayers and vows. We are however to be pitied. We do not know the word of the Great Spirit. All is darkness as yet to us, but to-day I hope we shall see the light shine. Speak, Black-gown, I have done—every one is anxious to hear you." I spoke to them for two hours on salvation and end of man's creation, and not one person stirred from his place the whole time of the instruction. As it was almost sunset, I recited the prayers that I had translated into their language a few days before. After which I took some refreshments, consisting of fragments of dried meat, and a piece of cooked moss, tasting like soap, and as black as pitch. All this however was as grateful to my palate as though it had been honey and sugar, not having eaten a mouthful since day-break. At their own request I then continued instructing the chiefs and their people until the night was far advanced. About every half hour I paused, and then the pipes would pass around to refresh the listeners and give time for reflection. It was during these intervals that the chiefs conversed on what they had heard, and instructed and advised their followers. On awakening the next morning, I was surprised to find my lodge already filled with people. They had entered so quietly that I had not heard them. It was hardly day-break when I arose, and they all following my example, placed themselves on their knees, and we made together the offering of our hearts to God, with that of the actions of the day. After this the Chief said: " Black-gown, we come here very early to observe you—we wish to imitate what you do. Your prayer is good; we wish to adopt it. But you will leave us after two nights more, and we have no one to teach us in your absence." I had the bell rung for morning prayers, promising him at the same time that the prayers should be known before I left them.

After a long instruction on the most important truths of religion, I collected around me all the little children, with the young boys and girls; I chose two from among the latter, to whom I taught the Hail Mary, assigning to each one his own particular part; then seven for the Our Father; ten others for the Commandments, and twelve for the Apostles' Creed. This method, which was my first trial of it, succeeded admirably. I repeated to each one his part until he knew it perfectly; I then made him repeat it five or six times. These little Indians, forming a triangle, resembled a choir of angels, and recited their prayers, to the great astonishment and satisfaction of the savages. They continued in this manner morning and night, until one of the chiefs learned all the prayers, which he then repeated in public. I spent three days in instructing them. I would have remained longer, but the savages were without provisions. There was scarcely enough for one person in the whole camp. My own provisions were nearly out, and I was still four days' journey from Fort Coleville. The second day of my stay among them, I baptized all their small children, and then twenty-four adults, who were infirm and very old. It appeared as though God had retained these good old people on earth to grant them the inexpressible happiness of receiving the sacrament of baptism before their death. They seemed by their transports of joy and gratitude at this moment, to express that sentiment of the Scripture: "My soul is ready, O God, my soul is ready." Never did I experience in my visits to the savages so much satisfaction as on this occasion, not even when I visited the Flat Heads in 1840; nor have I elsewhere seen more convincing proofs of sincere conversion to God. May He grant them to persevere in their virtuous resolutions. Rev. Father Point intends passing the winter with them to confirm them in their faith. After some advice and salutary regulations, I left this interesting colony, and I must acknowledge, with heartfelt regret. The great chief allowed himself scarcely a moment's repose for three nights I spent amongst them; he would rise from time to time to harangue the people, and repeat to them all he was able to remember of the instructions of the day. During the whole time of my mission, he continued at my side, so anxious was he not to lose a single word. The old chief, now in his eightieth year, was baptized by the name of Jesse. In the spring the territory of this tribe enchants the traveller who may happen to traverse it. It is so diversified with noble plains, and enamelled with flowers, whose various forms and colors offer to experienced botanists an interesting *parterre.* These plains are surrounded by magnificent forests of pine, fir and cedar. To the west their country is open, and the view extends over several days' journey. To the south, east and north, you see towering mountains, ridge rising above ridge, robed with snow, and mingling their summits with the clouds, from which, at a distance, you can hardly distinguish them. The lake forms a striking feature in this beautiful prospect, and is about thirty miles in circumference. It is deep, and abounds in fish, particularly in salmon trout, common trout, carp, and a small, oily fish, very delicious, and tasting like the smelt. The Spokan river rises in the lake, and crosses the whole plain of the Cœur d'Alenes. The valley that borders above the lake is from four to five miles wide, exceedingly fertile, and the soil from ten to fifteen feet deep. Every spring, at the melting of the snow, it is subject to inundations, which scarcely ever last longer than four or five days; at the same time augmenting, as in Egypt, the fertility of the soil. The potatoe grows here very well, and in great abundance.

The Spokan river is wide, swift and deep in the spring, and contains, like all the rivers of Oregon, many rapid falls and cascades. The navigation of the waters of this immense territory is generally dangerous, and few risk themselves on them without being accompanied by experienced pilots. In descending Clark's river, we passed by some truly perilous and remarkable places, where the pilots have full opportunity to exhibit their dexterity and prudence. The rapids are numerous, and the roar of the waters incessant, the current sweeping on at the rate of ten or twelve miles an hour; the rugged banks and projecting rocks creating waves resembling those of the troubled sea. The skilful pilot mounts the waves, which seem ready to engulf us, the canoe speeds over the agitated waters, and with the aid of the paddle, skilfully plied, bears us unharmed through numberless dangers. The most remarkable spot on this river is called the *cabinets;* it consists of four apartments, which you have hardly time to examine, as you are scarcely half a minute passing by them. Represent to yourself chasms between two rocky mountains of a stupendous height, the river pent in between them in a bed of thirty or forty feet, precipitating itself down its rocky channel with irresistible fury, roaring against its jagged sides, and whitening with foam all around it. In a short space it winds in four different directions, resembling very much, forked lightning. It requires very great skill, activity, and presence of mind, to extricate yourself from this difficult pass. The Spokan lands are sandy, gravelly, and badly calculated for agriculture. The section over which I travelled consisted of immense plains of light, dry, and sandy soil, and thin forests of gum pines. We saw nothing in this noiseless solitude but a buck, running quickly from us, and disappearing almost immediately. From time to time, the melancholy and piercing cry of the wood snipe increased the gloomy thoughts which this sad spot occasioned. Here, on a gay and smiling little plain, two ministers have settled themselves, with their wives, who had consented to share their husbands' soi-disant apostolical labors. During the four years they have spent here, they have baptized several of their own children. They cultivate a small farm, large enough, however, for their own maintenance and the support of their animals and fowls. It appears they are fearful that, should they cultivate more, they might have too frequent visits from the savages. They even try to prevent their encampment in their immediate neighborhood, and therefore they see and converse but seldom with the heathens, whom they have come so far to seek. A band of Spokans received me with every demonstration of friendship, and were enchanted to hear that the right kind of Black-gowns intended soon to form an establishment in the vicinity. I baptized one of their little children who was dying.

It was in these parts that in 1836 a modern Iconaclast, named Parker, broke down a cross erected over the grave of a child by some Catholic Iroquois, telling us emphatically, in the narrative of his journey, that he did not wish to leave in that country an emblem of idolatry.

Poor man!—not to know better in this enlightened age! Were he to return to these mountains, he would hear the praises of the Holy Name of Jesus resounding among them; he would hear the Catholics chaunting the love and mercies of God from the rivers, lakes, mountains, prairies, forests and coasts of the Columbia. He would behold the Cross planted from shore to shore for the space of a thousand miles—on the loftiest height of the Pointed Heart territory, on the towering chain which separates the waters of the Missouri from the Columbia rivers; in the plains of the Wallamette, Cowlitz and Bitter Root—and, whilst I am writing to you, the Rev. Mr. Demers is occupied in planting this same sacred symbol amongst the different tribes of New Caledonia. The words of Him who said that this holy sign *would draw all men to Himself,* begin to be verified with regard to the poor destitute sheep of this vast continent. Were he who destroyed that solitary, humble Cross now to return, he would find the image of Jesus Christ crucified, borne on the breast of more than 4000 Indians; and the smallest child would say to him: "Mr. Parker, we do not adore the cross; do not break it, because it reminds us of Jesus Christ who died on the cross to save us—we adore God alone."

In the beginning of May I arrived at Fort Coleville on the Coleville river; this year the snow melted away very early. The mountain torrents had overflowed, and the small rivers that usually moved quietly along in the month of April, had suddenly left their beds and assumed the appearance of large rivers and lakes, completely flooding all the lowlands. This rendered my journey to Vancouver by land impossible, and induced me to wait, nolens volens, at the Fort, for the construction of the barges which were not ready until the 30th of the same month, when I was again able to pursue my journey on the river. On the same day that I arrived among the Shuyelpi or Chaudiere tribe, who resided near the Fort, I undertook to translate our prayers into their language. This kept me only one day as their language is nearly the same as that of the Flat Heads and Kalispels, having the same origin. They were all very attentive in attending my instructions, and the old, as well as the young, tried assiduously to learn their prayers. I baptized all the younger children who had not received the sacrament before, for Mr. Demers had already made two excursions amongst them, with the most gratifying success. The great chief and his wife had long sighed for baptism, which holy sacrament I administered to them, naming them Martin and Mary. This chief is one of the most intelligent and pious I have become acquainted with.

The work of God does not, however, proceed without contradictions; it is necessary to prepare oneself for them beforehand when undertaking any enterprise amongst the tribes. I have had some hard trials in all my visits. I expected them, when on the 13th of May, I started to see the Okinakane tribe, who were desirous to meet a priest. The interpreter, Charles, and the chief of the Shuyelpi, wished to accompany me. In crossing the Columbia river my mule returned to the shore, and ran at full speed into the forest; Charles pursued her, and two hours afterwards I was told that he had been found dead in the prairie. I hastened immediately, and perceived from a distance a great gathering of people. I soon reached the spot where he was lying, and, to my great joy, perceived that he gave signs of life. He was however, senseless, and in a most pitiful state. A copious bleeding and some days of rest restored him and we resumed our journey. This time the mule had a large rope tied around her neck, and we crossed the river without any accidents ; we took a narrow path that led us by mountains, valleys, forests and prairies, following the course of the river Sharameep. Towards evening we were on the borders of a deep impetuous torrent, having no other bridge than a tree which was rather slight and in constant motion from the rushing of the waters. It reminded me of the bridge of souls spoken of in the Potowattamie legends. These savages believe that souls must traverse this bridge before they reach their elysium in the west. The good, they say, pass over it without danger; the bad, on the contrary, are unable to hold on, but stumble, stagger and fall into the torrent below, which sweeps them off into a labyrinth of lakes and marshes; here they drag out their existence; wretched, tormented by famine and in great agony, the living prey of all sorts of venomous reptiles and ferocious animals, wandering to and fro without ever being able to escape. We were fortunate enough to cross the trembling bridge without accident. We soon pitched our camp on the other side, and in spite of the warring waves which in falls and cascades thundered all night by our side, we enjoyed a refreshing sleep. The greater part of the next day the path conducted us through a thick and hilly forest of fir trees; the country then became more undulating and open. From time to time we perceived an Indian burial ground, remarkable only for the posts erected on the graves, and hung with kettles, wooden plates, guns, bows and arrows, left there by the nearest relatives of the deceased—humble tokens of their grief and friendship.

We encamped on the shore of a small lake called the Sharrameep, where was a Shuyelpi village; I gave these savages several instructions and baptized their infants. At my departure the whole village accompanied me. The country over which we travelled is open; the soil, sterile and sandy, and the different chains of mountains that traverse it seem to be nothing but sharp pointed rocks, thinly covered with cedars and pines. Towards evening we came up with the men of the first Okinekane encampment, who received us with the greatest cordiality and joy. The chief who came out to meet us was quite conspicuous, being arrayed in his court dress—a shirt made of a horse skin, the hair of which was outside, the mane partly on his chest and back, giving him a truly fantastic and savage appearance. The camp also joined us, and the fact of my arrival having been soon noised abroad in every direction, we saw, issuing from the defiles and narrow passes of the mountains, bands of Indians who had gone forth to gather their harvest of roots. Many sick were presented to me for baptism, of which rite they already knew the importance. Before reaching the rendezvous assigned us, on the borders of the Okinakane lake, I was surrounded by more than 200 horsemen, and more than 200 others were already in waiting. We recited together night prayers, and all listened with edifying attention to the instruction I gave them. The interpreter and Martin continued the religious conversation until the night was far advanced ; they manifested the same anxiety to hear the word of God that the Stiel Shoi had shown. All the next day was spent in prayer, instructions and hymns—I baptized 106 children and some old people, and in conclusion named the plain where these consoling scenes occurred, the "plain of prayer." It would be impossible for me to give you an idea of the piety, the happiness of these men, who are thirsting for the life-living waters of the Divine word. How much good a missionary could do, who would reside in the midst of a people who are so desirous of receiving instruction, and correspond so faithfully with the grace of God. After some regulations and advice, I left this interesting people, and pursuing my journey for three days over mountains and through dense forests, arrived safely at Fort Coleville.

Amongst the innumerable rivers that traverse the American continent, and afford means of communication between its most distant portions, the Columbia river is one of the most remarkable, not only on account of its great importance, west of the mountains, but also from the dangers that attend its navigation. At some distance from the Pacific ocean, crossing a territory which exhibits, in several localities, evident marks of former volcanic eruptions, its course is frequently impeded by rapids, by chains of volcanic rocks, and immense detached masses of the same substance which, in many places, obstruct the bed of the river.

I embarked on this river, on the 30th of May, in one of the barges of the Hudson Bay Company; Mr. Ogden, one of the principal proprietors, offered me a place in his. I shall never forget the kindness and friendly manner with which this gentleman treated me throughout the journey, nor the many agreeable hours I spent in his company. I found his conversation instructive, his anecdotes and bon mots entertaining and timely; it was with great regret that I parted from him. I will not detain you with a description of the rapids, falls and cascades, which I saw on this celebrated river; for, from its source in the mountains to the cascades it is but a succession of dangers. I will endeavour, however, to give you some idea of one of its largest rapids, called by the Canadian travellers, "great dalles." A dalle is a place where the current is confined to a channel between two steep rocks, forming a prolonged narrow torrent, but of extraordinary force and swiftness. Here the river is divided into several channels separated from one another by masses of rocks, which rise abruptly above its surface. Some of these channels are navigable at certain seasons of the year, although with very great risk, even to the most experienced pilot. But when, after the melting of the snow, the river rises above its usual level, the waters in most of these channels make but one body, and the whole mass of these united streams descend with irresistible fury. At this season the most courageous dare not encounter such dangers, and all navigation is discontinued. In this state the river flows with an imposing grandeur and majesty, which no language can describe. It seems at one moment to stay its progress; then leaps forward with resistless impetuosity, and then rebounds against the rock-girt islands of which I have already spoken, but which present only vain obstructions to its headlong course. If arrested for a moment, its accumulated waters proudly swell and mount as though instinct with life, and the next moment dash triumphantly on, enveloping the half smothered waves that preceded them as if impatient of their sluggish course, and wild to speed them on their way. Along the shore, on every projecting point, the Indian fisherman takes his stand, spreading in the eddies his ingeniously worked net, and in a short time procures for himself an abundant supply of fine fish. Attracted by the shoals of fish that come up the river, the seals gambol amid the eddying waves—now floating with their heads above the river's breast, and anon darting in the twinkling of an eye from side to side, in sportive joy or in swift pursuit of their scaly prey. But this noble river has far other recollections associated with it. Never shall I forget the sad and fatal accident which occurred on the second day of our voyage, at a spot called the "little dalles." I had gone ashore and was walking along the bank, scarcely thinking what might happen; for my breviary, papers, bed, in a word, my little all, had been left in the barge. I had proceeded about a quarter of a mile, when seeing the bargemen push off from the bank and glide down the stream with an easy, careless air, I began to repent having preferred a path along the river's side, so strewn with fragments of rocks that I was compelled at every instant to turn aside or clamber over them. I still held on my course, when all at once, the barge is so abruptly stopped that the rowers can hardly keep their seats. Regaining, however, their equilibrium, they ply the oars with redoubled vigour, but without any effect upon the barge. They are already within the power of the angry vortex: the waters are crested with foam; a deep sound is heard which I distinguish as the voice of the pilot encouraging his men to hold to their oars—to row bravely. The danger increases every minute, and in a moment more all hope of safety has vanished. The barge—the sport of the vortex, spins like a top upon the whirling waters—the oars are useless—the bow rises—the stern descends, and the next instant all have disappeared. A death-like chill shot through my frame—a dimness came over my sight, as the cry "we are lost!" rung in my ears, and told but too plainly that my companions were buried beneath the waves. Overwhelmed with grief and utterly unable to afford them the slightest assistance, I stood a motionless spectator of this tragic scene. All were gone, and yet upon the river's breast there was not the faintest trace of their melancholy fate. Soon after the whirlpool threw up, in various directions, the oars, poles, the barge capsized, and every lighter article it had contained. Here and there I beheld the unhappy bargemen vainly struggling in the midst of the vortex. Five of them sunk never to rise again. My interpreter had twice touched bottom and after a short prayer was thrown upon the bank. An Iroquois saved himself by means of my bed; and a third was so fortunate as to seize the handle of an empty trunk, which helped him to sustain himself above water until he reached land. The rest of our journey was more fortunate. We stopped at Forts Okinakane and Walla-walla, where I baptized several children.

The savages who principally frequent the borders of the Columbia river are from the lakes; the chief of whom, with several of the nation, have been baptized; also the Shuyelpi or Chaudieres, the Okinakanes, Cingpoils, Walla-wallas, Pierced Noses, Kayuses, Attayes, Spokanes, the Indians from the falls and cascades, and the Schinouks and Classops.

We arrived at Fort Vancouver on the morning of the 8th June. I enjoyed the happiness and great consolation of meeting in these distant parts, two respectable Canadian priests—the Rev. Mr. Blanchet, grand vicar of all the countries west of the mountains claimed by the British crown, and the Rev. Mr. Demers. They are laboring in these regions for the same object that we are trying to accomplish in the Rocky Mountains. The kindness and benevolence with which these Reverend gentlemen received me are proofs of the pure zeal which actuates them for the salvation of these savages. They assured me that immense good might be done in the extensive regions that border on the Pacific, if a greater number of Missionaries, with means at their command, were stationed in these regions; and they urged me very strongly to obtain from my Superiors some of our Fathers. I will try to give you in my next some extracts from the letters of these Missionaries, which will make the country known to you, its extent, and the progress of their mission. The Governor of the Honorable Company of Hudson Bay, Dr. McLaughlin, who resides at Fort Vancouver, after having given me every possible proof of interest, as a good Catholic, advised me to do every thing in my power to gratify the wishes of the Canadian Missionaries. His principal reason is, that if Catholicity was rapidly planted in these tracts where civilization begins to dawn, it would be more quickly introduced thence into the interior. Already a host of ministers have overrun a part of the country, and have settled wherever they may derive some advantages for the privations their philanthropy imposes on them. Such is the state of these regions of the new world, as yet so little known: you perceive that our prospects are by no means discouraging. Permit me therefore to repeat the great principle you have so often recommended to me, and which I have not forgotten: " Courage and confidence in God!" With the mercy of God, the church of Jesus Christ may soon have the consolation of seeing her standard planted in these distant lands on the ruins of idolatry and of the darkest superstition. Pray then that the Lord of such a rich harvest may send us numerous fellow laborers; for in so extensive a field we are but five, and beset with so many dangers, that at the dawn of day we have often reason to doubt whether we will live to see the sun go down. It is not that we have any thing to fear from the climate; far from it—for, if here death came only by sickness, we might indeed count upon many years, but water, fire, and the bow, often hurry their victims off when least expected. Of a hundred men who inhabit this country, there are not ten who do not die by some or other fatal accident. The afternoon of the 30th June I resumed my place in one of the barges of the English Company, and took my leave of the worthy and respectable Governor.— To my great joy I found that the Rev. Mr. Demers was one of the passengers, being about to undertake an apostolic excursion among the different tribes of New Caledonia, who, according to the accounts of several Canadian travellers, were most anxious to see a Blackgown, and hear the word of God. The wind being favorable, the sails of the barge were unfurled and the sailors plying their oars at the same time, the 11th of July saw us landed safely at Fort Wallawalla. The next day I parted, with many regrets, from my esteemed friends, Rev. Mr. Demers, and Mr.

Ogden. Accompanied only by my interpreter, we continued our land route to the 19th, through woods and immense plains. The high plains which separate the waters of the Snake river from those of the Spokan, offer some natural curiosities. I fancied myself in the vicinity of several fortified cities, surrounded by walls and small forts, scattered in different directions. The pillars are regular pentagons, from two to four feet in diameter, erect, joined together, forming a wall from forty to eighty feet high, and extending several miles in the form of squares and triangles, detached from one another, and in different directions. On our road we met some Pierced Noses, and a small band of Spokanes, who accosted us with many demonstrations of friendship, and although very poor, offered us more salmon than we could carry. The Pointed Hearts (a tribe which shall ever be dear to me) came to meet us, and great was the joy on both sides, on beholding one another again. They had strictly observed all the rules I had laid down for them at my first visit. They accompanied me for three days, to the very limits of their territory. We then planted a cross on the summit of a high mountain, covered with snow, and after the example of the Flat Heads, all the people consecrated themselves inviolably to the service of God. We remained there that night. The next morning, after reciting our prayers in common, and giving them a long exhortation, we bad them farewell. The 20th I continued my journey over terrific mountains, steep rocks, and through apparently impenetrable forests. I could scarcely believe that any human being had ever preceded us over such a road. At the end of four days' journey, replete with fatigue and difficulties, we reached the borders of the Bitter Root river, and on the evening of the 27th I had the happiness of arriving safely at St.

Mary's, and of finding my dear brethren in good health.—
The Flat Heads, accompanied by Father Point, had left
the village ten days before, to procure provisions. A few
had remained to guard the camp, and their families awaited
my return. The 19th, I started to rejoin the Flat Heads on
the Missouri river. We ascended the Bitter Root to its
source, and the 1st of August, having clambered up a high
mountain, we planted a cross on its very summit, near a
beautiful spring, one of the sources of the Missouri. The
next day, after a forced march, we joined the camp where
we had such a budget of news to open, so many interesting
facts to communicate to each other, that we sat up a greater
part of the night. The Rev. Father Point and myself, accompanied our dear neophytes, who to obtain their daily
bread, are obliged to hunt the buffalo, even over the lands
of their most inveterate enemies, the Black Feet. On the
15th of August, the feast of the Assumption, (the same on
which this letter is dated) I offered up the sacrifice of the
Mass, in a noble plain, watered by one of the three streams
that form the head waters of the Missouri, to thank God for
all the blessings He had bestowed on us during this last
year. I had the consolation of seeing fifty Flat Heads approach the holy table in so humble, modest and devout a
manner, that to my, perhaps partial eye, they resembled
angels more than men. On the same day I determined, for
the interest of this mission, which seems so absolutely to
require it, to traverse for the fourth time the dangerous
American desert. If heaven preserves me, (for I have to
travel through a region infested by thousands of hostile
savages) I will send you the account of this last journey.—
You see then, Rev. Father, that in these deserts we must
more than ever keep our souls prepared to render the fearful
account, in consequence of the perils that surround us; and

as it would be desirable that we could be replaced immediately, in case of any accident occurring—again I say to you, pray that the Lord may send us fellow laborers. "Rogate ergo Dominum messis ut mittat operarios in messem suam." And thousands of souls, who would otherwise be lost, will bless you one day in eternity. Rev. Father Point has expressed a desire to be sent amongst the Blackfeet. Until they are willing to listen to the word of God, which I think will be before long, he intends to preach the gospel to the Pointed Hearts and the neighboring tribes. I trust we shall be able to make as cheering a report of these as we have already done of our first neophytes. I have found them all in the best dispositions. The Rev. Father Mengarini remains with the Flatheads and Pends d'oreilles. On my first journey, in the autumn of 1841, which ended at Fort Coleville, I baptized 190 persons of the Kalispel tribe. On my visit, last spring, to the various distant tribes, (of which I have just finished giving you the account) I had the consolation of baptizing 418 persons, 60 of whom were of the Pends d'oreille tribe of the great lake; 82 of the Kœtnays or Skalzi; 100 of the Pointed Hearts; 56 of the Shuyelpi; 106 of the Okenakanes, and 14 in the Okenakanes and Wallawalla Forts.—These, with 500 baptized last year, in different parts of the country, mostly amongst the Flat Heads and Kalispels, and 196 that I baptized on Christmas day, at St. Mary's, with the 350 baptized by Rev. Fathers Mengarini and Point, make a total of 1654 souls, wrested from the power of the devil. For what the Scripture calls the "spirit of the world" has not wherewith to introduce itself amongst them. These poor people find their happiness even in this world in the constant practice of their christian duties. We may almost say of them, that all who are baptized are saved.—

Since God has inspired you with a zealous desire to second the views of the Association for the Propagation of the Faith, entreat those pious persons to whom you may communicate your designs, to redouble their prayers in our behalf. I conclude by beseeching you earnestly to remember me frequently and fervently in the Holy Sacrifice.

I remain, very Rev. and dear Father,
  Your affectionate servant
   and brother in Christ,
    P. J. DE SMET, S. J.

LETTER XIV.

St. Mary, June 28th, 1842.

Rev. Father:

THANKS be to God, our hopes have at length begun to be realized; the tender blossom has been succeeded by precious fruit, daily more and more visible in our colony; the chief and people, by their truly edifying conduct, give us already the sweetest consolation. Pentecost was for us and for our beloved neophytes a day of blessings, of holy exultation. Eighty of them enjoyed the happiness of partaking for the first time of the bread of Angels. Their assiduity in assisting during a month at the instructions we gave them, three times a day, had assured us of their zeal and favor; but a retreat of three days, which served as a more immediate preparation, contributed still more to convince us of their sincerity. From an early hour in the morning repeated discharges of musketry announced afar the arrival of the great, the glorious day. At the first sound of the bell a crowd of savages hurried towards our church. One of our Fathers, in a surplice and stole, preceded by three choristers, one of whom bore aloft the banner of the Sacred Heart of Jesus, went out to receive them, and conduct them in procession, and to the sound of joyous canticles, into the Temple of the Lord. What piety—what religious recollection, amidst that throng! They observed a strict silence, but at the same time the joy and gladness that filled their hearts, shone on their happy countenances. The ardent love which already animated these innocent hearts, was inflamed afresh by the fervent aspirations to the adorable Sacrament, which were recited aloud by one of our Fathers, who also intermingled occasionally some stanzas of canticles. The tender devotion, and the profound faith with which these Indians received their God, really edified and affected us. That morning at 11 o'clock they renewed their baptismal vows, and in the afternoon they made the solemn consecration of their hearts to the Blessed Virgin, the tutelar patroness of this place.— May these pious sentiments which the true religion alone could inspire, be preserved amongst our dear children. We hope for their continuance, and what increases our hope is, that at the time of this solemnity, about one hundred and twenty persons approached the tribunal of penance, and since that truly memorable occasion, we have from thirty to forty communions, and from fifty to sixty confessions every Sunday.

The feast of Corpus Christi was solemnized by another ceremony not less touching, and calculated to perpetuate the gratitude and devotion of our pious Indians towards our amiable Queen. This was the solemn erection of a statue to the Blessed Virgin, in memory of her apparition to little Paul. The following is a brief account of the ceremony. From the entrance of our chapel to the spot where little Paul received such a special favor—the avenue was simply the green sward, the length of which on both sides was bordered by garlands, hung in festoons—triumphal arches, gracefully arranged, arose at regular distances. At the end of the avenue, and in the middle of a kind of repository, stood the pedestal, which was destined to receive the statue. The hour specified having struck, the procession issued from the chapel in this order. At the head was borne aloft the banner of the Sacred Heart followed closely by little Paul carrying the statue and accompanied by two choristers, who profusely strewed the way with flowers. Then came the two Fathers, one vested in a cope, and the other in a surplice.— Finally the march was closed by the chiefs and all the members of the colony emulating each other in their zeal to pay their tribute of thanksgiving and praise to their blessed Mother. When they reached the spot one of our Fathers, in a short exhortation, in which he reminded them of the signal prodigy and assistance of the Queen of Heaven, encouraged our dear neophytes to sentiments of confidence in the protection of Mary. After this address and the singing of the Litany of the Blessed Virgin, the procession returned in the same order to the church. Oh! how ardently we desired that all the friends of our holy religion could have witnessed the devotion and recollection of these new children of Mary. It was also our intention not to dismiss them until we had given them the Benediction of the Blessed Sacrament, but unfortunately not possessing a Remonstrance we were obliged to defer this beautiful ceremony until the Feast of the Sacred Heart of Jesus. At that time the Sacred Host was carried in solemn procession, and since then each Sunday after Vespers, the faithful enjoy the happiness of receiving the Benediction.

May the blessing of God really descend upon us and our colony. We hope for it through the assistance of your prayers and those of all our friends.

I remain, Rev. Father,
Your very humble friend and servant,
GREG. MENGARINI, S. J.

LETTER XV.

Fort Vancouver, 28th September, 1841.

Reverend Father:

BLESSED be the Divine Providence of the all-powerful God who has protected, preserved and restored you safely to your dear neophytes.

I congratulate the country upon the inestimable treasure it possesses by the arrival and establishment therein of the members of the Society of Jesus. Be so kind as to express to the Reverend Fathers and Brothers my profound veneration and respect for them. I beg of God to bless your labours, and to continue your successful efforts. In a few years you will enjoy the glory and consolation of beholding through your means all the savages residing on the head waters of the Columbia, ranging themselves under the standard of the Cross. I do not doubt but that our excellent governor, Dr. McLaughlin, will give you all the assistance in his power. It is very fortunate for our holy religion, that this noble-hearted man should be at the head of the affairs of the honorable Hudson Bay Company, west of the Rocky Mountains. He protected it before our arrival in these regions. He still gives it his support by word and example, and many favors. As we are in the same country, aiming at the same end, namely, the triumph of the holy Catholic faith throughout this vast territory, the Rev. Mr. Demers and myself will always take the most lively interest in your welfare and progress, and we are convinced that, whatever concerns us will equally interest you. The following is an account of our present situation:

The Catholic establishment of Wallamette consists of nearly 80 families. The one at Cowlitz of only five,—twenty-two at Nez-quale on Puget-sund, which is from 25 to 30 leagues above Cowlitz. Besides these stations we visit from time to time, the nearest Forts where the Catholics in the service of the Hudson Bay Company reside. This is what takes up almost all our time. We are much in want of lay brothers and nuns, of school masters and mistresses. We have to attend to every spiritual as well as temporal affair, which is a great burden to us. The wives of the Canadians, taken from every quarter of the country, cause throughout the families a diversity of languages. They speak almost generally a rude jargon of which we can scarcely make any use in our public instructions—hence proceed the obstacles to our progress,—we go along slowly. We are obliged to teach them French and their catechism together, which occasions much delay. We are really overwhelmed with business. The savages apply to us from all sides. Some of them are indifferent, and we have not time to instruct them. We make them, occasionally, hasty visits, and baptize the children and the adults who happen to be in danger of death. But we have no time to learn their languages, and until now have been without an interpreter to translate the prayers we wish them to learn. It is only lately that I have succeeded in translating them into the Tchinoux language. Our difficulties are greatly increased by this variety of languages; each of the following tribes has a different dialect: The Kalapouyas, towards the head waters of the Wallamette; the Tchinoux of the Columbia river; the Kaijous from Walla-walla; the Pierced Noses, Okanakanes, Flat Heads, Snakes, Cowlitz, the

Klickatates from the interior, north of Vancouver; the Tcheheles, to the north of the mouth of the Columbia river; the Nez-quales, and those from the interior or of the Puget sund Bay, those of the Travers river, the Khalams of the above mentioned bay, those of Vancouver Island, and those from the northern posts on the sea shore, and from the interior of the part of the country watered by the tributary streams of the Travers river, all have their different languages.

Such are the difficulties we have daily to overcome. Our hearts bleed at the sight of so many souls who are lost under our eyes, without our being able to carry to them the word of Life. Moreover, our temporal resources are limited. We are but two, and our trunks did not arrive last spring by the vessel belonging to the honorable Hudson Bay Company. We have exhausted our means. The savages, women and children, ask us in vain for Rosaries. We have no more Catechisms of the diocess left to distribute among them; no English Prayer Books for the Catholic Irish; no controversial books to lend. Heaven appears to be deaf to our prayers, supplications and most ardent wishes. You can judge of our situation and how much we are to be pitied. We are in the mean time surrounded by sects who are using all their efforts to scatter every where the poisonous seeds of error, and who try to paralyze the little good we may effect.

The Methodists are, first, at Wallamette, which is about eight miles from my establishment; second, near the Klatraps, south of the mouth of the Columbia river; third, at Nez Quali, or Puget-sund; fourth, at the Great Dulles, south of Wallawalla; and fifth, at the Wallamette Falls. The Presbyterian Missions are at Wallawalla, as you approach Coleville. In the midst of so many adversaries we try to keep our ground firmly; to increase our numbers, and to visit various parts, particularly where the danger is most pressing. We also endeavor to anticipate the others, and to inculcate the Catholic principles in those places where error has not as yet found a footing, or even to arrest the progress of evil, to dry it up at its source. The conflict has been violent, but the savages now begin to open their eyes as to who are the real ministers of Jesus Christ. Heaven declares itself in our favor. If we had a priest to hold a permanent station amongst the savages, the country would be ours in two years. The Methodist Missions are failing rapidly; they are losing their credit and the little influence they possessed. By the grace of God, our cause has prevailed at Wallamette. This spring, Mr. Demers withdrew from the Methodists a whole village of savages, situate at the foot of the Wallamette Falls. Mr. Demers also visited the Schinouks, below the Columbia river. They are well disposed towards Catholicity. I have just arrived from Carcader, which is eighteen leagues from Vancouver. The savages at this place had resisted all the insinuations of a pretended Minister. It was my first mission, and only lasted ten days. They learned in that time the sign of the cross, the offering of their hearts to God, the Lord's Prayer, the Angelical Salutation, the Apostles' Creed, the ten Commandments, and those of the Church. I intend to revist them soon, near Vancouver, and to baptize a considerable number. Rev. Mr. Demers has been absent these two months, on a visit to the savages at the Bay of Puget-sund, who have long since besought him to come amongst them. I have not been able to visit since the month of May, my catechumens at Flackimar, a village whose people were converted last spring, and who had turned a deaf ear to a Mr. Waller, who is established at Wallamette. Judge then, sir, how great are our labors, and how much it would advance our mutual interest, were you to send hither one of your Rev. Fathers, with one of the three lay brothers. In my opinion, it is on this spot that we must seek to establish our holy religion. It is here that we should have a college, convent, and schools. It is here that one day a successor of the Apostles will come from some part of the world to settle, and provide for the spiritual necessities of this vast region, which, moreover, promises such an abundant harvest.— Here is the field of battle, where we must in the first place gain the victory. It is here that we must establish a beautiful mission. From the lower stations the Missionaries and Rev. Fathers could go forth in all directions to supply the distant stations, and announce the word of God to the infidels still plunged in darkness and the shadows of death. If your plans should not permit you to change the place of your establishment, at least take into consideration the need in which we stand of a Rev. Father, and of a lay brother, to succor us in our necessities. By the latest dates from the Sandwich Islands, I am informed that the Rev. Mr. Chochure had arrived there, accompanied by three priests, the Rev. Mr. Walsh making the fourth. A large Catholic Church it was hoped would have been ready last autumn for the celebration of the Holy Mysteries. The natives were embracing our everlasting faith in great numbers, and the meeting houses were almost abandoned.

The Bishop of Juliopolis, stationed at Red River, writes to me that the savages dwelling near the base of the eastern part of the Rocky Mountains have deputed to him a half blood who resides amongst them, to obtain from his Grace a priest to instruct them. Rev. Mr. Thibault is destined for this mission.

I remain, Rev. Father, yours,

F. N. BLANCHET.

LETTER XVI.

University of St. Louis, 1st Nov. 1842.

Very Rev. Father:

In my last letter of August, I promised to write to you from St. Louis, should I arrive safely in that city. Heaven has preserved me, and here I am about to fulfil my promise. Leaving Rev. Father Point and the Flat Head camp on the river Madison, I was accompanied by twelve of our Indians. We travelled in three days, a distance of 150 miles, crossing two chains of mountains, in a section of country frequently visited by the Black Feet warriors, without, however, meeting with any of these scalping savages. At the mouth of the Twenty-five Yard River, a branch of the Yellow Stone, we found 250 huts, belonging to several nations, all friendly to us—the Flat Heads, Kalispels, Pierce Noses, Kayuses, and Snakes. I spent three days among them to exhort them to perseverance, and to make some preparations for my long journey. The day of my departure, ten neophytes presented themselves at my lodge to serve as my escort, and to introduce me to the Crow tribe. On the evening of the second day we were in the midst of this large and interesting tribe. The Crows had perceived us from a distance; as we approached, some of them recognised me, and at the cry of "the Blackgown! the Blackgown!" the Crows, young and old, to the number of three thousand, came out of their wigwams. On entering the village, a comical scene occurred, of which they suddenly made me the principal personage. All the chiefs, and about fifty of their warriors, hastened around me, and I was literally assailed by them. Holding me by the gown, they drew me in every direction, whilst a robust savage of gigantic stature, seemed resolved to carry me off by main force. All spoke at the same time, and appeared to be quarrelling, whilst I, the sole object of all this contention, could not conceive what they were about. I remained passive, not knowing whether I should laugh or be serious. The interpreter soon came to my relief, and said that all this uproar was but an excess of politeness and kindness towards me, as every one wished to have the honor of lodging and entertaining the Blackgown. With his advice I selected my host, upon which the others immediately loosed their hold, and I followed the chief to his lodge, which was the largest and best in the camp. The Crows did not tarry long before they all gathered around me, and loaded me with marks of kindness. The social calumet, emblem of savage brotherhood and union, went round that evening so frequently, that it was scarcely ever extinguished. It was accompanied with all the antics for which the Crows are so famous, when they offer the calumet to the Great Spirit, to the four winds, to the sun, fire, earth and water. These Indians are unquestionably the most anxious to learn; the most inquisitive, ingenious, and polished of all the savage tribes east of the mountains. They profess great friendship and admiration for the whites. They asked me innumerable questions; among others, they wished to know the number of the whites. Count, I replied, the blades of grass upon your immense plains, and you will know pretty nearly the number of the whites. They all smiled, saying that the thing was impossible, but they understood my meaning. And when I explained to them the vast extent of the "villages" inhabited by white men (viz. New York,

Philadelphia, London, Paris) the grand lodges (houses) built as near each other as the fingers of my hand, and four or five piled up, one above the other—(meaning the different stories of our dwellings;) when I told them that some of these lodges (speaking of churches and towers) were as high as mountains, and large enough to contain all the Crows together; that in the grand lodge of the national council (the Capitol at Washington) all the great chiefs of the whole world could smoke the calumet at their ease; that the roads in these great villages were always filled with passengers, who came and went more thickly than the vast herds of buffalos that sometimes cover their beautiful plains; when I explained to them the extraordinary celerity of those moving lodges (the cars on the rail road) that leave far behind them the swiftest horse, and which are drawn along by frightful machines, whose repeated groanings re-echo far and wide, as they belch forth immense volumes of fire and smoke; and next, those fire canoes, (steamboats) which transport whole villages, with provisions, arms and baggage, in a few days, from one country to another, crossing large lakes, (the seas) ascending and descending the great rivers and streams; when I told them that I had seen white men mounting up into the air (in balloons) and flying with as much agility as the warrior eagle of their mountains, then their astonishment was at its height; and all placing their hands upon their mouths, sent forth at the same time, one general cry of wonder. "The Master of life is great," said the chief, "and the white men are His favorites." But what appeared to interest them more than aught else, was prayer (religion;) to this subject they listened with the strictest, undivided attention. They told me that they had already heard of it, and they knew that this prayer made men good and wise on earth, and insured their happiness in the future life. They begged me to permit the whole camp to assemble, that they might hear for themselves the words of the Great Spirit, of whom they had been told such wonders. Immediately three United States flags were erected on the field, in the midst of the camp, and three thousand savages, including the sick, who were carried in skins, gathered around me. I knelt beneath the banner of our country, my ten Flat Head neophytes by my side, and surrounded by this multitude, eager to hear the glad tidings of the gospel of peace. We began by intoning two canticles, after which I recited all the prayers, which we interpreted to them: then again we sang canticles, and I finished by explaining to them the Apostles' Creed and the ten Commandments. They all appeared to be filled with joy, and declared it was the happiest day of their lives. They begged me to have pity on them—to remain among them and instruct them and their little children in the knowledge, love and service of the Great Spirit. I promised that a Blackgown should visit them, but on condition that the chiefs would engage themselves to put a stop to the thievish practices so common amongst them, and to oppose vigorously the corrupt morals of their tribe. Believing me to be endowed with supernatural powers, they had entreated me from the very commencement of our conversation, to free them from the sickness that then desolated the camp, and to supply them with plenty. I repeated to them on this occasion that the Great Spirit alone could remove these evils—God, I said, listens to the supplications of the good and pure of heart; of those who detest their sins, and wish to devote themselves to His service—but He shuts his ear to the prayers of those who violate His holy law. In His anger, God had destroyed by fire, five infamous "villages" (Sodom, Gomorrah, etc.) in consequence of their horrid abominations—that the Crows walked in the ways of these wicked men, consequently they could not complain if the Great Spirit seemed to punish them by sickness, war and famine. They were themselves the authors of all their calamities—and if they did not change their mode of life very soon, they might expect to see their misfortunes increase from day to day—while the most awful torments awaited them, and all wicked men after their death. I assured them in fine that heaven would be the reward of those who would repent of their evil deeds and practice the religion of the Great Spirit.

The grand orator of the camp was the first to reply: " Black Gown," said he, " I understand you. You have said what is true. Your words have passed from my ears into my heart—I wish all could comprehend them." Whereon, addressing himself to the Crows, he repeated forcibly, " Yes, Crows, the Black Gown has said what is true. We are dogs, for we live like dogs. Let us change our lives and our children will live." I then held long conferences with all the chiefs assembled in council. I proposed to them the example of the Flat Heads and Pends-d'orielles, whose chiefs made it their duty to exhort their people to the practice of virtue, and who knew how to punish as they deserved all the prevarications against God's holy law. They promised to follow my advice, and assured me that I would find them in better dispositions on my return. I flatter myself with the hope, that this visit, the good example of my neophytes, but principally the prayers of the Flat Heads will gradually produce a favourable change among the Crows. A good point in their character, and one that inspires me with almost the certainty of their amendment, is, that they have hitherto resisted courageously all attempts to introduce spirituous liquors among them. "For what is this fire-water good?" said the chief to a white man who tried to bring it into their country, "it burns the throat and stomach; it makes a man like a bear who has lost his senses. He bites, he growls, he scratches and he howls, he falls down as if he were dead. Your fire-water does nothing but harm—take it to our enemies, and they will kill each other, and their wives and children will be worthy of pity. As for us we do not want it, we are fools enough without it." A very touching scene occurred during the council. Several of the savages wished to examine my Missionary Cross; I thence took occasion to explain to them the sufferings of our Saviour, Jesus Christ, and the cause of His death on the Cross—I then placed my Cross in the hands of the great chief; he kissed it in the most respectful manner; raising his eyes to heaven, and pressing the Cross with both his hands to his heart, he exclaimed, "O Great Spirit, take pity on me and be merciful to Thy poor children." And his people followed his example. I was in the village of the Crows when news was brought that two of their most distinguished warriors had fallen victims to the rage and cruelty of the Black Feet. The heralds or orators went round the camp, proclaiming in a loud voice the circumstances of the combat and the tragic end of the two brave men. A gloomy silence prevailed every where, only interrupted by a band of mourners, whose appearance alone was enough to make the most insensible heart bleed, and rouse to vengeance the entire nation. This band was composed of the mothers of the two unfortunate warriors who had fallen, their wives carrying their new born infants in their arms, their sisters, and all their little children. The unhappy creatures had their heads shaven and cut in every direction; they were gashed with numerous wounds, whence the blood constantly trickled. In this pitiable state they rent the air with their lamentations and cries, imploring the warriors of their nation to have compassion on them—to have compassion on their desolate children— to grant them one last favour, the only cure for their affliction, and that was, to go at once and inflict signal vengeance on the murderers. They led by the bridle all the horses that belonged to the deceased. A Crow chief mounting immediately the best of these steeds, brandished his tomahawk in the air, proclaiming that he was ready to avenge the deed. Several young men rallied about him. They sung together the war-song, and started the same day, declaring that they would not return empty-handed (viz: without scalps).

On these occasions the near relations of the one who has fallen, distribute every thing that they possess, retaining nothing but some old rags wherewith to clothe themselves. The mourning ceases as soon as the deed is avenged. The warriors cast at the feet of the widows and orphans the trophies torn away from the enemies. Then passing from extreme grief to exultation, they cast aside their tattered garments, wash their bodies, besmear themselves with all sorts of colours, deck themselves off in their best robes, and with the scalps affixed to the end of poles, march in triumph round the camp, shouting and dancing, accompanied at the same time by the whole village.

On the 29th I bade adieu to my faithful companions, the Flat Heads, and the Crows. Accompanied by Ignatius, Gabriel, and by two brave Americans, who, although Protestants, wished to serve as guides to a Catholic Missionary, I once more plunged into the arid plains of the Yellow Stone. Having already described this region, I have nothing new to add concerning it. This desert is undoubtedly dangerous, and has been the scene of more tragic deeds, combats, stratagems, and savage cruelties, than any other region. At each step, the Crow interpreter, Mr. V. C. who had sojourned eleven years in the country, recounted different transactions; pointing, meanwhile, to the spots where they had occurred, which, in our situation, made our blood run cold, and our hair stand erect. It is the battle ground where the Crows, the Black Feet, Scioux, Sheyennes, Assiniboins, Arikaras ,and Minatares, fight out their interminable quarrels, avenging and revenging, without respite, their mutual wrongs. After six days' march, we found ourselves upon the very spot where a combat had recently taken place. The bloody remains of ten Assiniboins, who had been slain, were scattered here and there—almost all the flesh eaten off by the wolves and carniverous birds. At the sight of these mangled limbs—of the vultures that soared above our heads, after having satiated themselves with the unclean repast, and the region round me, which had so lately resounded with the savage cries of more savage men, engaged in mutual carnage—I own that the little courage I thought I possessed, seemed to fail me entirely, and give place to a secret terror, which I sought in vain to stifle or conceal from my companions. We observed in several places the fresh tracks of men and horses, leaving no doubt in our minds as to the proximity of hostile parties; our guide even assured me that he thought we were already discovered, but by continuing our precautions he hoped we might perhaps elude their craftiness and malicious designs, for the savages very seldom make their attacks in open day. The following is the description of our regular march until the 10th of September. At day-break we saddled our horses and pursued our journey; at 10 A. M. we breakfasted in a suitable place, that would offer some advantage in case of an attack. After an hour and a half, or two hours' rest, we resumed our march a second time, always trotting our horses, until sunset, when we unsaddled them to dine and sup; we then lighted a good fire, hastily raised a little cabin of branches, to induce our ever watchful foes, in case they pursue us, to suppose that we had encamped for the night; for, as soon as the inimical videttes discover any thing of the kind, they make it known by a signal to the whole party. They then immediately assemble, and concert the plan of attack. In the meantime, favored by the darkness, we pursued our journey quietly until 10 or 12 o'clock at night, and then, without fire or even shelter, each one disposed himself as well as he might, for sleep. It appears to me that I hear you ask: But what did you eat for your breakfast and supper? Examine the notes of my journal, and you will acknowledge that our fare was such as would excite the envy of the most fastidious gastronome. From the 25th of August to the 10th September, 1842, we killed, to supply our wants, as we journeyed on, three fine buffalo cows, and two large bulls; (only to obtain the tongue and marrow bones) two large deer, as fat as we could have wished; three goats, two black-tail deer, a big-horn or mountain sheep, two fine grey bears, and a swan—to say nothing of the pheasants, fowls, snipes, ducks and geese.

In the midst of so much game, we scarcely felt the want of bread, sugar or coffee. The haunches, tongues and ribs replaced these. And the bed? It is soon arranged. We were in a country where you lose no time in taking off your shoes; you wrap your buffalo robe around you, the saddle serves as a pillow, and thanks to the fatigues of a long journey of about forty miles, under a burning sun, you have scarcely laid your head upon it before you are asleep.

The gentlemen of Fort Union, at the mouth of the Yellow Stone, received me with great politeness and kindness. I rested there during three days. A journey so long and continuous, through regions where the drought had been so great that every sign of vegetation had disappeared, had very much exhausted our poor horses. The 1800 miles that we had yet to travel, were not to be undertaken lightly. After having well considered every thing, I resolved to leave my horses at the Fort, and to trust myself to the impetuous waters of the Missouri in a skiff, accompanied by Ignatius and Gabriel. The result was most fortunate, for, on the third day of our descent, to our great surprise and joy, we heard the puffing of a steamboat. It was a real God-send to us; accordingly, our first thought was to thank God, in all the sincerity of our hearts. We soon beheld her majestically ascending the stream. It was the first boat that had ever attempted to ascend the river in that season of the year, laden with merchandize for the Fur Trade Company. Four gentlemen from New York, proprietors of the boat, invited me to enter and remain on board. I accepted with unfeigned gratitude their kind offer of hospitality; the more so, as they assured me that several parties of warriors were lying in ambush along the river. On entering the boat I was an object of great curiosity—my blackgown, my missionary cross, my long hair, attracted attention. I had thousands of questions to answer, and many long stories to relate about my journey.

I have but a few words to add. The waters were low, the sand-banks and snags everywhere numerous; the boat consequently encountered many obstacles in her passage. We were frequently in great danger of perishing. Her keel was pierced by pointed rocks, her sides rent by the snags. Twenty times the wheels had been broken to pieces. The pilot's house had been carried away in the tempest; the whole cabin would have followed if it had not been made fast by a large cable. Our boat appeared to be little more than a mere wreck, and in this wreck, after forty-six days' navigation from the Yellow Stone, we arrived safely at St. Louis.

On the last Sunday of October, at 12 o'clock, I was kneeling at the foot of St. Mary's Altar, in the Cathedral, offering up my thanksgiving to God for the signal protection He had extended to his poor, unworthy servant. From the beginning of April I had travelled five thousand miles. I had descended and ascended the dangerous Columbia river. I had seen five of my companions perish in one of those life-destroying whirlpools, so justly dreaded by those who navigate that stream. I had traversed the Wallamette, crossed the Rocky Mountains, passed through the country of the Black Feet, the desert of the Yellow Stone, and descended the Missouri; and in all these journeys I had not received the slightest injury. "Dominus memor fuit nostri et benedixit nobis." I recommend myself to your good prayers, and have the honor to remain

Your very humble and obedient
son in Jesus Christ,
P. J. DE SMET, S. J.

Crown of life for that which he has been proved, he shall receive the crown which God has promised to them that love him.
S James 1. 12. v.

Rom.X.18.
Their Sound went into all the earth

And their words unto the Ends of the world.

Mount Lebanon
Cyprus
Egypt
Abissinia Ind.
Potowatomies
&Domine
Batavia
India
New Zeland
Marquesas Cr.
Israel
Wallis Lakes
Tibet
Sandwich Is.
Abissinia
Oceanica
Guinea
Brit.Guinea
Algiers
Jamaica
Tartary
The Levant
China
Ma...

Nantrone, Okinaganes Kheytenais, 1 Blackfoot Chief
Flatheads, Pended'oreille. Kispenes Thinteal heads.
W Pikes and Paul, Chief of the { Flatheads and
                                  Andersville.
All Baptists the Chief of the Nigness and Lake Indians
visited; and baptized great numbers of Stranger
along the coast of the Pacific.
Many Potowatamies converted and northern
Indians bordering on Red River.
Sandwich Islands, New Zeland etc.etc.

Point Mengarini // Lay Brothers ///
                   P. J. De Smet /
Blanchet   De Mers //

Councils.

Nice, Constantinople, Ephesus,
Chalcedon, Constantinople, Constantinople,
Nice, Constantinople, Latran, Latran,
Latran, Latran, Lyons, Lyons, Vienna,
Constance, Basle, Florence, Trente.

Jamaica
The Levant China
Indoustan Siam
Mathura Tong-King
             Cochinchina
             Su-Tchuen

Africa
Asia
America
Europe

China etc
Paraguay etc.
India
Abissinia
Bosniana
Tartary
the Goths
Sweden
Hungary
Russia
Saxony
Germany etc
Britany
Ireland
Persia
Englandis Conv.
Spain
Rome

Ecumenical Councils

Holy Fathers of Christ's Church.

And behold I am with you all days even to the consummation of the world. Math. 28.

St. Matt. c. XVIII. v. 17.

And if he will not hear the Church let him be to thee as the heathen and Publican.

Mormons
Wesley   Campbell
Jansenius   Geo Fox
Zwinglius   Baine
Luther   Henry
             Calvin

Modern Heretics.

Four Great schisms.
Donatist
Greecke
West
England

Ancient Heretics:
Mahomet
Iconoclasts
Berenger
Albigenses
Photius
Michel
Cerulaire
Wickleff.

Faith, Hope, Charity
Prayer. Good works.

the end of man. Death
Judgment
Heaven
Hell

Sacraments

Descent of the H.Ghost

Ascension

Resurrection

· Last Supper.
· Entrance into Jerusalem.
· Transfiguration.
· Promise made to Peter.
· Choosing his Apostles.
· John the B. beheaded.
· fasting 40 days.
· Baptized by John the B.

Carrying the cross

To gain heaven:
You must believe in the twelve
articles of the Apostles creed.
observe the ten Command-
ments of God and of the
church.
To obtain the assistance
of God's grace:

12 Apostles
Commandments of the Church.
Peter | | | | | | | | | | | Judas
Crowning

Scourging

Scourging

Agony in the Garden

by one's grace : practise good works and sanctify yourself by the reception of the holy sacraments.

Jesus
Joseph
Mary

///
Zachary, Elisabeth
St. John the Baptist

Minor
//////
Osina, Joel
Amos, Abdias,
Jonas
Micheas.

Teaching the doctors.

Flight to Egypt.
Presentation.
Circumcision.
/ Death of the Holy innocents.

/// Kings

Prophets
//////
Nahum,
Habaccuc
Sophonias,
Aggeus, Zachar..
&c.

Descent of the Holy Ghost

Assumption of the B V Mary

/ Herod

Annunciation to the B V Mary

Great / Isaias
Prophets Jeremias
//// Ezechiel
Daniel

//// Kings Saul, Solomon
David, Roboam
/ Solomon

////// Machabees
/ Eleazar
Antiochus

Temple of

////// Judges Josue, Jephte
Debora, Samson
Heli Samuel

over Judea 19 kings.

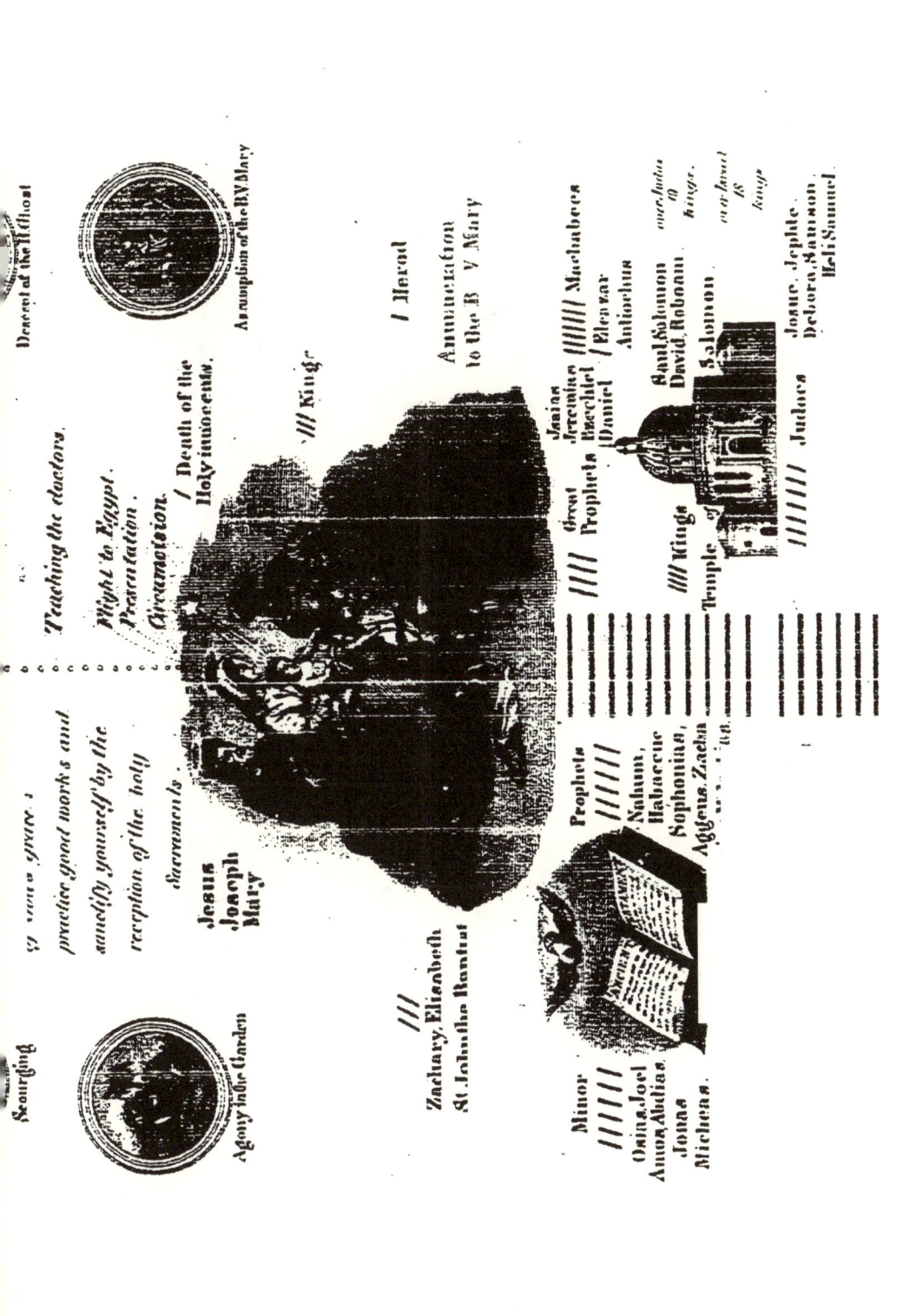

over Israel 18 kings

Sodom & Gomorrha etc. destroyed
/ Lot

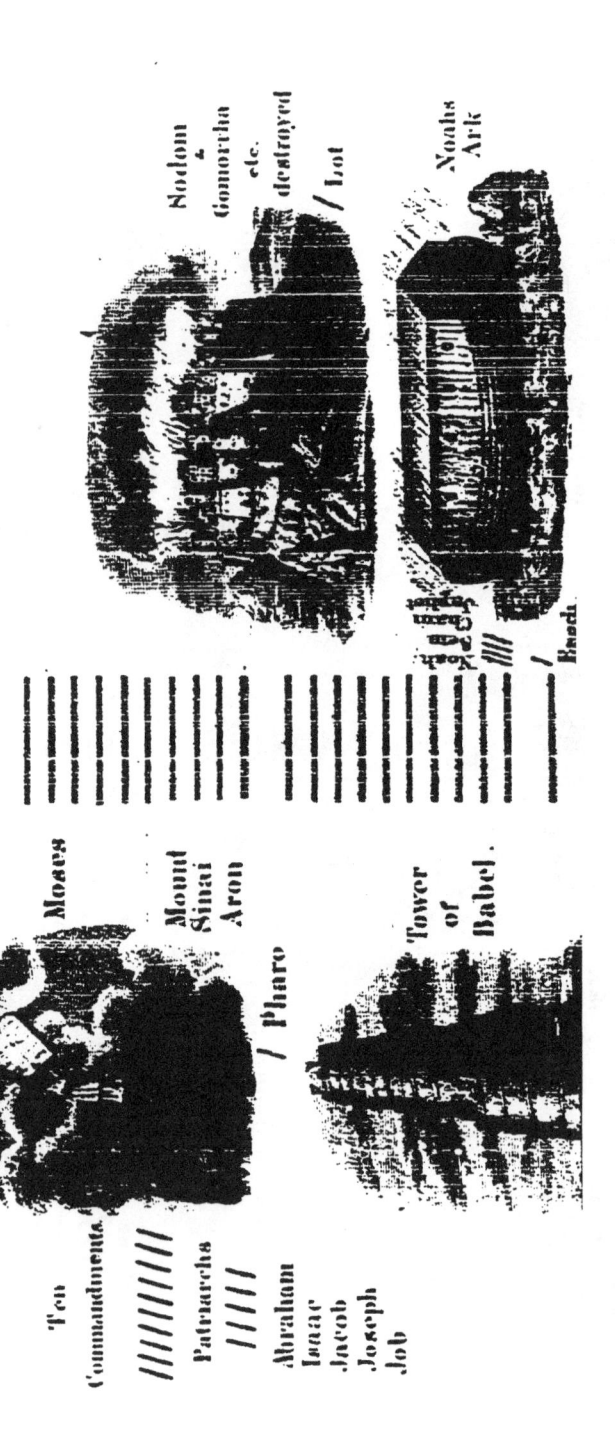

Noahs Ark

Noah Shem Japhet
/ Enoch

||||||| ||||||| ||||||| ||||||| ||||||| ||||||| ||||||| ||||||| ||||||| |||||||

Moses
Mount Sinai Aron
/ Pharo

Tower of Babel.

Ten Commandments
///////
Patriarchs
/////
Abraham
Isaac
Jacob
Joseph
Job

Before all Ages God alone.

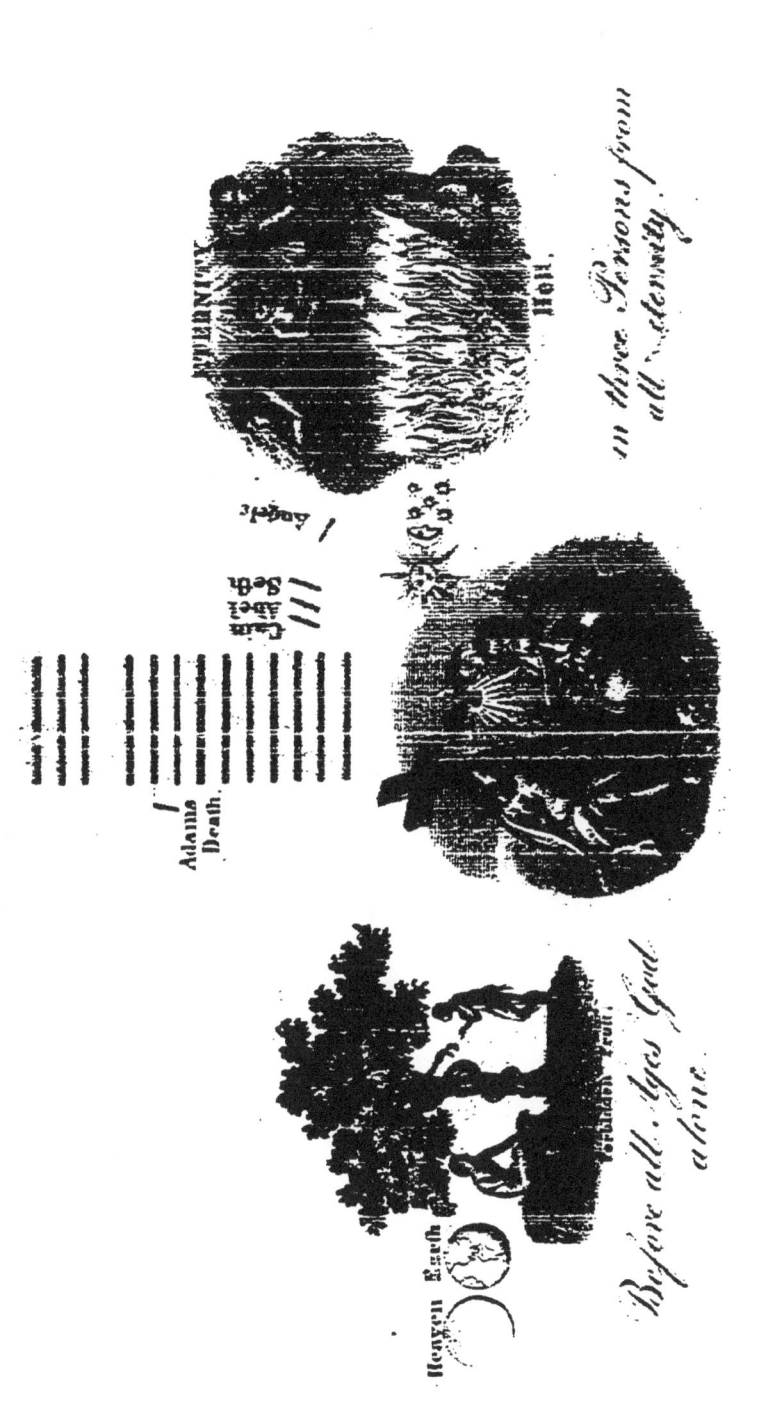

Heaven | Earth
forbidden fruit.

Adam's
Death.
Cain.
Abel.
Seth.
I beget.

in three Persons from all eternity.

ETERNITY
Hell.

EXPLANATION

OF THE

INDIAN SYMBOLICAL CATECHISM.

1. Four thousand years from the creation of the world to the coming of the Messiah. 1843 years from the birth of Jesus Christ to our times. (On the map, each blank line represents a century.) *Instruction.*—There is but one God; God is a spirit; He has no body; He is everywhere; He hears, sees and understands every thing; He cannot be seen, because he is a spirit. If we are good we shall see Him after our death, but the wicked shall never behold Him; He has had no beginning, and will never have an end; He is eternal; He does not grow old; He loves the good, whom he recompenses; He hates the wicked, whom he punishes. There are three persons in God; each of the three is God—they are equal in all things, &c.

2. The heavens, the earth, Adam and Eve, the tree of the knowledge of good and evil, the serpent, the sun, moon, stars, the angels, and hell. *Instruction.*—God is all powerful; He made the heavens and earth in six days. The first day he created matter, light, the angels. The fidelity of some and the revolt of others. Hell. The second day, the firmament, which is called heavens; the third day, the seas, plants, and trees of the earth; fourth day, the sun,

moon, and stars; fifth day, the birds and fishes; sixth day, the animals, Adam and Eve, the terrestrial paradise, and the tree of the knowledge of good and evil. The seventh day was one of rest. A short time after the seventh day, the serpent tempted Eve. The fall of Adam, original sin; its consequences. Adam driven from Paradise, the joy of the Devil. The promise given of a future Saviour, the Son of God. He did not come immediately, but 4000 years afterwards.

N. B. It is not well to interrupt too frequently the explanation of the figures on the chart. The necessary remarks on the history of religion in general may be made more advantageously apart, and in a continuous manner. Pass at once to the Incarnation of Jesus Christ, the mystery of Redemption, &c.

3. Death of Adam.

4. Henoch taken up into heaven; he will return at the end of the world.

5. Noah's Ark, in which four men and four women are saved; all the others perish in the deluge. *Instruction.*— The history of the deluge. The preaching of Noah. The ark was 450 feet long, 75 wide, and 45 high. Deluge lasts 12 months. The Rainbow. Sem, Cham and Japhet.

6. The Tower of Babel, built by Noah's descendants. *Instruction.*—About 150 years after the deluge; 15 stories high. Confusion of languages.

7. Abraham, Isaac, Jacob, Joseph, Job, Moses, Aaron, Pharaoh. *Instruction.*—The history of Abraham, Isaac, Jacob and Joseph. His dreams. He is sold at the age of 16. Jacob passes over to Egypt about 22 years after his son. The Israelites reside in that country 205 years. The history of Moses, the ten plagues of Egypt. The Passo-

ver. The Israelites leaving Egypt. The passage of the Red Sea. Pharaoh's army.

8. Sodom, Gomorrah, five cities destroyed by fire from heaven. Lot saved by two angels. *Instruction.*—Three angels visit Abraham. Two angels go to Sodom. The wife of Lot changed into a pillar of salt.

9. The ten commandments of God given to Moses alone on Mount Sinai. *Instruction.*—Fifty days after the Israelites have crossed the Red Sea. The promulgation of the Commandments on two tables.. First fast of Moses, idolatry of the people, prayer of Moses, golden calf, &c. Second fast of Moses. Second tables of the law, 40 years in the desert, the manna, the water issuing from the rock, the brazen serpent. Caleb and Josua. Moses prays with his arms extended. Josua. The passage of the Jordan. Fall of the walls of Jericho. The twelve Tribes. Government of God by means of Judges for the space of three to four hundred years. Josua, Debora, Gideon, Jephte, Samson, Heli, Samuel, Saul, David, Solomon, Roboam. *Instruction.*—The kingdom of Israel formed of ten tribes; it subsisted for 253 years, under 18 kings. That of Juda, formed of two tribes, subsisted 386 years, under 19 kings.

12. The Temple of Solomon. *Instruction.*—It was built in 7 years. Its dedication. What it contained. It was burned about the 16th year of the 34th age. It was re-built at the end of the captivity. This last building was very inferior, and it was at last destroyed forty years after the death of Jesus Christ. Julian, the apostate, was instrumental in accomplishing the prediction of our Saviour.

11. The four great and the twelve minor prophets.

12. Elias taken up into heaven; will return at the end of the world. Eliseus his disciple. Jonas three days in a whale's belly.

13. The captivity of Babylon. *Instruction.*—This captivity lasted for 70 years. It commenced on the 16th of the 34th age, and terminated about 86th of the 35th.

14. History of Susana, Tobias, Judith, Esther. Nabuchodonozer reduced for the space of 7 years to the condition of a brute. The three children in the furnace.

15. The Old Testament. *Instruction.*—The history of the book of the law, destroyed in the commencement of the captivity. Re-placed at the end of this time by the care of Esdras. Destroyed again under the persecution of Antiochas.

16. The holy man Eleazar. The seven Machabees and their mother; Antiochus, St. Joachim, and St. Anne.

17. Zacharias, Elizabeth, Mary, Joseph. The apparition of the angel Gabriel to Zacharias. Birth of St. John the Baptist. The angel Gabriel appears to Mary. Mystery of the Incarnation of the Word. Fear of Joseph. The visitation. Mary and Joseph leave for Bethlehem. Jerusalem is 30 leagues from Nazareth, Bethlehem is 2 leagues from Jerusalem, Emmaus 3 leagues.

18. Jesus Christ, the Son of God, made man for us. The history of the Annunciation.

19. Jesus Christ is born on Christmas day, at Bethlehem. The history of His birth; the angels and shepherds. The circumcision at the end of eight days. The name of Jesus.

20. The star of Jesus Christ seen in the East, predicted by Balaam.

21 The three kings (Magi.) Gaspard, Balthazar and Melchior, having seen the star, come to adore the infant Jesus. *Instruction.*—The star disappears. The Magi visit Herod. King Herod consults the priests. They point out Bethlehem. The star re-appears. The

adoration and presents of the Magi twelve days after our Saviour's birth.

22. Herod wishes to kill the infant Jesus. Herod's fears; his hypocrisy; his recommendation to the Magi.

23. An angel orders the three kings not to return by Herod's dominions, but by another road. The infant Jesus is carried to the temple of Jerusalem forty days after his birth. The holy man Simeon, and the holy widow Anne acknowledge Him as God. This fact comes to Herod's ears; his anger; his strange resolution with regard to the children of Bethlehem, where he thought the infant Jesus had returned.

24. An angel orders Joseph to fly into Egypt with the infant Jesus and Mary his mother. *Instruction.*—What happened the night after the presentation in the Temple. By the command of Herod all the little children in the town and environs of Bethlehem are put to death.

26. He falls sick and dies at the end of a month, devoured by worms. (Croiset, 18 vol. page 17.)

27. An angel orders St. Joseph to carry the infant Jesus, and Mary his mother, back into their own country. They return to Nazareth.

28. Jesus, Mary and Joseph, go up every year to the temple to celebrate the Passover.

29. Mary and Joseph lose the infant Jesus at the age of twelve years, and find him at the end of three days, in the temple, in the midst of the doctors of the law. *Instruction.*—Fear of Joseph and Mary. Words of his mother. Answer of Jesus.

30. Jesus Christ dwelt visibly on earth for more than 33 years.

31. He taught men the manner of living holily. He

gave them the example, and obtained for them the grace to follow it, by his sufferings and death.

32. St. John baptizes Jesus Christ. *Instruction.*—The birth of the precursor; his life and fasting; his disciples. He declares he is not the Messiah. He points Him out as the Lamb of God. His death. The heavens open at the baptism of Jesus Christ. The Holy Ghost descends. The Eternal Father speaks. Jesus Christ goes into the desert. He fasted for forty days. He is tempted by the devil. The preaching of Christ during three years. His life, His doctrine, His miracles.

33. The twelve Apostles of Jesus Christ—Peter, Andrew, James, John, Philip, Bartholomew, Thomas, Matthew, James, Jude, Simon, Judas.

34. St. Peter, the chief of the Apostles, the Vicar of Jesus Christ on earth, and the first Pope.

35. The Apostles the first Bishops.

36. Judas sells his master for thirty pieces of money. Hatred of the Jews. The treason of Judas.

37. Mount Calvary. The cross of Jesus Christ. The other crosses and the robbers.

38. Jesus Christ died on Good Friday. History of the Passion of Jesus Christ. Crucified at 12 o'clock and died at 3. Darkness over the earth. Miracles. Repentance of the executioners. His soul descends into hell. His body is embalmed and laid in the sepulchre, and guarded by Roman soldiers.

39. Jesus Christ rises from the dead on Easter day. History of the Resurrection. He appears to Mary, to St. Peter, to the two disciples going to Emmaus, to the Apostles. Incredulity of St. Thomas. Christ's apparition eight days after. Then also at the lake of Tiberias. The

confession of St. Peter. The mission of the Apostles.

40. Jesus Christ ascends into heaven on Ascension day, 40 days after His resurrection. He sends the Holy Ghost to His Church 10 days after His ascension. Wonders and mysteries of the day.

41. He will return to the earth at the end of the world for the general judgment.

42. The seven Sacraments, instituted by our Lord Jesus Christ for our sanctification. The three Sacraments that can be received but once. The five Sacraments of the living. The two of the dead.

43. Prayer in order to obtain the assistance of the grace of God. St. Paul and St. Matthias.

44. Our duties for every day, every week, every month, every year.

45. The six Commandments of the Church.

46. The Church of Constantine the great.

47. The cross of Jesus Christ found on Calvary by St Helen, after having sought it for three years. The miraculous cross of Constantine. The invention of the Holy Cross. The cross carried by Heraclius in the seventh century. Julian the Apostate.

48. The New Testament. The arrangement of the Canon. The discipline ordained by the Council of Nice.

50. St. Augustine converts the English and teaches them the religion of Christ or the Catholic religion.

51. The English follow the religion of Christ, or the Catholic religion, for 900 years.

52. Luther, Calvin, Henry VIII. wander from the way of Christ, reject His religion, that is, the Catholic church. The by-road and its forks represent the Reformation, with its divisions or variations for the last 300 years. The straight road of Jesus Christ existed a long time before.

Lucifer or Satan, the first to take a wrong road—he seduces Adam and Eve and their descendants to accompany him. Jesus Christ comes to conduct us into the right road, and enable us to keep it by the grace of redemption. The devil is enraged at the loss he suffers; but he succeeded in the following ages, by inducing men to walk in a new, bad road, that of the pretended Reformation.

53. Arius, Macedonius, Pelagius, Nestorius, Eutyches, Monothelites.

54. Mahomet, Iconoclasts, Berenger, Albigenses, Photius, Wicleff.

55. The four great schisms—of the Donatists, the Greeks, the West, and of England

56. Luther, Calvin, Henry VIII.

57. Baius, Jansenius, Wesley.

58. The sacred phalanx of the Œcumenical councils.

59. The priests came into the Indian country to teach the Indians the right road or the religion of Jesus Christ, to make them the children of the Catholic church.

60. History of the Catholic Missions now flourishing throughout the world.

CPSIA information can be obtained
at www.ICGtesting.com
Printed in the USA
LVHW102247310123
738370LV00002B/5

9 781432 609740